Event Design

Events are becoming more complex as their range of functions grows, as meeting places, creative spaces, economic catalysts, social drivers, community builders, image makers, business forums and network nodes. Effective design can produce more successful business models that can help to sustain cultural and sporting activities even in difficult economic times. This process requires creative imagination, and a design methodology or in other words 'imagineering'.

This book brings together a wide range of international experts in the fields of events, design and imagineering to examine the event design process. It explores the entire event experience from conception and production to consumption and co-creation. By doing so it offers insight into effective strategies for coping with the shift in value creation away from transactional economic value towards social and relational value which benefit a range of stakeholders from the community to policy makers. Mega-events, small community events, business events and festivals in eight different countries are examined providing an international view of social issues in event design.

A wide selection of current research perspectives is employed, integrating both theoretical and applied contributions. The multidisciplinary nature of the material means that it will appeal to a broad academic audience, such as art and design, cultural studies, tourism, events studies, sociology and hospitality.

Greg Richards is Professor of Leisure Studies at the University of Tilburg and Professor of Events at NHTV Breda University of Applied Science in the Netherlands. He has worked on projects for numerous national governments, national tourism organizations and municipalities, and he has extensive experience in tourism research and education.

Lénia Marques is a Lecturer in Imagineering at NHTV Breda University of Applied Sciences, the Netherlands.

Karen Mein is a Lecturer in Business Administration at NHTV Breda University of Applied Sciences, the Netherlands.

Routledge advances in event research series
Edited by Warwick Frost and Jennifer Laing
Department of Marketing, Tourism and Hospitality,
La Trobe University, Australia

Events, Society and Sustainability
Edited by Tomas Pernecky and Michael Lück

Exploring the Social Impacts of Events
Edited by Greg Richards, Maria deBrito and Linda Wilks

Commemorative Events
Warwick Frost and Jennifer Laing

Power, Politics and International Events
Edited by Udo Merkel

Event Audiences and Expectations
Jo Mackellar

Event Portfolio Planning and Management
A holistic approach
Vassilios Ziakas

Conferences and Conventions
A research perspective
Judith Mair

Fashion, Design and Events
Edited by Kim M. Williams, Jennifer Laing and Warwick Frost

Food and Wine Events in Europe
Edited by Alessio Cavicchi and Cristina Santini

Event Volunteering
Edited by Karen Smith, Leonie Lockstone-Binney, Kirsten Holmes and Tom Baum

The Arts and Events
Hilary du Cros and Lee Jolliffe

Sports Events, Society and Culture
Edited by Katherine Dashper, Thomas Fletcher and Nicola McCullough

The Future of Events and Festivals
Edited by Ian Yeoman, Martin Robertson, Una McMahon-Beattie, Elisa Backer and Karen A. Smith

Exploring Community Events and Festivals
Edited by Allan Jepson and Alan Clarke

Event Design
Social perspectives and practices
Edited by Greg Richards, Lénia Marques and Karen Mein

Rituals and Traditional Events in the Modern World
Edited by Warwick Frost and Jennifer Laing

Forthcoming:

Events in the City
Using public spaces as event venues
Andrew Smith

Approaches and Methods in Events Studies
Tomas Pernecky

Event Design

Social perspectives and practices

Edited by
**Greg Richards, Lénia Marques and
Karen Mein**

Routledge
Taylor & Francis Group

LONDON AND NEW YORK

First published 2015
by Routledge
2 Park Square, Milton Park, Abingdon, Oxon OX14 4RN

and by Routledge
711 Third Avenue, New York, NY 10017

Routledge is an imprint of the Taylor & Francis Group, an informa business

© 2015 selection and editorial matter, Greg Richards, Lénia Marques and
Karen Mein; individual chapters, the contributors

British Library Cataloguing in Publication Data
A catalogue record for this book is available from the British Library

Library of Congress Cataloging in Publication Data
Event design: social perspectives and practices / edited by Greg Richards,
Lénia Marques, Karen Mein.
    pages cm. – (Routledge advances in event research series)
    1. Special events industry. 2. Special events–Management.
    3. Special events–Planning. I. Richards, Greg. II. Marques, Lénia.
    III. Mein, Karen.
    GT3405.E89 2014
    394.2–dc23   2014012607

ISBN: 978-0-415-70464-9 (hbk)
ISBN: 978-0-203-76190-8 (ebk)

Typeset in Times New Roman
by Wearset Ltd, Boldon, Tyne and Wear

Contents

List of figures   ix
List of tables   x
Notes on contributors   xi
Preface   xvi

1 **Introduction: designing events, events as a design strategy**   1
   GREG RICHARDS, LÉNIA MARQUES AND KAREN MEIN

2 **Imagineering events as interaction ritual chains**   14
   GREG RICHARDS

3 **Service design methods in event design**   25
   SATU MIETTINEN, ANU VALTONEN AND
   VESA MARKUKSELA

4 **The role of imagineering as an event design strategy in the
   business event industry**   37
   FRANK OUWENS

5 **From visitor journey to event design**   50
   DOROTHÉ GERRITSEN AND RONALD VAN OLDEREN

6 **The discourse of design as an asset for the city: from
   business innovation to vernacular event**   65
   MARCO BEVOLO

7 **How to slay a dragon slowly: applying slow principles to
   event design**   78
   ILJA SIMONS

8 Designing events for socio-cultural impacts: the Holy Week
   in Puglia (Italy)   92
   ANNA TRONO AND KATIA RIZZELLO

9 Design processes around dynamic marketing
   communications for event organizations   109
   ANNE-MARIE HEDE AND PAMM KELLETT

10 Co-creative events: analysis and illustrations   122
   PHIL CROWTHER AND CHIARA OREFICE

11 Classical music, liveness and digital technologies   137
   ARTHUR MARIA STEIJN

12 The transformation of leisure experiences in music festivals:
   new ways to design imaginative, creative and memorable
   leisure experiences through technology and social networks   161
   JUNE CALVO-SORALUZE AND
   ROBERTO SAN SALVADOR DEL VALLE

13 Traditional gastronomy events as tourist experiences: the
   case of Santarém Gastronomy Festival (Portugal)   181
   MARTA CARDOSO, GORETTI SILVA AND CARLOS FERNANDES

14 Event design: conclusions and future research directions   198
   GREG RICHARDS, LÉNIA MARQUES AND KAREN MEIN

   Index   213

Figures

5.1	Staged versus customer experience	52
5.2	Touchpoints from the visitor's perspective	53
5.3	Value fit between organization and visitor	54
8.1	The places of the Holy Week in Puglia	96
8.2	The city of Taranto and pollution from the steel industry	98
8.3	Pairs of confrères from the Confraternity of Our Lady of Sorrows and of Our Lady of Mount Carmel	99
8.4	'Troccola'	100
8.5	Procession dedicated to the Addolorata	102
8.6	Procession of the Mysteries	103
9.1	The three phases of iterative events	111
11.1	Illustration of the performance radius in relation to live concerts	142
11.2	A generic story structure graph	145
11.3	Illustration of the strength of various A/V parameter components	145
11.4	A fragment of A/V parameters	147
11.5	A continuous sound-inspired illustration	148
11.6	Motion graphics designed to stay within borders of the 2-D screen space	149
11.7	Principles and illustration of translating tracked movement into live-generated motion graphics	151
11.8	Poster proposals for the moon-concerts	153
11.9	Technical drawing of the sound portal with three video projectors	154
11.10	Sketch of underground metro station	156
11.11	Preliminary schematic construction of a design-laboratory	159
12.1	The impact of technology in leisure experiences approaches	166
14.1	The space–time expansion of event design	203

Tables

5.1	Overview of case study respondents	55
5.2	Importance of touchpoints from the organizers' perspective	57
5.3	Plus and minus points of Paaspop identified by mystery guests	58
5.4	Touchpoints that were positively rated and seen as important by visitors to Paaspop Den Hout 2011	59
5.5	Touchpoints experienced as important by both the organizers and the visitors	60
5.6	Top four touchpoints and related motivations	62
5.7	Top five touchpoints in the direct-exposure phase and related experience ratings for the study trip of the platform of museum locations	62
9.1	Dynamic marketing communications, HPWS, event stage and key points for consideration	118
11.1	A selection of points, including some directions for possible solutions	139
11.2	A selection of guidelines that need consideration for how audiences experience music	140
11.3	A selection of expected results from the activity *Spatial and Interactive Experience Design and Classical Live Music*	141
11.4	A selection of the historical development of the concept of *liveness*	144
11.5	The five main A/V parameter components	146
11.6	Indexed focus points derived from previous tables related to Case 1	152
11.7	Indexed focus points derived from previous tables related to Case 2	152
11.8	Indexed focus points derived from previous tables related to Case 3	155
11.9	A selection of moving image properties	157
13.1	Profile of the sample	188
13.2	Main reasons for attending the event	189
13.3	Items and indicators	190
13.4	Correlation between experience outcomes and transcending expectations	192
13.a.1	Significant differences between groups	194

Contributors

Marco Bevolo is Lecturer in International Leisure Management/Sciences at NHTV University of Applied Sciences in the Netherlands. Until 2009 he was a Director at Philips Design headquarters, where he was the driving force behind CultureScan, the cultural futures research programme. He primarily works in the areas of strategic design, people research and thought leadership. He graduated with honours in Psychology at the Faculty of Literature and Philosophy from the University of Turin and he is completing his PhD at the University of Tilburg, the Netherlands. He published his work with Emerald, Palgrave, Gower, AVEdition and EMAP.

June Calvo-Soraluze, as well as being a singer-songwriter, studied Business Management specialising in Strategic Management at DBS. She extended her knowledge of management at UIBE in Beijing and at ASB in Denmark. In the latter, she received her MBA degree and developed the idea of her Master's thesis entitled *Understanding Leadership in Music Festivals: The Analysis of Management Dilemmas*, published by Lambert Academic Publishing in which she combines her two specialist areas: leadership and music. She is currently doing her PhD with a grant from the Basque Government on the new professional profile needed by music festival managers.

Marta Cardoso is a researcher at the Polytechnic Institute of Viana do Castelo, Portugal. She has conducted research into cultural and creative tourism and event experiences at the Santarém Gastronomy Festival and presented papers at scientific conferences in Spain and Portugal.

Phil Crowther enjoyed an 11 year private sector career managing large leisure and event venues. In 2006 he joined Sheffield Hallam University as a lecturer in Event Management and now holds the role of Principal Lecturer with responsibilities for research and business engagement. In addition to his teaching and consultancy work, he has published in international journals around the topic of events and strategy. His specific research interest focuses upon the strategic application of events primarily in a market context, and it is in this area that he is completing his PhD. He teaches mainly in the areas of event outcomes and event design in the public, private and third sectors.

Carlos Fernandes is the lead faculty in Tourism Studies at the Polytechnic Institute of Viana do Castelo, Portugal. He obtained his PhD at Bournemouth University (UK). His interests include tourism as a strategy for community development, heritage, cultural and creative tourism and tourism destination management. He is course leader of the BA in Tourism (UNWTO Tedqual certified). He also cooperates in World Tourism Organization activities including training courses in Angola, Zimbabwe and Mozambique and with the Council of Europe in Ukraine and Moldova. He is on the board of advisers of the International Institute of Gastronomy, Culture, Arts and Tourism (IGCAT).

Dorothé Gerritsen has been a Lecturer in Event Management at the Academy for Leisure of NHTV Breda University of Applied Sciences since 1995. She has a Master's degree in communication science (Radboud University, Nijmegen). In the specialist area of Event Management, she initiates and supervises research projects in the field of event marketing. In 2011 she wrote the book *Events as a Strategic Marketing Tool* together with Ronald van Olderen. Originally published in Dutch, this volume was published in English by CABI in 2014. The book has already been used at different universities in the Netherlands since 2012.

Anne-Marie Hede is an Associate Professor (Marketing) in the School of International Business and Associate Dean (Research and Research Training) in the Faculty of Business and Law, Victoria University (Melbourne, Australia). She is an experienced researcher in the field of events, and has undertaken a number of studies on events, using theories and models of marketing and management, to explore issues of significance to the event sector. Her research on events has been published and presented in a number of international journals and conferences.

Pamm Kellett is an Associate Professor in the School of Management and Marketing and Coordinator of the Postgraduate Sport Management Program at Deakin University (Melbourne, Australia). She holds a PhD in Sport Management from Griffith University (Australia). The objective of her research is to formulate and test intervention strategies that contribute to the development and optimal effectiveness of organizations in the sport and recreation sector. Ultimately, her research aims to enhance the quality of working life for those who work and participate in such organizations.

Vesa Markuksela, DSocSci (Management), LicSc (Econ), is a university lecturer in management, particularly in service design, at the University of Lapland, Finland. His current research interest is to explore community bonding practices, through senses and embodiment in consumer culture, especially with methodical solution of sensory ethnography.

Lénia Marques is Lecturer in Imagineering and Research at NHTV Breda University of Applied Sciences, the Netherlands and member of the research centres CELTH (the Netherlands) and CEMRI (Portugal). After obtaining her PhD in Literature in 2007 at Universidade de Aveiro (Portugal), she did a post-doctoral project on Travel and Arts. She lectured at the Universidade Aberta (Lisbon) and collaborated with the University of Barcelona and IBERTUR in Cultural Tourism projects. She has published widely in the fields of comparative and travel literature, intercultural relations, cultural tourism and events. Her current research focuses on creative tourism, cultural events and place narrative.

Karen Mein lectures in Business Administration at the NHTV University in Applied Sciences in Breda, the Netherlands. She has an MSc in Finance and Accounting from Teesside University, UK. She has worked in banking and at the University of Teesside, both as project manager in the field of SME and entrepreneurship, and as a lecturer in accounting and finance. She was later a senior lecturer at the Hogeschool Rotterdam Business School. She worked as a consultant delivering training, mentoring and coaching to business start-ups in the creative industries. Her current research interest lies in the development of networks in the creative industries.

Satu Miettinen DA (Doctor of Arts) is a Professor of applied art and design at the University of Lapland. She works in the area of service design as a researcher, teacher and a designer. Her current research projects look at the use of service design in citizen engagement and service prototyping when developing online digital services.

Ronald van Olderen lectures in Event Management and coordinates Event Management programmes at the NHTV University of Applied Sciences in Breda, the Netherlands. He has been involved in the development of content for the Event Management specialist area since 2011, focusing on corporate events in particular. He initiates and supervises research in the field of event marketing in close cooperation with industry. In 2011 he wrote the book *Events as a Strategic Marketing Tool* together with Dorothé Gerritsen. Originally published in Dutch, this volume was published in English by CABI in 2014. The book has already been used at different universities in the Netherlands since 2012.

Chiara Orefice, before joining Sheffield Hallam University in 2008, acquired experience in business events, working in the private and public sector and in international organizations in Italy, Thailand, Switzerland, France, Belgium and the UK. She is course leader for the MSc International Events and Conference Management and the faculty Erasmus coordinator. She is a member of the European Association of International Educators and of Meeting Professional International and she is involved in international projects aimed at developing the role of event professionals. Teaching and research interests centre on event design, return on investment and the impact of culture in international events.

Frank Ouwens has been engaged as a professional event specialist in the international corporate events industry since 1996. As a creative director for leading international agencies such as Jack Morton Worldwide and de Otter Creators he conceptualized and realized numerous live communication projects for clients such as Volkswagen, Mercedes, Philips, KPN and NIKE. For the past five years he has combined his creative work with lecturing in Imagineering, Concepting and Event Management at the NHTV in Breda, the Netherlands, as well as coaching students at the Pop Academy of ARTeZ, Enschede, the Netherlands, in the area of brand concepting.

Greg Richards is Professor of Leisure Studies at Tilburg University, Professor of Events at NHTV Breda and President of the International Institute for Gastronomy, Culture, Arts and Tourism (IGCAT) in Barcelona.

Katia Rizzello is Research Fellow in Economic and Political Geography at the Department of Cultural Heritage, University of the Salento (Lecce) in Italy. She obtained her PhD at the University of Bologna. Her research interests include European regional development policies, religious tourism and pilgrimage, social nature of events experience and innovative event measurement methodologies.

Roberto San Salvador del Valle holds a BA in History and a PhD in Leisure Studies. He is currently Lecturer at the University of Deusto, Bilbao. He teaches courses on Tourism, Leisure Management and Congress, Event and Trade Fair Management, including: Leisure and Tourism (BA), Leisure Policies (MALM), Leisure, City and Event Policies (MACETM) and Leisure Theory (PhD). His publications mainly focus on leisure phenomenon, policies, innovation and the city. He is part of the Leisure and Human Development research team, officially recognized by the Basque Government. Other research interests include social trends, time and space evolution.

Goretti Silva has lectured in Tourism Studies at the Polytechnic Institute of Viana do Castelo, Portugal, since 2002. Her interests include tourism as a strategy for rural development, particularly in peripheral regions, SMEs in tourism, tourism destination sustainable development and special interest tourism. She obtained her PhD at Bournemouth University (UK). Additionally she has collaborated with several organizations and has been involved in research and development projects, and has presented papers at several national and international conferences.

Ilja Simons is a Lecturer in the Academy for Leisure at the NHTV Breda, University of Applied Sciences in Breda, the Netherlands. She holds a Master's degree in Sociology from Erasmus University Rotterdam and she specializes in the sociology of culture. Her research interests include narratives, communities, power relations and silent voices within the context of leisure and tourism. Recently, she started a PhD project at Tilburg University, about contemporary events as social practices in which social cohesion is created and maintained.

Arthur Maria Steijn is an artist, lecturer and PhD-fellow at the Royal Danish Academy of Fine Arts, School of Design in Copenhagen, Denmark. He teaches production design, compositing, motion graphics and animation at the Department of Communication Design. His ongoing research project 'Motion graphics in spatial experience design' aims at developing design methods relevant for designing and involving motion graphics in spatial contexts. He also has over 15 years of experience as a designer in the field of performance, dance, opera, theatre, event and exhibition design. A selection of his artistic work can be viewed at: www.arthursteijn.dk.

Anna Trono is Associate Professor in Political and Economic Geography at the Department of Cultural Heritage, University of the Salento (Lecce) Italy. She studies regional policies and local development issues. These skills and competencies have also been developed during study visits at the Geography Departments of the London School and Political Science and University of Glasgow. For 15 years she has researched cultural tourism and environmental sustainability issues and has published numerous essays and books on these themes. She prepares and manages national and international (EU) research projects as chief scientist or work-group member.

Anu Valtonen, PhD (Econ.) is Professor of Marketing at the University of Lapland, Finland. Her research interests relate to cultural theories and methodologies in marketing and consumer research. Her current research projects explore sleep, embodiment and senses.

Preface

This book is the result of a series of activities by the ATLAS Events Research Group. Following the inaugural meeting of the group in Breda, the Netherlands in 2011, a second meeting was convened in Peniche, Portugal in 2013 to concentrate on the theme of event design. Some of the presentations made to that meeting were later developed into chapters for the current volume. In addition a number of international experts were invited to contribute with chapters on their areas of interest in the field of event design.

In keeping with the research line developed by the ATLAS Group, this volume approaches the design of events from a social and a network perspective. This builds on the previous publications developed by the group, which include the volume *Exploring the Social Impact of Events* (Routledge, 2013) and a forthcoming Special Issue of the *Journal of Policy Research in Tourism, Leisure and Events* on Monitoring and Evaluating Cultural Events (2014). Ongoing research activities of the ATLAS Group include an Expert Meeting on Event Engagement (Sheffield, UK, 2014) and a workshop on Events and Quality of Life at the ATLAS Conference in Budapest, Hungary (2014). For further information on the activities of the ATLAS Events Research Group, see https://independent.academia.edu/gregrichards/ATLAS-Events-Group.

We are very grateful to ATLAS for the support offered to the group over the past three years, without which this book would not have been possible. In particular our thanks go to the ATLAS Coordinator Leontine Onderwater for her hard work in making this research project possible. We are also grateful to the Polytechnic Institute of Leiria in Peniche for hosting the 2013 meeting, and to Nuno Almeida for making this meeting possible.

Greg Richards, Lénia Marques and Karen Mein
Tilburg and Breda, the Netherlands, March 2014

1 Introduction

Designing events, events as a design strategy

Greg Richards, Lénia Marques and Karen Mein

Events are becoming increasingly important as social, cultural and economic phenomena, to the extent that many of us live in 'eventful cities' (Richards and Palmer 2010) or traverse 'eventscapes' (Ferdinand and Shaw 2012) in our daily lives. Events are also becoming more complex as their range of functions grows; as meeting places, creative spaces, economic catalysts, social drivers, community builders, image makers, business forums and network nodes.

Events are therefore being designed to fulfil particular roles in society and business, and this process requires creative imagination, and a design methodology which can be framed according to different perspectives such as 'Service Design', 'Design Thinking' (Lockwood 2010) or 'Imagineering' (Nijs and Peters 2002). Events do not just happen; they are carefully crafted to weave narratives (content) into places (context) through processes of experience design. Effective design of an event can produce more successful business models that can help to sustain cultural and sporting activities even in difficult economic times. Effective design of an event can also become a key element in adapting to changing external conditions and can even create new opportunities where there was a threat (or nothing else) before.

This volume brings together a range of different perspectives on the factors that shape the way in which events are designed. It is less about the practical, micro aspects of design and far more about how events are designed to meet a range of different needs and aspirations for their organizers, visitors and other stakeholders. We examine these issues in a range of different events including mega-events, small community events, business events and festivals. These events are analysed in eight different countries, providing an international view of social issues in event design.

Why do events need to be designed?

Getz (2007: 18) defines an event as 'an occurrence at a given place and time; a special set of circumstances; a noteworthy occurrence'. This idea of events as a special set of circumstances is developed by Greg Richards in Chapter 2, where he analyses events as special times and spaces in which specific rituals or practices can be developed and maintained. These practices are designed to meet particular objectives (such as building social cohesion or stimulating economic impact or image change) related to individual events or to the places and communities in which they take place. The purposive nature of such events requires that they be designed to produce the desired outputs as effectively as possible.

Modern societies have increasingly recognized the power of events as economic, social and cultural tools, and this has arguably led to a growing number of events being purposefully staged. This has led to the emergence of an 'events industry' that was estimated to be worth over £36 billion in the UK alone in 2010 (Business Visits and Events Partnership 2010). This is witness to the growing size, influence and professionalism of the events industry. This growth in itself places new emphasis on the events themselves, which are now usually expected to be professionally organized, managed and marketed.

Essentially events have become value creation platforms in contemporary society. They are a vehicle or format for a wide range of value creation activities and they generate different kinds of value(s): economic, cultural, social, creative, environmental. They are ideally suited to the contemporary knowledge economy because they can generate, concentrate and disseminate knowledge among large numbers of people quickly and effectively. Because they usually depend on face to face contact, events can be a powerful value creation tool.

Events as value creation platforms can also be conceptualized as living organisms: they are born of fertile connections between people, they grow, creating more value in the process, they change, they reproduce (producing a ripple effect or instigating copycat events) and they eventually die. Event design in this sense can be seen as relying on the 'DNA' of the event that provides the code for the processes of growth and change which correspond to the event itself, but also to the organizations involved and society in general. This DNA is composed of different elements that include leading strategic internal decisions which concern, for example, a vision, a mission and strategic goals for the organizations involved. Linking events to the DNA of places ensures a good 'fit' between events and needs of stakeholders, and also ensures that events are 'anchored' in the places that created them.

Clear choices in terms of DNA are also important, such as the analysis of music festivals (e.g. the Tomorrowland festival in Belgium), village celebrations (e.g. Draaksteken, as described by Simons, Chapter 7) or conferences (e.g. the FRESH conference as described by Crowther and Orefice, Chapter 10) underline. The success of such events is related to clear vision, mission and strategic objectives that respond to challenges and adapt to the context of the event. Even where tradition lies at the core of an event, it can no longer be designed in a purely traditional way, as is shown by the examples provided by Trono and Rizzello (Chapter 8) and Cardoso, Silva and Fernandes (Chapter 13).

The design of events also needs to take their particular nature into account. For example, the fact that most events are based on 'live' content and the co-presence of large numbers of people means that timing becomes a design issue, as do problems of access, and dealing with waste and nuisance. The effective use of events as value creation platforms in the knowledge economy therefore raises a range of design-related issues for events. Design processes are therefore applied to events in order to:

- increase effectiveness and efficiency;
- increase recognition of events among stakeholders;
- ensure the production of discrete effects, such as social practices, social cohesion, cultural processes and economic impacts;
- minimize undesirable effects of events, such as noise, nuisance, environmental damage;
- optimize the success of the event, in terms of visitors numbers, the quality of the experience and other outputs.

As Brown (2005: 2) points out, the event process really needs to start with design, because 'events that are designed badly start out wrong and can't be made better by good management processes and a great risk management plan'. Event design is therefore far more than just décor and the 'look' of events – it is a basic process that needs to be integrated into the development of all events in order to ensure their longevity. Brown (2005: 2) defines event design as 'the creation, conceptual development and design of an event to maximize the positive and meaningful impact for the event's audience and/or participants'. However, as this volume illustrates, the implications of event design go far beyond the event audience and participants. For example, events have a relationship with the places in which they are held, which also raises issues of identity and image (Bevolo, Chapter 6; Simons, Chapter 7). Events can also be linked to religious rituals (Trono and Rizzello, Chapter 8), to the use of Web 2.0 (Hede and Kellett, Chapter 9) and technological advances (Calvo-Soraluze and San Salvador del Valle, Chapter 12) or by their influence in the cultural landscape (Steijn, Chapter 11).

This volume provides therefore examples of how these design processes work in relation to different types of physical content, locations and types of events.

What is design?

As the Design Council (2006) put it 'Design is everywhere – and that's why looking for a definition may not help you grasp what it is.' The diversity of design and design approaches is certainly evident from the range of contributions to the current volume. However, there are some widely held ideas about what design is and what function it has in social and economic processes. For example, as Cox (2005: 2) states, 'design is what links creativity and innovation. It shapes ideas to become practical and attractive propositions for users or customers. Design may be described as creativity deployed to a specific end.'

This also dovetails neatly with the network approach to events developed by the ATLAS Events Group (Richards *et al.* 2013), which views events as a means for reaching a wide range of social, economic and cultural ends. In this view, however, the design process is also wider than the creation of products or experiences for users or customers. As the chapters in this volume show, the range of stakeholders and actors involved in event design includes many other parties, including residents, public authorities, voluntary associations and commercial operators.

In this broader context, events are far more than a practical proposition or product. They can also be catalysts, symbols, conduits and lenses that enable people to function within and reflect upon their own role in society. In the context of the knowledge economy, for example, events could be viewed as generators, containers and disseminators of knowledge. So Grudin's (2010: 62) broader definition of design as the agency that 'shapes, regulates, and channels energy, empowering forces that might otherwise be spent chaotically', is pertinent, particularly as he views design as 'embodied knowledge', which can be transferred into practice. In order for the embodied, implicit knowledge of design to be applied more widely, that knowledge has to be made explicit through processes of externalization and combination with other forms of knowledge (Nonaka and Takeuchi 1995). This is effectively what has happened in different areas of design in recent decades, which we can also see reflected in the different approaches to event design.

Imagineering

The combination of knowledge from different fields is most clearly illustrated by the concept of imagineering. Long thought to have been originated by Walt Disney, imagineering refers to the combination of imagination and engineering. According to Paleo-Future (2007) the word was actually coined in 1942 to describe work being done in the laboratories of the Aluminium Company of America. Quoting from a 1942 newspaper article, imagineering was seen as a 'combination of imagination and engineering', it is defined as 'the fine art of deciding where we go from here'. This original definition also fits very well with Ratcliffe and Krawczyk's (2004) analysis of imagineering for cities as a process of 'Imagine ahead – plan backwards'.

The imagineering concept was later applied by Disney to the design and development activities at his theme parks. Imagineering therefore became more centrally related to the development of experiences, an idea later translated into a definition of imagineering as value creation from an experience perspective by Nijs and Peters (2002). In the realm of events, imagineering was seen as 'creating and managing worlds of experience, based in internal values (DNA) on the one hand and/or values of the target groups on the other, with the objective of creating the emotional involvement of all stakeholders' (Hover 2008: 43).

An example of the imagineering perspective on business events is developed by Frank Ouwens in Chapter 4 and examples of the use of the customer journey in events are provided by Gerritsen and van Olderen (Chapter 5).

Service design

The rise of the service economy in the 1980s created a need to effectively design and manage service delivery. Early work on service design (Shostak 1982) therefore used a 'service blueprint' as a means of visualizing and designing services. As Miettinen, Valtonen and Markuksela (Chapter 3) describe in their analysis of service design at Raunta Zoo in Finland, the field has developed considerably in the past three decades. Interaction between participants or customers and different elements of a service lie at the heart of the service design approach. This is also the basic starting point for another more specific application of service design that has evolved around the notion of the customer journey. As Gerritsen and van Olderen point out in Chapter 5, the customer journey can be a very useful design tool that allows the service provider to understand better how the consumer interacts with the different 'touchpoints' provided.

Nonetheless, the service design concept can be extended much further, as Miettenen, Valtonen and Markuksela show in their discussion of service design and design thinking in Chapter 3. As Osterwalder and Pigneur (2009: 59) argue, a

> designer's job is to extend the boundaries of thought, to generate new options, and, ultimately, to create value for users. This requires the ability to imagine 'that which does not exist.' We are convinced that the tools and attitude of the design profession are prerequisites for success in the business model generation.

Design thinking

As Miettenen, Valtonen and Markuksela point out in Chapter 3, design thinking seeks to be a human-centred approach that defines strategy according to the embeddedness in the context. The examples are manifold and, as Lockwood (2010) shows, it can be an approach used by businesses that are looking for new models in order to survive in a competitive context. Therefore, events can be part of the strategy and act as catalyst where emotional energy is an important event output (Richards, Chapter 2). Moreover, the design of the event itself is developed using a design thinking approach, which results in new strategic guidelines for organizations and managers. An illustration in the field of events related to city branding can be found in Bevolo's analysis of Eindhoven (Chapter 6).

Experience design

The transition from the service economy to the experience economy described by Pine and Gilmore (1999) heralded a new focus on the way in which experiences are designed. Pine and Gilmore argued that experiences revolve far more around the consumer. Whereas the management and design of services had tended to focus on the actions of the supplier, experiences can only be created in the presence of the consumer, and each experience is therefore individually mediated.

Ek *et al.* (2008) developed four definitions of experience design, located on a continuum from a static starting point to a dynamic endpoint. They argued that most previous studies of experience design had concentrated on relatively static concepts related to design as a noun (shaping something static) or experience as a noun (observation of or participation in an event), whereas less attention has been paid to the more dynamic aspects of design as a verb (dynamically shaping something) or experience as a verb (to undergo emotional sensations). In their view, much more attention needs to be paid to the dynamic aspects of experience design, because this is where the experience actually 'happens'.

In the field of events, experience design is described by Berridge (2012: 278), who argues that 'if the core phenomenon of an event is the experience then event design effectively becomes the platform upon which it is built'. Storytelling is an important aspect of many experiences, and it is becoming increasingly integrated into event experiences as well.

As Mossberg *et al.* (2010: 4) point out:

> the design phase involves more concrete concept development: creating the story line, designing the servicescape (i.e. physical location), packaging and programming the activities, for instance offering a number of storytelling activities in combination with a meal and accommodation or making a programme for on-stage storytelling activities, music and other performances. Creating awareness for the storytelling offer with point of departure in a marketing plan as well as prolonging the storytelling experience through souvenirs and other relevant products (e.g. food) are also central activities of the design phase.

This indicates that storytelling is often linked to the more physical aspects of experience design. However, storytelling may also become part of the more intangible design elements, being central to the DNA of the organization and/ or the event. This process may include creating a vision or a storyline that seeks to involve audiences through identification processes (Hover 2008). Some festivals are very good at this, such as Glastonbury (UK), Andanças (Portugal), Roskilde Festival (Denmark) or Tomorrowland (Belgium). In addition, the Dragon Slaying event described by Ilja Simons in Chapter 7 is not just based on the historical story of George and the Dragon; it also tells a story about the contemporary community that (re)created the event. The fact that the event is endogenous means that it is not only about creating and telling a story, but also about having a narrative identity that permeates the event. Narrative is also being used as a central pillar in the experience design of events thorough the means of technology, such as the classical music events analysed by Steijn in Chapter 11.

Social design

Beyond the personal experience of events, nowadays, also in design thinking studies, more attention is being given to social contexts and social change (Brown and Wyatt 2010). The development of design thinking towards social innovation has resulted in social design. The concept of social design can be approached from the point of view of design, which usually relates to the social responsibilities of designers, or from the social perspective of designing the social world or promoting social innovation. Events have often been used as catalysts for social change, because as Sewell (1996) points out, an event is essentially produced by a gap between expectation and reality. Events can therefore become a means of changing social structures and creating new realities. Consider for example the role of Live Aid in changing perceptions of famine in Africa and convincing governments of the need for action (Rojek 2013). Increasingly more businesses and non-profit organizations (often NGOs but also educational organizations) are designing events for social innovation.

As Richards and Palmer (2010) point out, events can be used as a means of social design for spaces in the city. This is a strategy that has been extensively used in Barcelona, for example, to open up and 'pacify' run-down areas of the inner city. By staging cultural events in areas where little mixing of different social groups occurs, it is hoped that more civic and responsible uses of public space can be promoted and at the same time more contact created by individuals and social groups (cf. Bevolo, Chapter 6).

Designing events – an emerging social practice?

Brown and James (2004) argue that design has often been ignored in the practice of event management, even though design is often crucial to the success of an event. They identify five basic design principles for events: scale, shape, focus, timing and build. The final term 'build' emphasizes the largely physical approach that is often taken to event design.

In this volume we argue for a broader approach to design, which recognizes the social role of events and also the social factors that shape those events. A growing number of cities are beginning to use events proactively as a strategic and tactical tool to achieve a range of different aims (e.g. Dubai, Eindhoven, Edinburgh, Melbourne, Montreal, Singapore). A small, but influential group of event designers is therefore emerging at the interface between urban policy, spatial planning and cultural and economic development.

For example, events umbrella organizations such as Rotterdam Festivals and Antwerpen Open now play an increasing role as event designers. For example, having identified the 'food' theme as an important aspect of the urban landscape of Rotterdam, Rotterdam Festivals proceeded to organize the World Food Festival in 2013 to link up the different parts of the food sector in the city. These included restaurants and cafés, food producers, scientists and chefs, as well as a range of related areas such as hospitality, event management, city marketing, the municipality and creative entrepreneurs.

The principles described by Richards and Palmer (2010) in relating events to urban management and revitalization can be applied more widely to the events design field as a whole. These principles include:

- vision
- risk-taking
- programming
- engagement
- equity.

Vision is an essential aspect of design – without a vision of the future nothing new can be created. Defining a vision is about more than creativity; it is also an essential tool for galvanizing people to work towards a common goal, and ensuring that specific aims are reached. Very often, to be effective, the vision also needs to involve taking certain risks; at the very least the risk of failure, but also potential economic, social and cultural risks as well. Unless an event offers something new and innovative it will quickly become tired and uninteresting as a value creation platform. This is also the reason why events must be able to reinvent themselves, although without changing their vision (as the Draaksteken described by Simons, Chapter 7).

The increasing use of events to generate social cohesion (Richards *et al.* 2013) also makes the question of engagement crucial in event design. Events need to implicate people as well as entertain them if they want to make a difference. But the way in which engagement is achieved also needs careful design in order to ensure a certain level of equity, at least at programme level. If the ultimate aim of the event programme is to improve the quality of life, then this should apply equally to everybody.

These elements have been increasingly incorporated into different events in different ways. For example the use of storytelling or the adoption of a strong ritual form are strategies for ensuring engagement and projecting a certain vision. This is evident in the way in which many mega-events have begun to incorporate stylized design elements, such as carefully staged opening and closing ceremonies (Tomlinson 1996). For example, in the case of the Beijing Olympics, Luo (2010: 771) describes how 'China attempted to use the opening and closing ceremonies as public rituals for realizing its dream of reinventing itself as a nation.' In such instances it becomes clear that the design and form of an event itself can become a means of communication.

The careful design of events as a form of expression becomes increasingly important as the competition for attention from consumers and other stakeholders increases (Richards 2013). Events and event programmes increasingly need to be spectacular and distinctive in order to stand out and attract attention from publics and the media. The success of events is therefore also often measured in terms of attendance and/or media coverage. The need to attract attention is also linked to the growing role of narrative and storytelling in events. Events need to have a story in order to engage audiences and make themselves interesting. For example Ziakas (2013: 27) describes how events can be seen as 'dramatic stories that express versions of a community's social order', hence 'allowing the expression of different aspects of community life'. The telling of stories through events is also a means of confronting and dealing with social and cultural challenges and contributing to social cohesion and community identity (Bevolo, Chapter 6 and Simons, Chapter 7).

As Simons shows in Chapter 7, and, to a certain extent also Calvo-Soraluze and San Salvador del Valle (Chapter 12) and Crowther and Orefice (Chapter 10), in addition to this top-down approach, there is also more evidence of bottom-up, ad hoc events which are not designed professionally, but which emerge through collaborative action.

Emergent design

Gore (2010) examines the development of 'flash mob' dance performances, which are often designed to look spontaneous, even though they are usually carefully planned (a phenomenon Marcuse (2004: 109) described as 'organized spontaneity'). This is also a good example of how the design of events has begun to change under the influence of expanding technological possibilities. Flash mobs depend on rapid decentralized communication through extended networks and visual technologies that allow such impromptu performances to be filmed and displayed via the Internet. This type of event, quite recent in the eventscape, results from the high impact of technology as a major force on event design (Adema and Roehl 2010). The same description could be used for other developing phenomena such as described by Steijn (Chapter 11).

Increasing friction and clashes between top-down and bottom-up modes of event organization (often starkly visible during major global events such as the G20 summit) highlights the practice of designing events as a kind of 'thirdspace' between local and global, old and new, large and small. As Sewell (1996) suggests, this can also be a means of announcing and overcoming disjuncture, and perhaps of creating new and different visions of the world.

Contributions to this volume

In the following chapter Greg Richards presents a theoretical consideration of the role of 'interaction ritual chains' (Collins 2004) as design tools for events. The co-presence implicit in events can be used to focus attention, create a feeling of belonging to a group and so generate 'emotional energy'. Richards argues that rituals are triggers and therefore should be thought of in the design process. Ritual design is an element to be taken into account in successful events programmes or portfolios.

Continuing the presentation of different theoretical perspectives to event design, Satu Miettinen, Anu Valtonen and Vesa Markuksela outline in Chapter 3 the ways in which principles of service design can be applied to events. In this relatively new field, experiments are being used to design services, looking at the customer journey and touchpoints to improve the experience of events. They define touchpoints as something physical through which one uses the service, such as objects, places and interfaces.

In Chapter 4, Frank Ouwens provides another perspective focusing on the role that imagineering can play in event design strategy, in particular in the business event industry. Outlining the evolution of the concept of imagineering, Ouwens argues that event organizers need to adopt new design methods in order to meet the increasing demands of clients and the external environment.

Also from an imagineering perspective, in Chapter 5, Dorothé Gerritsen and Ronald van Olderen analyse the use of the visitor journey in events. Throughout an event the visitor journey is marked out by a series of touchpoints at the interface between consumer and producer (also referred to by Miettinen, Valtonen and Markuksela in Chapter 3). These touchpoints can also imply that the visitor is touched at an emotional level, creating real contact between supplier and consumer.

The importance of events is being increasingly recognized by policy makers and also being integrated as strategy in city planning and branding, as underlined in Chapter 6 by Marco Bevolo. He examines the ways in which design has influenced the city of Eindhoven and in particular its flagship event, the Dutch Design Week. Bevolo explores the way in which design became part of the cultural DNA of the city, and how this has enabled it to stage a very successful design event, as well as to export its own design model to other cities.

The link between event design and place is also the subject of Chapter 7, by Ilja Simons. Using Collins' (2004) interaction ritual chains as theoretical basis, Simons analyses the case of the Draaksteken Beesel event. This event is only staged once every seven years by the inhabitants of a small village in the south of the Netherlands. The effort involved in the staging of this event by a small community means that they have to take their time and 'slowly' design an event that is rich in tradition. However, at the same time, the long time period reveals the changes that are taking place in the local community and the local culture, which are embraced and decided by the community in a bottom-up process.

The rites of Holy Week in the Puglia region of Italy are also based on tradition, as Anna Trono and Katia Rizzello explain in Chapter 8. On the other hand, the rituals and the emotional energy attached to these are strong elements of this religious celebration. These traditional rituals are still very conservative, even if spectacular elements have been highlighted for tourist consumption.

Anne-Marie Hede and Pamm Kellett investigate the technological impacts on event design in Chapter 9. These authors look into the ways that Web 2.0 is allowing events to be imagineered, in particular in terms of human resource management. Events are extended in time and space through the use of 'dynamic marketing communications', which means that new skills have to be integrated into event design. This, the authors argue, is particularly important for events, which are subject to temporal fluctuation as they develop through phases of regeneration, activation and dormancy.

The interactive potential of new technology to market events is a theme also analysed in Chapter 10 by Phil Crowther and Chiara Orefice. Examining how events work as mutual value creation spaces, they demonstrate how events have previously been seen as relatively peripheral in marketing, but that they have the potential to become much more central 'value creation spaces' if they are used effectively.

Another perspective on the use of digital media and technological advances in event design, namely in live classical music events, is analysed by Arthur Maria Steijn in Chapter 11. Using experience design as a framework, the author describes an ongoing project designed to improve and expand the experience of classical music events, taking the music outside the concert hall and into new spaces, including a metro station.

Technology has also been having an influence on the design of music festivals, a topic studied by June Calvo-Soraluze and Roberto San Salvador del Valle in Chapter 12. This study illustrates the way technology is influencing the pace and style of events and is impacting on the welfare and well-being dimensions of leisure experiences.

Focusing on the traditional aspect of another type of event, the gastronomic festival, Marta Cardoso, Goretti Silva and Carlos Fernandes investigate the Santarém National Gastronomy Festival (Portugal) in Chapter 13. Although the festival has been running for more than 30 years, little has changed in the design of the event. With the numbers of visitors decreasing, their research highlights the challenges of designing the visitor experience in order to increase satisfaction and generate repeat visits to the festival.

The final chapter by Greg Richards, Lénia Marques and Karen Mein outlines the main findings of the research presented in this volume and presents some remaining challenges for event design research. The potential future research areas discussed include the extension of event design in both space and time, as organizers and participants co-create experiences beyond the location and timeframe of the event itself. They also underline the growing need for research into the co-creation process itself. This is often cited as being important in event research, but few studies have yet tackled how the co-creation process works or what effects this has on event design.

References

Adema, K.L. and Roehl, W.S. (2010) 'Environmental scanning the future of event design', *International Journal of Hospitality Management*, 29(2): 199–207.

Berridge, G. (2012) 'Designing event experiences', in S. Page and J. Connell (eds) *The Routledge Handbook of Events*, London: Routledge, pp. 273–288.

Brown, G. and James, J. (2004) 'Event design and management: ritual sacrifice?' in I. Yeoman, M. Robertson, J. Ali-Knight, S. Drummond and U. McMahon-Beattie (eds) *Festival and Event Management*, London: Routledge, pp. 53–64.

Brown, S. (2005) 'Event design: an Australian perspective', Paper presented at the second International Event Management Body of Knowledge Global Alignment Summit in Johannesburg, South Africa, July 2005.

Brown, T. and Wyatt, J. (2010) 'Design thinking for social innovation', *Stanford Social Innovation Review*, 28: 29–35.

Business Visits and Events Partnership (2010) 'Britain for events', London: BVEP. Online, available at: www.businesstourismpartnership.com/research-and-publications/research/

category/4-bvep-research?download=151:britain-for-events-report-october-2010 (accessed 11 October 2013).

Collins, R. (2004) *Interaction Ritual Chains*, Princeton, NJ: Princeton University Press.

Cox, G. (2005) 'The Cox review of creativity in business: building on the UK's strengths', Norwich: HMSO.

Design Council (2006) 'What is design?' Online, available at: www.designcouncil.org.uk/webdav/harmonise?Page/@id=6011&Section/@id=1033 (accessed 2 October 2013).

Ek, R., Hornskov, S.B., Larsen, J. and Mansfeldt, O.K. (2008) 'A dynamic framework of tourist experiences: space-time and performances in the experience economy', *Scandinavian Journal of Hospitality and Tourism*, 8: 122–140.

Ferdinand, N. and Shaw, S.J. (2012) 'Events in our changing world', in N. Ferdinand and P. Kitchin (eds) *Events Management: An International Approach*, London: Sage, pp. 5–22.

Getz, D. (2007) *Event Studies: Theory, Research and Policy for Planned Events*, Oxford: Butterworth Heinneman.

Gore, G. (2010) 'Flash mob dance and the territorialisation of urban movement', *Anthropological Notebooks*, 16(3): 125–131.

Grudin, R. (2010) *Design and Truth*, New Haven, CT: Yale University Press.

Hover, M. (2008) 'Imagine your event: imagineering for the event industry', in U. Wünsch (ed.) *Facets of Contemporary Event Management-Theory and Practice for Event Success*, Bad Honne: Verlag K.H. Bock, pp. 37–62.

Lockwood, T. (ed.) (2010) *Design Thinking: Integrating Innovation, Customer Experience, and Brand Value*, New York: Allworth Press.

Luo, J. (2010) 'Betwixt and between: reflections on the ritual aspects of the opening and closing ceremonies of the Beijing Olympics', *Sport in Society*, 13(5): 771–783.

Marcuse, H. (2004) 'Die Unterschiede zwischen alter und neuer Linker', in *Nachgelassene Schriften*, Vol. 4, Springe: Zu Klampen.

Mossberg, L., Therkelsen, A., Huijbens, E.H., Björk, P. and Olsson, A.K. (2010) *Storytelling and Destination Development*, Oslo: Nordic Innovation Centre.

Nijs, D. and Peters, F. (2002) *Imagineering. Het creëren van belevingswerelden*, Amsterdam: Uitgeverij Boom.

Nonaka, I. and Takeuchi, H. (1995) *The Knowledge-Creating Company*, Oxford: Oxford University Press.

Osterwalder, A. and Pigneur, Y. (2009) 'Business model generation'. Online, available at: www.businessmodelgeneration.com/downloads/businessmodelgeneration_preview.pdf (accessed 2 October 2013).

Paleo-Future (2007) 'Word origins: imagineering, continued' (1942) Thursday 17 May 2007. Online, available at: http://paleo-future.blogspot.com.es/2007/05/word-origins-imagineering-continued.html (accessed 11 October 2013).

Pine, J. and Gilmore, J. (1999) *The Experience Economy*, Boston, MA: Harvard Business School Press.

Ratcliffe, J. and Krawczyk, E. (2004) *Imagineering Cities: Creating Liveable Urban Futures in the 21st Century*, Dublin: Futures Academy, Dublin Institute of Technology.

Richards, G. (2013) 'Events and the means of attention', *Journal of Tourism Research & Hospitality*, 2(2). Online, available at: www.scitechnol.com/2324-8807/2324-8807-2-118.pdf (accessed 11 October 2013).

Richards, G. and Palmer, R. (2010) *Eventful Cities: Cultural Management and Urban Revitalization*, London: Routledge.

Richards, G., de Brito, M. and Wilks, L. (eds) (2013) *Exploring the Social Impact of Events*, London: Routledge.

Rojek, C. (2013) *Event Power: How Global Events Manage and Manipulate*, London: Sage.

Sewell, W.H. (1996) 'Historical events as transformations of structures: inventing revolution at the Bastille', *Theory and Society*, 25: 841–881.

Shostack, L.G. (1982) 'How to design a service', *European Journal of Marketing*, 16(1): 49–63.

Tomlinson, A. (1996) 'Olympic spectacle: opening ceremonies and some paradoxes of globalisation', *Media Culture Society*, 18(4): 583–602.

Ziakas, V. (2013) 'A multidimensional investigation of a regional event portfolio: advancing theory and praxis', *Event Management*, 17(1): 27–48.

2 Imagineering events as interaction ritual chains

Greg Richards

Concepts of event design

As many of the chapters in this volume make clear, the design process implies a relationship between the objectives of an event and the outcomes that are generated. A successful event is arguably one that is designed in such a way that it generates positive outcomes and value for all stakeholders involved. This model fits closely with the idea of a ritual as developed by Randall Collins (2004), borrowing heavily from the ideas of Durkheim. In Collins' view, the way rituals are organized, or in other words, designed, is important in securing positive outcomes of the ritual. This chapter looks at how Collins' model can be used to think through processes of event design.

The subject event design touches on many different fields, including design, service design, urban design and imagineering. It is important first to examine what these different approaches to the field imply. Many of the chapters in this book deal with different concepts of design, such as design as a 'language' (Bevolo, Chapter 6), service design or design thinking (Miettenen *et al.*, Chapter 3) or imagineering (Ouwens, Chapter 4). Design, for example, can simply be a strategic approach to achieving a desired aim or output. If the output of the design process is the unique experience desired by consumers, this also suggests that the design of each event, or event programme, also needs to think about uniqueness. It might be argued that uniqueness for the participant depends on creating a gap between expectation and reality. As discussed in Chapter 1, Sewell (1996) sees this gap as being an essential element in events. The implication is that an 'event' is created by doing something outside the stream of everyday experience, which implies also an active and creative role in design for the event organizer. This is interesting as it appears to contrast with the service design approach, because as Miettenen *et al.* explain in Chapter 3, service design usually revolves around the needs of users. This assumes that the wants or needs of the user are paramount, whereas creating something that is different from their expectations actually involves thinking about things that users don't even know they want. This seems to suggest that the process of creating events that are memorable and which have lasting effects is somewhat different from the standard service design approach.

Another way of thinking about event design can be linked to the apparently more specialized field of 'imagineering'. Imagineering, according to Nijs and Peters (2002) entails value creation and value innovation from an experience perspective. Value can only be created through the interaction of different stakeholders in an experience. This process of exchange can be organized, as Hover (2008: 39) states, by 'creating and managing worlds of experience, based in internal values (DNA) on the one hand and/or values of the target groups on the other, with the objective of creating the emotional involvement of all stakeholders'. In order to be successful, Hover argues, experiences need to be meaningful, unique, have enduring appeal, be multilayed and timely.

One of the limitations of both imagineering and service design approaches, however, is that they tend to focus on the stakeholders involved. In fact, one can argue that design and the creation of events are essentially collective, social activities. The knowledge that is applied in design can be conceived of as embodied, tacit knowledge that needs to be deployed through social networks (Bevolo, Chapter 6). Although we tend to think about creators and designers as individuals working away in splendid isolation to produce a masterpiece, the truth is that the social context for design, creativity and innovation is paramount. As Scott (2010) demonstrates, creativity needs the support of social structures in order to circulate ideas and generate knowledge. These collective processes are increasingly being recognized in the study of creative networks (Potts *et al.* 2008) and social innovation. This means that events are always produced in a concrete social context, and this chapter aims to link the design of events to the concrete contexts in which they are produced.

The social context of events

We are used to thinking about events, almost by definition, as isolated happenings separated from their surroundings. In fact, if there is no separation between an event and its temporal or spatial context, it cannot be considered an event. This approach, however, also often spills over into events research. Much of what is written about events, for example, is framed in terms of event management, a largely self-contained field of enquiry in which the link to wider society is analysed in terms of the role of different 'stakeholders'. Even though many researchers have pointed out the intimate relationships between contemporary staged events and the social festivity of traditional events, there is often an assumption that the modern version has been ripped from its traditional social roots to become something 'inauthentic' or 'commodified' (e.g. Greenwood 1989). Rojek has gone further in exposing what he sees as a design process aimed to achieve global emotional management through megaevents.

Events are important links in the chain of communication power that influential social networks deploy to regulate global populations. [...] They stir up a

global media *mazurka* that unintentionally obscures the structural transformations that are necessary to make the world (or the corporation) a better place.

(2013: xii)

Event management refers to the targeting and managing of designed public
events geared to invest emotional energies and economic resources to
selected goals. [...] [I]t is most useful to think of them as components of
lifestyle architecture through which we now build competent, relevant, credible images of ourselves.

(2013: 1–2)

Events, Rojek (2013: 34) argues, are created to fulfil a series of 'moral designs'.
Interestingly, Rojek titles his critique of events as 'event management', even
though he very clearly tries to locate events within a broader social, economic
and political context.

Urry (2002) also emphasizes the important social role of events in underpinning contemporary relationships. In his analysis of 'mobilities' he sees the need
for physical co-presence as one of the important driving forces for physical
movement. Even though we are almost permanently connected via virtual means
these days, we still feel the need to connect physically via events.

These more critical approaches to event studies emphasize the fact that events
cannot be studied in isolation from their context, but rather must be seen as
having a recursive relationship with that context. They are devices which enable
groups of people to cope with, and perhaps influence, their surroundings. The
most essential quality of an event is its ability to re-frame time and space.
Bakhtin (1941) conceptualized this as the subversion of the established order of
things through carnival, and Turner (1969) referred to the change of state made
possible by the liminal qualities of events.

However, the important thing about the transformational role of events is not
just the fact that things change, but also the new possibilities that are offered by
the transformational moment of the event. For example, an event can be the
window to a new sort of time, in which the objective, sequential passage of time
or *chronos*, where the passing of time is measured by the clock, transforms into
kairos, a time between, or a special moment in which something happens. The
shift towards *kairos* is exemplified by Csíkszentmihályi's (1990) concept of
'flow', where our concentrated engagement in an experience causes us to lose
our perception of time. This temporal shift gives the pre-conditions for creativity, and for new ways of seeing the world.

Sewell (1996) frames this quality of events as their ability to produce a difference between expectation and reality, which makes them 'special' because they
result in a change in social structures and practices. Changing structures create a
moment in which perceptions and models of social life can change. This gives a
power to events that is widely, if often implicitly, recognized. As Bevolo
(Chapter 6) shows events can be designed in such a way that they influence the
future of a city. Many cities have used events to transform their reality and/or

their image, such as Barcelona (Olympic Games, World Expo), Lille, Glasgow (European Capital of Culture) and Helsinki (World Design Capital).

The change implied by events is not always transformational, in the sense of generating a sudden change in structures. However, the fact that an event has to be marked off in some way from the everyday context means that every event, no matter how modest in scale, is likely to produce some degree of change. This can produce a degree of cultural shift or drift over time – a process that is made more obvious when the interval between event editions becomes greater (see Simons, Chapter 7).

At the level of event programme design, therefore, we may often see a dichotomy emerging between those events which are supposed to act as a stimulus for change (pulsar events) and those events that are designed to sustain the status quo, or 'organic' events (Trono and Rizzello, Chapter 8). Places increasingly need to think about the balance between those events that maintain things as they are (and arguably help to support identity and social cohesion) and those events that introduce the potential for change. Too much reliance on organic events may create stagnation, whereas too many pulsar events may create an unsettling sensation of constant change. In fact, it often seems that the whole process of creating, designing, bidding for and staging events has become part of an (urban) ritual that links politics, media and people into a marketing machine that needs change and dynamism to feed it (Rennen 2007). In the end, the disappointment of not capturing a major pulsar event may also be a gap between expectation and reality that stimulates change as well (Richards, 2014).

So the whole process of event or event programme design is intimately linked to the wider social context in which it is rooted and the ritual functions that events serve within society.

Events as ritual design

The essential qualities of events that make them fruitful carriers of design and imagineering are basically related to their ritual qualities; to their ability to focus the attention of social groups. Collins (2004) has used the work of Durkheim and others to analyse the ways in which rituals work in modern societies, and how they can provide the motivation for people to engage in a wide range of different activities. Collins argues that for rituals to be successful, they need to be able to generate 'ritual entrainment', which has four essential elements:

1   Two or more people in co-presence: bodily assembled and, through neuro-logical feedback loops, able to charge up a situation with excitement and significance.
2   A boundary that demarcates insiders from outsiders, lending participants a privileged sense of inclusiveness.
3   All parties to the encounter have a common focus of attention.
4   Participants share 'a common mood or emotional experience'.

When the ritual is performed successfully, this in turn produces a number of outcomes:

1   Individuals feel solidarity with one another; they imagine themselves to be members of a common undertaking.
2   They are infused with 'emotional energy' (EE), a feeling of exhilaration, achievement and enthusiasm which induces initiative.
3   Ritual membership generates collective symbols that are defended and reinforced.
4   Violations of these symbols provoke righteous indignation towards, and sanctions against, those guilty of transgression.

Collins also argues that participation of individuals in successful rituals stimulates them to repeat the experience, entering into successive new rituals in what he terms an 'Interaction Ritual Chain'.

It can be argued that Collins' model of Interaction Ritual Chains (IRC) can be effectively transferred to the field of ritual or event design. Successful event design will entail the principle elements prescribed in the IRC model (co-presence, shared focus, boundaries and shared mood), and this in turn should produce increased emotional energy, stimulating people to become involved in another ritual or event. For example many festival visitors return year after year to the same event, and they gain a particularly high level of emotional energy from being 'insiders' at the event and feeling that they are situated at the centre of the ritual. This also mirrors the model of event space developed by Quinn and Wilks (2013), which suggests that some actors in the event are more central than others in the event space, and therefore gain greater benefits from the ritual.

Re-framing event design and imagineering in these essentially social terms has some important implications for the design of events. In particular, the fact that events imply co-presence with other people emphasizes the role of trust in the design of events. Events can only take place where trust in others exists, or where it can be created and maintained. Events often constitute important 'trusting spaces' in which the normal boundaries of everyday life are transformed, and new possibilities emerge (Richards and Palmer 2010). This is particularly important in the contemporary 'network society' (Castells 2009) that is characterized by increasing physical distance between individuals connected by networks. Events represent important temporal nodes in the network society that provide moments of co-presence in a society increasingly challenged by unsynchronized individual agendas.

The design or imagineering of events can therefore potentially achieve more than satisfying customers or producing 'meaningful experiences' for users. The argument made here is that events, and therefore event design are essentially social processes that contain the potential for change. To realize their full potential, event designers also need to be fully aware of social context and be able to develop engaging narratives to link event content to that context.

The following section briefly examines some of the implications of a 'ritual design approach' through case studies of two events: the *Festes de Gràcia* in Barcelona and the Hieronymus Bosch 500 celebrations in Den Bosch in the Netherlands.

Festes de Gràcia, Barcelona

The Festes de Gràcia is essentially a locally based festival which has mush-roomed into an annual ritual for the entire population of Barcelona, and increas-ingly for visitors as well. Held each year in mid-August, it consists of a series of decorated streets in the neighbourhood of Gràcia, close to the centre of Barcelona.

Pablo (1998: 33–38) argues that:

> we invent tradition every day [...] only about 15 per cent of the festivals are more than 25 years old. In Gràcia and Sants over 70 per cent are less than 15 years old. For Barcelona as a whole, 53.6 per cent of festivals are less than 15 years old. Even so, many of these *festas* are based on traditional ele-ments, which points to the reinvention of old traditions rather than the cre-ation of new ones.

The event has been held annually since the mid 1800s, and has changed relat-ively little in its basic concept (or content), but significantly in its context and design. For example, there is a constant flux in the specific streets taking part in the event, as some groups of neighbours wax and wane in their enthusiasm for the event. New groups of people also bring new ideas about design and new themes emerge which are then 'borrowed' by others streets and embroidered upon.

The decoration of the streets essentially turns the neighbourhood inside out; local people live their lives outside and receive around two million visits from people who come to look at their creative decorations and celebrate with them. Even though the street is effectively transformed into an open-air living room through which people constantly pass, there are markers and boundaries setting off specific spaces for the locals. Tables and chairs are set out to provide social spaces for insiders, and people are respectfully asked not to touch the decora-tions (often an impossible feat in the crush of a late night music performance). The barrier to outsiders is maintained (however precariously) through defence of the collective symbols (the decorations). People who damage decorations are the subject of anger and disapproval. Often, the concept of 'outsiders' is not related to spatial distance, as Richards (2007: 243) notes that 'residents of one decorated street complained about interference from "outsiders". These outsiders were not foreign tourists, or even people from other parts of Barcelona, but rather people from the next street.'

This opening up of the street immediately transforms the 'normal' spheres of public and private, and turns the resident into performer and host. Status is negotiated through creativity, through the quality of the decorations. This creativity, today based on recycled materials, is framed by the everyday, a supreme example of relational aesthetics (Bourriaud 2002). The creative hierarchy is maintained by a contest held among the streets to see who is crowned with the accolade of best decorated street. The competition is one of the elements that help to sustain the ritual all year long, as locals collect and work on the material needed for the decorations and think about their designs.

The physical layout of the festival itself, squeezed into narrow streets made even narrower by the bars and impromptu dining spaces that spring up, adds to the atmosphere. As Bachelard argues, the role of space is to contain compressed time (quoted in Mandanipour 2003: 74). The creation of bounded space therefore also creates a container for compressed time, which is also one of the main features of the event. The concentration of time produces excitement, flow, and the concentration of space (clustering, crowding, co-presence) provides the social aspect of shared experience, excitement and communion, as suggested by Collins.

So the *Festa* has all the elements of Collins' IRC: co-presence, shared focus, boundaries and shared mood. The resulting emotional energy stimulates investment of time and resources in the decorations rather than any financial incentive. For example, the amount of work invested in the decorations varies enormously between the different streets, but there is a direct relationship between hours invested and the number of prizes won by each street (Richards and Palmer 2010). The prizes are not monetary, but rather expressed in terms of pride and joy in the recognition of the effort made.

This effect also underlines the important role of mutual attention in the ritual system. Local residents take a great deal of pride in displaying their creativity, and their investment in the decorations is reciprocated by the attention paid to the decorations by visitors. This effectively means that the apparently passive role of the spectators is actually an essential part of the whole creation of the event.

So in this local, 'traditional', organic event, the way in which the event is designed becomes important in ensuring positive outcomes for both residents and visitors. A large part of the work that goes into making the event is effectively submerged, hidden from view apart from a few short days in summer. The temporal and spatial boundaries of the event create a ritual space or a container for compressed time, heightening the shared focus of attention, the shared mood and ultimately delivering more emotional energy.

Hieronymus Bosch 500

The Hieronymous Bosch 500 celebrations (or Jeroen Bosch, to give him his Dutch name) have been created in honour of the 500th anniversary of the death of the famous painter in 2016. The creation of this event is mainly thanks to the fact that the city that gave the painter his name, the Dutch city of 's-Hertogenbosch or Den Bosch, has until recently ignored the most important figure in its history. The reason for this is simple – none of Bosch's paintings remain in the city. His work is now spread around the globe in museums in Bruges, Madrid, Vienna, New York, Los Angeles and other cities.

Recovering Bosch's legacy and linking him to the city has therefore been an important process of rediscovery, recovery and renovation. Importantly for the city, however, Bosch gives for the first time a common focus of attention for its inhabitants. In a 2008 survey 83 per cent of residents said they saw Bosch as a suitable figurehead for such an event (Marques 2013).

The idea was to design a series of 'new traditions' for the city around the theme of Bosch. The painter was seen not just as a historical figure, but also as a creative inspiration for contemporary culture. In order to develop the programme, a Project Bureau was established as an independent foundation, although it has strong links to the city council.

The first stage in the design process was to establish the outcomes that the city wanted to achieve through the event programme. In addition to the important economic impacts that were anticipated from a major exhibition of Bosch artworks, the organizers also wanted to make a contribution to identity building, social cohesion and creative capacity in the city. So a multifaceted programme was devised, including events aimed at tourists (the blockbuster Bosch exhibition in 2016), at local residents (collective activities in open spaces in the city) and at the creative sector (arts and new media events).

The design elements related to the IRC have been particularly evident in the events aimed at local residents. Specific events have been created in the Bosch 500 programme to bring local people together. For example a 'Bosch Dinner' was organized in the main square, featuring a cooking contest between teams from the different neighbourhoods of the city, and recreating the medieval banquet scenes reminiscent of paintings by Bosch and his contemporaries. Parts of this event are modelled on the Palio horse races in Sienna, as the system of neighbourhoods competing is replicated in the cooking contest. The teams wear coloured hats and aprons that also mirror the costumes of the riders in the Palio.

A Bosch Parade is held on the river circling the inner city, with weird and wonderful craft designed by local artists. This provides a spectacle that unites the residents with the river and makes people aware of the route it takes around the city centre (in many places underground). As with the Bosch Dinner it helps to create a shared mood and collective focus of attention for residents, as well as creating attention for the city itself.

One of the most important elements of the design of the programme has been the formation of a club of 'Bosch Cities' which do have artworks by Hieronymous Bosch, such as Madrid, Lisbon and Vienna. This network has provided the leverage for bringing some of his work to Den Bosch for the major exhibition in 2016. The other Bosch Cities have promised to lend these works in return for participation in a restoration and research project, and also the possibility of staging their own Bosch exhibition at a later date. This part of the project helps to support the emotional energy generated by the local events, because it also helps to focus attention on the city of Den Bosch as the centre of an important international network. All of this is designed to create a shared mood and the generation of emotional energy among residents and those who visit the city.

In comparison with the Festes de Gràcia, which are effectively self-organized by local residents, the Jeroen Bosch 500 celebrations are a top-down and highly designed attempt to generate value from the Bosch legacy. There is an emphasis on applying the creativity of Bosch in a modern context, developing the creative capacity of the city and making Bosch, and therefore the city, relevant to a range of contemporary audiences. Innovation is inherent in the development of new events such as the Bosch Dinner or the Bosch Parade, even though these new traditions are created by recycling or borrowing from old ones, such as the Palio.

The experience of Den Bosch suggests that ritual form is still very important in event design – in fact the whole emphasis is on creating new rituals for the city. The new events have a similar form that is repeated each year to emphasize the ritual content and to ensure that they become 'traditions' after a while. Even so, the main question might be whether traditions kick started by a major pulsar event will take hold rapidly among the local population, or whether they will be seen as largely external and peripheral by the majority of people. If these new traditions do not take hold fast enough, a feeling of deflation may occur among local residents, actually reducing rather than increasing the stock of emotional energy.

Discussion

The social, network-based view of events provides us with a different concept of how events can relate to the people who create the event and the places that host them. This approach goes beyond the narrow concept of service design as a production of events from a people-centred perspective: in the IRC people make the event, the event makes new people of them.

The case studies presented here illustrate the continuing value of a ritual focus in the study of events and event design. The IRC approach helps us to understand how events should be designed in order to increase the output of emotional energy, without which the event will not be sustainable in the long term. The rituals created help to ensure that all those involved will continue to invest resources in the maintenance of the event. But we also need to be aware of potential pitfalls as well. Because ritual structures are long-lasting, we are also presented with the problem of how to change rituals and adapt them to new circumstances. This is why the organic recreation or reinvention of ritual is so important in the case of the Festes de Gràcia, and why the injection of innovative ideas is so important in the creation of new pulsar events such as Jeroen Bosch 500.

Perhaps what needs to be considered at the end of the day, however, is the output of the design process – what are we trying to achieve in designing events? A traditional management approach might talk about designing for satisfaction, or to maximize impacts. However satisfaction-based approaches are very one-dimensional, and impact studies, as Evans and van Heur (2013) point out, are focused on what happens during and after the event, rather than before.

A design perspective, however, places a lot of focus on the front end of events. We can incorporate social issues into the way the event is designed in order to tackle them. Collins' IRC also make clear that there is an important link between events over time: each successive ritual or event has an important effect on what follows. The design of events therefore must not take place in a temporal or spatial vacuum, but must be intimately related to the content and context of the event. Events should help to move not just audiences but also other stakeholders from *chronos* into *kairos*, providing the potential for change. Event designers therefore need to consider what changes the event is trying to achieve. Is this simply a change in state of mind or emotion, or a longer term change in attitudes or even in actions? If we want these things to happen we can learn a lot from traditional events like the Festes de Gràcia, but also from modern rituals such as the Jeroen Bosch 500. Both are designed not just to achieve short-term change, but also long-term shifts, for example in terms of social cohesion. To achieve this, such events need to work actively with a wide range of stakeholders and make sure that the event is designed around them, and designed to change them. In this sense the ritual can move from the simple production of emotional energy into the harnessing of that energy to induce change. In doing so we can learn much from the way in which rituals have been designed over time so that we can re-invent them again.

References

Bakhtin, M. (1941) *Rabelais and his World*, Bloomington, IN: Indiana University Press.

Bourriaud, N. (2002) *Relational Aesthetics*, Dijon: Les presses du réel.

Castells, M. (2009) *Communication Power*, Oxford: Blackwell.

Collins, R. (2004) *Interaction Ritual Chains*, Princeton, NJ: Princeton University Press.

Csíkszentmihályi, M. (1990) *Flow: The Psychology of Optimal Experience*, New York: Harper & Row.

Evans, G. and van Heur, B. (2013) 'European capital of culture: emancipatory practices and euregional strategies: the case of Maastricht Via 2018', in G. Richards, M. de Brito and L. Wilks (eds) *Exploring the Social Impact of Events*, London: Routledge, pp. 73–83.

Greenwood, D. (1989) 'Culture by the pound: an anthropological perspective on tourism as cultural commoditization' in V. Smith (ed.) *Hosts and Guests: The Anthropology of Tourism*, Philadelphia, PA: University of Pennsylvania Press, pp. 171–186.

Hover, M. (2008) 'Imagine your event: imagineering for the event industry', in U. Wünsch (ed.) *Facets of Contemporary Event Management-Theory and Practice for Event Success*, Bad Honne: Verlag K.H. Bock, pp. 37–62.

Madanipour, A. (2003) *Public and Private Spaces of the City*, London: Routledge.

Marques, L. (2013) 'Constructing social landscape through events: the glocal project of 's-Hertogenbosch', in G. Richards, M. de Brito, L. Wilks (eds) *Exploring the Social Impacts of Events*, London: Routledge, pp. 84–94.

Nijs, D. and Peters, F. (2002) *Imagineering: Het creëren van belevingswerelden*, Amsterdam: Uitgeverij Boom.

Pablo, J. (1998) 'Arxiu festiu de Gràcia', in Forum Barcelona Tradició (ed.) *Festa I Ciutat – volum 1*, Collecio L'Agulla n. 24, 33–38.

Potts, J., Cunningham, S., Hartley, J. and Ormerod, P. (2008) 'Social network markets: a new definition of the creative industries', *Journal of Cultural Economics*, 32: 167–185.

Quinn, B. and Wilks, L. (2013) 'Festival connections: people, place and social capital', in G. Richards, M. de Brito and L. Wilks (eds) *Exploring the Social Impacts of Events*, London: Routledge, pp. 15–30.

Rennen, W. (2007) *Cityevents: Place Selling in a Media Age*, Amsterdam: Amsterdam University Press.

Richards, G. (2007) 'Culture and authenticity in a traditional event: the views of producers, residents and visitors in Barcelona', *Event Management*, 11(1/2): 33–44.

Richards, G. (2014) 'Evaluating the European capital of culture that never was: the case of Brabantstad 2018', *Journal of Policy Research in Tourism, Leisure and Events*. DOI:10.1080/19407963.2014.944189.

Richards, G. and Palmer, R. (2010) *Eventful Cities: Cultural Management and Urban Revitalisation*, London: Routledge.

Rojek, C. (2013) *Event Power: How Global Events Manage and Manipulate*, London: Sage.

Scott, A.J. (2010) 'Cultural economy and the creative field of the city', *Geografiska Annaler, Series B, Human Geography*, 92: 115–130.

Sewell, W.H. (1996) 'Historical events as transformations of structures: inventing revolution at the Bastille', *Theory and Society*, 25: 841–881.

Turner, V.W. (1969) *The Ritual Process*, London: Penguin.

Urry, J. (2002) 'Mobility and proximity', *Sociology*, 36: 255–274.

3 Service design methods in event design

Satu Miettinen, Anu Valtonen and Vesa Markuksela

This chapter explores how to engage service design and event design in fruitful dialogue. It introduces the service design approach and, second, it exemplifies the use of this approach through references to existing studies. Finally, it offers a case study conducted at Ranua Zoo. Ranua Zoo is an open air zoo situated in Finnish Lapland that specializes in Arctic wildlife (www.ranuazoo.com). It aims at creating a new service concept for families visiting the zoo during the Christmas season. The case contains many typical features of tourist attractions such as seasonality and attendance. Unmanageable weather conditions challenge the design and delivery of the service. Moreover, in this case, the core products, animals, pose a further challenge in the sense that their behaviour cannot be fully planned beforehand. The design of interactive encounters, which lies at the heart of both service and event design, is therefore particularly interesting. The chapter shows how a set of service design methods enables the zoo to create a series of small events to attract more visitors outside the main season. As an outcome, the research paper proposes service design methods that can be used in event design.

Introduction to service design

Service design is establishing itself as both a practice and an academic discourse (Miettinen and Valtonen 2012). Service design, as a multidisciplinary field, has adopted working traditions from several fields. A variety of methods and tools derive from ethnographic research, marketing, industrial design, business and management (Tassi 2009). In the service design process, prototyping most clearly represents an activity stemming from industrial design. However, the immaterial nature of services, for example their simultaneous production and consumption and their heterogeneous production quality (Vargo and Lusch 2004), has called for new ways to concretize and illustrate new service concepts (Winhall 2011).

At the heart of the service design approach lies the idea of interaction (Zeithaml *et al.* 2009). The interaction may take place at cultural, social and personal levels. It is typical to acknowledge the existence of several stakeholders in a service design process. The use of different design methods, design research, design thinking and different visualization techniques connects different stakeholder views during the service development process. The service design process has characteristics from both iterative design process goals (Gould and Lewis 1985) and the International Organization for Standardization (ISO) principles for human-centred design (ISO 9241-210 Standard 2010). In service design, there is an iterative cycle of design, test and measure, and redesign. The service design process uses generative, formative and predictive methods (Fulton Suri 2008). The idea of innovation is implicit, and it can use several methods for concretizing new offerings or innovations even in the same development process. The process of service design enables concretizing and understanding of the overview and the detail. The designer's role as a communicator and a facilitator of a process is evident. This is in line with the recent marketing notion that emphasizes the role of the marketer as a facilitator of consumer experiences (Firat and Nikhlesh 2006).

Design thinking is an essential part of service design. Lockwood (2010) defined design thinking as a human-centred innovation process that emphasizes observation, collaboration, fast learning, visualization of ideas, rapid concept prototyping and concurrent business analysis, which ultimately influences innovation and business strategy. Design thinking also involves consumers, designers and business people in an integrative process, which can be applied to products, services or even business design. Service design offers a tool to influence thinking, and service prototyping can also positively affect concepts and business strategy development. The service design process starts with exploratory or immersive research to generate opportunities for innovation in strategy, rather than starting by defining strategy (Holmlid and Evenson 2008).

Furthermore, Lockwood (2010) emphasized the role of visualization, hands-on experimentation and creating quick prototypes, which are sufficiently simplified to generate usable feedback as an integral part of design thinking. Prototyping can provide a basis for dialogue to take place. These same elements are the core of the service design process. Service prototyping has the same focus as the purpose of prototypes in the design process: to make the intangible become tangible using various ways of visualization. These include concept sketches, rough physical prototypes, stories, role playing, storyboards and any form of visualization.

Commonly, service designers employ methods that aim at empowering the user, and the users are invited to actively take part to the service design process. Co-design work is carried out on a regular basis, and new innovative methods are developed to allow inclusion, creativity and engagement (Prahalad and Ramaswamy 2004; Moisander and Valtonen 2006; Miettinen and Koivisto 2009; Miettinen 2011; Miettinen and Valtonen 2012; Miettinen *et al.* 2012).

Service design and events

Events play a significant role in tourist intensive areas like Lapland; therefore, their proper design is vital for the economic and cultural development of the area in question. Getz (2007) conceives events as spatial-temporal phenomena: they happen during certain times (e.g. a season), last a limited amount of time and are situated in a symbolic and geographical place. In elaborating on specific features of events, Getz stresses that each event is unique due to the dynamic and complex interactions taking place between the setting, people (customers and workers) and management systems of the event. The same applies to service design. A service is first designed and then consumed through service moments (interactions) and through the customer's journey across a spatial-temporal experiencescape.

Consuming a service means consuming an experience; it is a process that extends over time. The customer's journey illustrates how the customer perceives and experiences the service interface along the time axis. It also considers the phases before and after actual interaction with the service. The first step in creating a customer journey is to decide its starting and stopping points. The customer journey serves as the umbrella under which the service is explored and, with various methods, systematized and visualized. Further service moments are experiences through service touch points that are the tangible, for example, spaces, objects, people or interactions (Moritz 2005), and make up the total experience of using a service. Touch points can take many forms, from advertising to personal cards, web and mobile interfaces, bills, retail shops, call centres and customer representatives. In service design, all touch points need to be considered in totality and crafted in order to create a clear, consistent and unified customer experience.

Mapping out a customer journey means identifying the processes that constitute the service, isolating possible fail points and establishing the timeframe for the journey. Service blueprinting is a process analysis methodology proposed by Shostack (1982, 1984). Shostack's methodical procedure draws upon time and motion method engineering, project programming and computer system and software design. The proposed blueprint allows for a quantitative description of critical service elements, such as time, logical sequences of actions and processes, and it specifies both actions and events that happen in the time and place of the interaction (front office) and actions and events that are out of the line of visibility for the users but fundamental for the service. Service blueprinting involves the description of all the activities for designing and managing services, including schedule, project plans, detailed representations (such as use cases), design plans or service platforms (Morelli 2002).

To illustrate the way event design and service design may be linked, we offer an example of developing a pop music event called 'Iskelmäniityt' by using service design methods. The event was held in a small village in the Lakeside of Finland. The development project had three main objectives: (1) highlight the strengths and differentiate the event from other festivals by developing the customer experience, (2) develop the event to suit better the users' needs and (3) improve service functionality and usability. The work was mainly done by using service design methods. The main goal for using service design was to improve the usability of the event and to generate design outputs from the user's point of view. During the project, the event organizer and the users were involved with design work on the different methods. In the first phase, they acquired knowledge and understanding about the current level of service and its users by using a variety of participatory research methods (interviews, questionnaires, participatory observation, identifying a service journey). During the first phase, a rough diagram of the service journey was produced. This was one of the main methods that communicated the value of service design for the stakeholders. Throughout the process, more information about the event was accumulated and a more accurate description of the service journey was made. This made the service delivery areas visible for the users. The service journier visualized the touch points of the service journey. This was a very effective way to examine brand identity and how it was delivered throughout the touch points. The second step was to create three different user profiles based on the story of how the users experienced the event. The stories illustrate the pre-event phase experienced by the users (online engagement, travel to event site, etc.) and alternative services that take into account customer's needs and objectives. Finally, in a use case scenario, the user profiles are employed to illustrate the development of new service ideas and service offerings based on user needs (Pikkula 2010).

Looking at event design through a service design lens enables us to use innovative methods and apply the service design approach during the design process. Service design looks at the event design from the users' point of view. This point of view can be studied through applied ethnography, so we observe and engage the users in the design process in order to create a deep understanding about their needs before, during and after the event. We can also determine the appropriate service channels to meet these needs. Service design helps us to analyse and visualize the interactions and processes needed to deliver the service. Visualizations concretize otherwise abstract contents and thus make it easier to communicate the service offerings to the stakeholders involved in the development process.

Creating a multi-channel service experience for tourism

The key point of many events is to offer a platform for the co-creation of unique and memorable experiences. In this sense, events lie at the centre of the contemporary experience economy (Pine and Gilmore 1999). In the recent business and management discourse, the focus of value creation has shifted to experiences, and experiences are increasingly created through services. Consumers are co-creating value with the firm (Prahalad and Ramaswamy 2004; Vargo and Lusch 2004, 2006, 2008; Grönroos 2008). Co-creation allows a customer to co-construct the service experience to suit his or her context, and the service design process offers methods to enable this (Miettinen 2009). Service design plays a strategic role in the co-creation of value. This is realized by using not only different service design methods but also a wider approach that integrates service thinking, understanding the user in connection with service rationales and relations and constructing service propositions (Miettinen 2012). The concept of user experience in design includes the needs, emotions and experiences of users and the products that contribute to the experience. According to Battarbee (2006), research on and involving co-experience should happen in the real context of the users' lives. In this way, design researchers can develop an understanding of the experiences relevant to the users and further their interaction with the products and their meanings (Miettinen 2007). Service design connects different silos and touch points into a unified experience (Polaine 2012). This approach is used in experience design, which is an approach to create emotional connection with guests or customers through careful planning of tangible and intangible service elements (Pullman and Gross 2004).

A service design process can act as a framework that enables a designer to work in tourism service production. Miettinen (2007) discussed the creative tourism experience, the use of design tools and methods to reveal this creative tourism experience. Traditional and innovative research methods served to analyse the creative tourism experience and help to produce new knowledge on the process of service design. According to Miettinen (2007), multiple research methods are needed in service design work related to tourism.

Niittymaa (2011) discusses how the use of service design methods helped find new opportunities for event development. Service design tools can help the company to determine who their clients are and whether their service portfolio meets the needs of customers. Niittymaa (2011) examines the company's service production system through a service design approach. This helps in defining the factors that most affect the service experience of the users and the relationships and interactions between these factors. Since service design is strongly based on visual models, this can help to illustrate, model and concretize the existing services. Niittymaa examines customer stories and experiences by creating user profiles and customer journeys. Service design demands both customer and employee participation in the development project. Both parties' involvement in the event development is needed to ensure that their perspectives and expertise are taken into account. The guest wants to be sure that the event organizer takes his or her wishes into account. To make this happen, customers should be encouraged and motivated to participate actively in the event design process. Service design gives us tools to engage the customers in this process.

Stickdorn and Frischhut (2012) discuss how service design tools are in use in more recent tourism research and development. Their publication focuses on the results of a research project where service design thinking was successfully applied to the tourism industry and particularly to prototype tourism-specific research methods, such as mobile ethnography. Kim and Miettinen (2012) introduce a new service proposal for authentic tourist experience, emphasizing the role of service design as a strategic tool both in tourist engagement and in creative tourism development as it relates to libraries.

Patrício *et al.* (2008) discuss how technology has revolutionized the way services are delivered. This is present in almost every aspect of service provision. Service offerings have evolved multi-interface systems where technology plays a central role both in frontstage interactions and in backstage support processes. Customer experiences are the result of all the moments of contact with the firm, using different service channels (people to people, digital, mobile, etc.). Services are complex. They are delivered by people, smart products and online services. Events are also an experience of these same overlapping service channels that together create the overall service experience.

Service design is a new competence area that helps in managing and developing multi-channel service experiences. The notion and contents of experience design are present in a service design process. The users and stakeholders participate in the service prototyping activity where service propositions are experienced, evaluated and developed further. The service design and service prototyping competencies are manifested through a multidisciplinary and facilitated working approach that can be applied in various fields. Furthermore, these competencies include a vast knowledge in different areas of design, such as strategic design, experience design, industrial design and interaction design. However, the most important ability is empathy connected with innovative and a solution-oriented approach.

Service design and prototyping are approaches and competences used to manage the design process of multi-channel service experiences. The prototyping approach gives us tools to concretize service offerings that are delivered through different channels and smart devices. Furthermore, prototyping gives us the means to look at how the service experience forms through the customer journey and different touch points.

Ranua Zoo case

Ranua Zoo is a wildlife park and one of the leading tourist attractions in Finnish Lapland. A service design project was conducted with the company, the aim of which was to create a new fascinating service concept for visiting tourist families during the Christmas season. The main goal of the service development project was to create a fantasy-driven storyline for the British tourists visiting Ranua Zoo during this season. As the zoo is an outdoor attraction, the weather plays a role in the way it is experienced and designed. The Christmas season represents the dark period when the presence or the absence of snow and the cold change the experience (Valtonen *et al.* 2010; Rantala *et al.* 2011).

During the first phase of the project, a service design team visited Ranua Zoo, interviewed employees and took the tour around the wildlife park with other visitors. They experienced the service environment themselves and also took notes of other people's actions during the tour. Empirical material was gathered for idea generation in the form of videos, photos and notes. Ranua Zoo representatives also gathered ideas in a workshop before the project, which they shared with the service design team to aid the generation of ideas (Miettinen *et al.* 2012).

After the visit, the team started to generate ideas for the new service and built an experience prototype for testing and evaluating. The idea of combining storytelling with this challenging environment to create a fairytale-like experience was recognized as a new kind of service opportunity for this otherwise strongly traditional service. Not only was the customer journey in the wildlife park defined, so were interactions between customers and 'the story' before and after visiting Ranua Zoo. For instance, the phases taking place in customers' homes before taking the trip to Finland were connected to the storyline through related marketing material and web content. The visitors browse the Internet for information about the site. During the development process, the versions of the experience prototype served as a platform for developing the concept, but they also served as a communication tool between the service design team, subcontractors and other stakeholders who played a crucial part in producing the new service concept. This also helped Ranua Zoo management to understand the benefits of design thinking and prototyping in creating new service concepts.

The storyboarding method can facilitate the product and service design processes. Storyboards can illustrate a visual storyline of a service or product use situation in its context(s) for users and clients. They can also help to illustrate customer interface interactions for the design team or users. The process of creating a storyboard helps designers put themselves in the shoes of the people for whom they are designing. It often prompts invention and ingenuity, as problems that end-users encounter are recognized and opportunities to solve them are devised. The story can serve as a 'user experience test bed' as prototypes are developed and critiqued. For example, take a proposed design for the system and run through the story imagining the protagonist using it. Does the system solve the problems the protagonist encounters? Does it 'fit in' with the story and the protagonist's environment? Does the solution provide the intended value to the people in the story? What changes to the system should be made so it does (Gruen 2000)?

Storyboards are sequences of images, which demonstrate the relationship between individual displays and actions within a system. A typical storyboard contains a number of images depicting features such as menus, dialogue boxes and windows. A sequence of these screen representations conveys further information about the structure, functionality and navigation options available within an intended system. The storyboard can be shown to colleagues in a design team and to potential users. This allows users and design team members to offer critical feedback about the composition and scope of the intended interface. Storyboarding can be used early in the design cycle. In this case, it supports the exploration of design possibilities and the early verification of user requirements (Landay and Myers 1996; Heinilä *et al.* 2005).

An experience prototype is a representation of a design made before the final solution exists. We need prototyping for electronics. We need to think about a total experience like designing a service or designing what happens with the digital chips and what they can enable for people. Then we need storytelling. We need to use video to tell a story, theatre for the enactment of a story or a computer for simulations. All of those become a necessary part of our prototyping vocabulary. The rapidness of a prototype cycle between trying something out and testing it with people is what makes the relationship between design and business successful. We can make a small prototype very inexpensively, we can try it out and, if it's successful, perhaps we'll move to the next stage. The aim of experience prototyping is to test the feasibility of the service, the logistics, customer experience and financial impact of the service product in a cheap and quick way. An experience prototype can be any kind of representation in any kind of medium that is designed to understand, explore or communicate what it might be like to engage with the product, space or system we are designing (Buchenau and Fulton Suri 2000).

The finalized experience prototype of the service concept was presented to Ranua Zoo representatives. After their positive feedback and approval, the concept was further developed. The service stage also had a role in prototyping different design concepts for the restaurant environment in Ranua Zoo. The service design team used techniques like digital image projection on table surfaces and servicescape images that were modified to match different settings. This gave a more concrete way to evaluate different options before proceeding to build physical prototypes of the elements for the service concept (Miettinen *et al.* 2012).

As an outcome of the service design process a story about 'saving Christmas' was developed, starting in the British travel agency and following the customer journey to Ranua Zoo. At the zoo exciting tasks linked to the animals had to be completed. The story ended at a dinner with Santa Claus. The service journey was experience prototyped with the management of the Ranua Zoo. They proceeded into more detailed design of the service touchpoints. All the graphic design elements related to the service journey, interior design elements related to dining with Santa Claus and costumes for the zoo guides were also designed.

Service design methods used in event design

The service stage is the place dedicated to acting out scenarios and experiencing the servicescape simulation. The stage itself has a strong analogy to a theatre stage, which facilitates acting. Acting the service moments throughout the service journey enables you to empathize with different situations, user roles and simulate different behaviours in the service moments. Role-playing has been recognized as a powerful method for observing and discovering aspects and elements in the service prototype (Buchenau and Fulton Suri 2000). We found a service stage with role accessories and prop building blocks to be an encouraging area even for people with no prior experience of role-playing.

Servicescape simulation with images and sounds can effectively simulate the user's situation at hand. The service stage allows the supplementing of the virtual content (for example images from the Google streetview, photographs or sounds from the service environment) with concrete spatial elements (for example prototypes for furniture, user interfaces of machines) and interactions needed for prototyping the service. The use of virtual and tangible elements enables the experimentation that helps to develop and define both the service moments and the service journey further. Servicescape simulation works as a development and learning environment for the service. Rough and unfinished tangible mock-up elements support the idea of the service stage as an informal place where wild ideas can be played out and incomplete experimentation is encouraged. This is important, especially in the early phases of the design process.

The service prototype made it possible for the service design team to generate ideas and test them out by themselves, thus developing the ideas through iterative phases. Without any worries of disturbing existing business processes, the students were able to test even wilder ideas. The first prototype was a quickly made, rough representation of the service environment, but the iterative cycles better specified the needs for changes, and so the physical fidelity of the prototype was increased during the process. The prototyping-based service design process also helped the client company to shift from a product-oriented idea to thinking about opportunities from the holistic experience (Miettinen *et al.* 2012).

In this case, we found service prototyping to be a useful activity for developing, evaluating and communicating ideas and emerging service concepts. It helps to concretize immaterial ideas and facilitates both user-centric thinking and out of box idea generation in participating stakeholders, including the design team, company staff, their subcontractors and end-users. A customer journey walkthrough augmented with servicescape simulation can also help the entrepreneur to see the undesirability of the status quo when it comes to the customer experience. Our research and development work considers how service prototyping can add value at various stages in the service design process to elicit customer insight and help communicate and evaluate new service concepts.

The case also opens up a platform to further develop the methods for designing events that take place outdoors and in nature. The development of such a wilderness servicescape (Markuksela 2013) calls for a set of methods that help to capture the way all the senses – touch, sight, audio, scents, taste – play a role in the creation of experiences.

Conclusion

Design is becoming a more important part of strategic and multidisciplinary innovation activities. This implies a broader role for designers because they can build bridges between different disciplines and transform knowledge into solutions. Service design is a new competence area that helps in managing and developing multi-channel service experiences. The notion and contents of event design are present in a service design process. The users and stakeholders participate in the service prototyping activity where service propositions are experienced, evaluated and developed further. The service design and service prototyping competencies are manifested and facilitated through a multidisciplinary, working approach that can be applied in various fields. Furthermore, these competencies include a vast knowledge of different areas of design, such as strategic design, experience design, industrial design and interaction design. However, the most important ability is empathy connected with an innovative and solution-oriented approach (Miettinen and Kuure 2013).

At Ranua Zoo the use of service design and experience prototyping was only a start. Ranua Zoo has been continuing to use service design methods as one of its development tools for event design. During 2013 Ranua Zoo was developing and implementing a design route called 'the Sparks of a Firefox' from the zoo towards the centre of Ranua. Ranua Zoo will utilize service design and design methods in this project.

Acknowledgement

The Ranua Zoo service design case was part of Service Innovation Corner research project realized at SINCO lab (www.sinco.fi) by research and service design team members Simo Rontti, Essi Kuure and Antti Lindström.

References

Battarbee, K. (2006) 'Co-experience: Understanding User Experiences in Social Interaction', 2nd edn, Academic Dissertation, Helsinki: University of Art and Design Helsinki A51.

Buchenau, M. and Fulton Suri, J. (2000) 'Experience Prototyping', San Francisco, CA: IDEO. Online, available at: www.ideo.com/images/uploads/thinking/publications/pdfs/FultonSuriBuchenau-Experience_Prototyping ACM_8-00.pdf (accessed 20 April 2009).

Firat, A.F. and Nikhlesh, D. (2006) 'Theoretical and Philosophical Implications of Post-modern Debates: Some Challenges to Modern Marketing', *Marketing Theory*, 6(2): 123–162.

Fulton Suri, J. (2008) 'Informing our Intuition, Design Research for Radical Innovation', *Rotman Magazine*, Winter: 53–55.

Getz, D. (2007) 'Event Tourism: Definition, Evolution, and Research', *Tourism Management*, 29: 403–428.

Gould, J.D. and Lewis, C. (1985) 'Designing for Usability: Key Principles and What Designers Think', *Communications of the ACM*, 28(3): 300–311.

Grönroos, C. (2008) 'Service Logic Revisited: Who Creates Value? And Who Co-creates?' *European Business Review*, 20(4): 298–314.

Gruen, D. (2000) 'Storyboarding for Design: An Overview of the Process', Lotus Research; IBM Research. Online, available at: http://domino.watson.ibm.com/cam-bridge/research.nsf/0/ebcd159a81a43e36852569200067d59e/$FILE/Techreport%20 2000.03.PDF (accessed 3 May 2009).

Heinilä, J. (ed.), Strömberg, H., Leikas, J., Ikonen, V., Iivari, N., Jokela, T., Aikio, K. P., Jounila, I., Hoonhout, J. and Leurs, N. (2005) 'User Centred Design Guidelines for Methods and Tools', VTT Information Technology; University of Oulu, Dept. of Information Processing Science; Philips Research, Philips Applied Technologies; Nomadic Media Consortium, November 2005. Online, available at: www.vtt.fi/inf/julkaisut/muut/2005/UCD_Guidelines.pdf (accessed 3 May 2009).

Holmlid, S. and Evenson, S. (2008) 'Bringing Service Design to Service Sciences, Management and Engineering', in B. Hefley and W. Murphy (eds) *Service Science, Management and Engineering: Education for the 21st Century*, Berlin-Heidelberg: Springer Verlag, pp. 341–345.

ISO 9241-210 Standard (2010) International Standard 'Ergonomics of Human–System Interaction, Part 210: Human-Centred Design for Interactive Systems'. First Version 2010-03-15. Reference number: ISO 9241-210:2010 (E).

Kim, S. and Miettinen, S. (2012) 'Helsinki Central Library as a Gateway to the City', *Touchpoint*, 4(1): 54–57.

Landay, J.A. and Myers, J.A. (1996) 'Sketching Storyboards to Illustrate Interface Behaviors', HCI Institute, School of Computer Science, Carnegie Mellon University. Online, available at: www.cs.cmu.edu/afs/cs.cmu.edu/user/landay/pub/www/research/publications/CHI96/short_storyboard.Ps (accessed 3 May 2009).

Lockwood, T. (ed.) (2010) *Design Thinking: Integrating Innovation, Customer Experience, and Brand Value*, New York: Allworth Press.

Markuksela, V. (2013) *Aisti kuin kala: Etnografia vetouistelun veljeskunnan kalastuskäytännöstä*. *Väitöskirja*, Rovaniemi: Lapin Yliopiston paino.

Miettinen, S. (2007) *Designing a Creative Tourism Experience*, Helsinki: University of Art and Design Helsinki, A 81.

Miettinen, S. (2009) 'Designing Services with Innovative Methods', in S. Miettinen and M. Koivisto (eds) *Designing Services with Innovative Methods*, Helsinki: University of Art and Design Helsinki, B 93. Kuopio Academy of Design. Taitemia Publication Series 33, Otava Keuruu, pp. 10–25.

Miettinen, S. (2011) 'Service Prototyping in Action!' *Touchpoint*, 3(2): 64–67.

Miettinen, S. (2012) 'Discussions on Change, Value and Methods', in S. Miettinen and A. Valtonen (eds) *Service Design with Theory: Discussions on Change, Value and Methods*, Rovaniemi: Lapland University Press, pp. 5–12.

Miettinen, S. and Koivisto, M. (eds) (2009) *Designing Services with Innovative Methods*, Helsinki: University of Art and Design Helsinki, B 93. Kuopio Academy of Design. Taitemia Publication Series 33, Otava Keuruu.

Miettinen, S. and Kuure, E. (2013) 'Designing a Multi-Channel Service Experience', *Design Management Review*, 24(3): 30–37.

Miettinen, S. and Valtonen, A. (eds) (2012) *Service Design with Theory: Discussion on Value, Societal Change and Methods*, Rovaniemi: Lapland University Press.

Miettinen, S., Rontti, S., Kuure, E. and Lindström, A. (2012) 'Realizing Design Thinking Through a Service Design Process and an Innovative Prototyping Laboratory: Introducing Service Innovation Corner (SINCO)', DRS 2012 Bangkok. Online, available at: http://drs2012bangkok.org (accessed 3 May 2009).

Moisander, J. and Valtonen, A. (2006) *Qualitative Marketing Research: A Cultural Approach*, London: Sage.

Morelli, N. (2002) 'Designing Product/Service Systems: A Methodological Exploration', *Design Issues*, 18(3): 3–17.

Moritz, S. (2005) *Service Design: Practical Access to an Evolving Field*, Cologne: Köln International School of Design.

Niittymaa, N. (2011) 'Tapahtuman suunnitteluprosessin kehittäminen palvelumuotoilua hyödyntäen: Laurea ammattikorkeakoulu.Hotelli- ja ravintola-alan Liikkeenjohdon koulutusohjelma Opinnäytetyö'. Online, available at: http://publications.theseus.fi/handle/10024/34143 (accessed 4 May 2013).

Patrício, L., Fisk, R. and Falcão e Cunha, J. (2008) 'Designing Multi-Interface Service Experiences: The Service Experience Blueprint', *Journal of Service Research*, 10(4): 318–334.

Pikkula, E. (2010) 'Iskelmäniityt – Tapahtuman kehittäminen palvelumuotoilun menetelmin: In Hyvinvointia edistävät käyttöliittymät- ja palvelualustat matkailussa ja vapaa-ajassa. Loppuraportti', in S. Miettinen (ed.) *Savonia Ammattikorkeakoulu*, Kuopion Muotoiluakatemia, Taitemia 34, ISSN 1238-4666.

Pine, J. and Gilmore, J. (1999) *The Experience Economy*, Boston, MA: Harvard Business School Press.

Polaine, A. (2012) 'Play, Interactivity and Service Design: Towards a Unified Design Language', in S. Miettinen and A. Valtonen (eds) *Service Design with Theory: Discussion on Value, Societal Change and Methods*, Rovaniemi: Lapland University Press, pp. 159–168.

Prahalad, C.K. and Ramaswamy, V. (2004) 'Co-Creating Unique Value with Customers', *Strategy and Leadership*, 32(3): 4–9.

Pullman, M. and Gross, M. (2004) 'Ability of Experience Design Elements to Elicit Emotions and Loyalty Behaviors', *Decision Science*, 35(3): 551–578.

Rantala, O., Valtonen, A. and Vesa, M. (2011) 'Materialising Tourist Weather: Weather-Wise Tourist Guide Practices', *Journal of Material Culture*, 16(3): 285–300.

Shostack, G.L. (1982) 'How to Design a Service', *European Journal of Marketing*, 16(1): 49–63.

Shostack, G.L. (1984) 'Designing Services that Deliver', *Harvard Business Review*, January/February, 133–139.

Stickdorn, M. and Frischhut, B. (eds) (2012) *Service Design and Tourism: Case Studies of Applied Research Projects on Mobile Ethnography for Tourism Destinations*, Norderstedt, Germany: Books on Demand GmbH.

Tassi, R. (2009) 'Service Design Tools: Tools Provenance Map'. Online, available at: www.servicedesigntools.org/sites/default/files/TOOLS_PROVENANCE.jpg (accessed 20 September 2011).

Valtonen, A., Markuksela, V. and Moisander, J. (2010) 'Doing Sensory Ethnography in Consumer Research', *International Journal of Consumer Studies*, 34(4): 375–380.

Valtonen, A., Miettinen, S. and Kuure, E. (2012) 'Sleep-Centric Service Design', *Touchpoint*, 4(4): 36–39.

Vargo, S.L. and Lusch, R.F. (2004) 'The Four Services Marketing Myths: Remnants from a Manufacturing Model', *Journal of Service Research*, 6(4): 324–335.

Vargo, S.L. and Lusch, R.F. (eds) (2006) *The Service-Dominant Logic of Marketing: Dialog, Debate and Directions*, Armonk, NY: M.E. Sharpe Inc.

Vargo, S.L. and Lusch, R.F. (2008) 'Why "Service"?' *Journal of the Academy of Marketing Science*, 36: 25–38.

Winhall, J. (2011) 'Case Study 11 Designing the Next Generation of Public Services', in A. Meroni and D. Sangiorgi (eds) *Design for Services*, London: Gower Publications, pp. 131–138.

Zeithaml, V.A., Bitner, M.J. and Gremler, D.D. (2009) *Services Marketing, Integrating Customer Focus across the Firm*, New York: McGraw-Hill/Irwin.

4 The role of imagineering as an event design strategy in the business event industry

Frank Ouwens

Introduction

The business event industry is facing challenging times. Due to the sustained economic crisis, not only the number of events but also revenues have dropped strongly over the last few years (NIDAP 2012). Major companies in the business events field have disappeared and event agencies are reviewing their portfolio and positioning. Moreover, the playing field of the event industry is evolving. Clients find themselves in an ever-changing business context: transparency, customer involvement and value-based entrepreneurship become crucial characteristics for the modern organization. Questions arise relating to the efficiency and effectiveness of events and their position within the marketing communication mix. The need for renewal in the business event industry becomes evident, both in terms of the (experience) communication mix, as well as the added value of events in the current competitive climate.

This chapter seeks to map the current landscape of the business event industry in the Netherlands and asks whether imagineering approaches can provide adequate responses to the changes taking place. In particular, the relevance of imagineering as an event design strategy within this business events sector is examined.

The first section of the chapter gives a theoretical overview of imagineering, and explores its relationship to closely related theoretical fields. The second section analyses the potential role of imagineering played as an event design strategy within the business events industry.

The origins of imagineering

Imagineering as a methodology has been subject to various interpretations over the years. The term was first applied by the Alcoa Corporation after the Second World War, who, in referring to imagineering, focused on using the imaginative mind in creating new business opportunities. Later, Walt Disney introduced the term to the world stage, by referring to imagineering in relation to the internal development process in the creation of Disney theme parks. For the few next decades, Disney's interpretation of the imagineering process, and its focus on *experiences* dominated and shaped its very meaning. Imagineering would become an experience-orientated process, used predominantly in the leisure industry, and over the years it filtered into other areas of the economic landscape.

As early as 1970, futurist Alvin Toffler predicted an ever-increasing need for intangible, emotional experiences. Being an experience-orientated process using the imaginative mind, imagineering quickly attracted interest from actors outside the leisure industry.

It was not so much imagineering's value-creation power (as utilized by Alcoa), but its focus on meaningful experiences that gained interest. It was, however, not until the 1990s that authors such as Schulze (1992), Pine and Gilmore (1999) and Wolf (1999), described this focus on experiences and entertainment in more general terms. They saw experiences as *the* desired consumption value for customers, providing an alternative to the prevailing business focus on products fulfilling consumer's needs.

This essential issue is acknowledged by Kuiper and Smit (2011), who claim that imagineering could be used for strategic innovation and for solving management problems. They emphasized not just the experience building capabilities of imagineering, or its creative 'out of the box' approach, but also the potential of imagineering as an overall business strategy. They argue that imagineering, applied in a strategic context, could be much more than simple experience design.

The evolution of imagineering

The redefinition of imagineering led to a renewed interest in the concept. In 2002, for example, Nijs and Peters redefined imagineering as an 'integral approach for the design of experiences'. They argued that the term that was until then often referred to in the context of Disney, needed to be redefined in a European context. In a European setting, they argued, experiences and imagineering are more closely related to *values* and *meaning* instead of the design of the (physical) experience, which could be argued to be the basis of Disney's interpretation. For Nijs and Peters, 'intangibles' such as consumer values became central to the imagineering process, instead of the actual physical design of experiences.

In this approach, imagineering takes the values of people as a starting point in order to create sustainable relationships with individuals and organizations (NHTV 2011). Meaning plays a central role in this process and through the use of an imaginative narrative or concept, it aims to inspire, include and direct people in a desired direction. In this context imagineering goes beyond sheer experience design and is closely related to corporate social responsibility (CSR), social design and innovation as well as organizational transformation. In other words, imagineering became a much wider term for all kinds of processes.

Kuiper and Smit (2011) argue that this 'wide' interpretation of imagineering could be used for different processes, levels and goals. According to them, imagineering can be applied in organizations at three different levels:

1   Strategy level. Imagineering is used 'in order to load, build and sustain a brand and its social function by offering an experience world which generates cohesion with groups of people'. Imagineering as a strategic driver for organizational innovation.

2   Process level. Imagineering is 'based on the use of multiple disciplines, talents and techniques and using their combined imaginative power to find an innovative solution'. Imagineering as a co-creative and imaginative process for existing challenges.

3   Instrument level. Imagineering is 'using the capacities of both the left and right side of the brain, so ratio and analysis combined with imagination, empathy and creativity in order to achieve synergy'. Imagineering as a creative tool for practical solution seeking.

Imagineering and marketing

Over the years, imagineering has also become more closely related to marketing. In common with imagineering, the concept of 'Experiential Marketing' (Schmitt 1999) also adopted customer experiences as its focus. The American Marketing Association (2007) even changed its definition of marketing in 2004 from an 'exchange' orientation to an orientation on 'value creation', focusing not only on customers but on clients, partners and society at large. Marketing guru Philip Kotler has meanwhile also acknowledged (Kartajaya *et al.* 2010) that values and idealism are key decisive elements in the consumer decision process.

This development is recognizable in many other publications and many contemporary authors address this changed business focus. David H. Pink (2006) introduces the concepts of High Touch and High Concept, which are closely related to the imaginative value-creation process and focus on people's values within imagineering:

High Concept involves the capacity to detect patterns and opportunities, to create artistic and emotional beauty, to craft a satisfying narrative, and to combine seemingly unrelated ideas into something new. High Touch involves the ability to empathize with others, to understand the subtleties of human interaction, to find joy in one's self and to elicit it to others, and to stretch beyond the quotidian in pursuit of purpose and meaning.

(Pink 2006: 2–3)

Other authors also emphasize the need for a new focus on people and values. Sinek (2009) describes the 'Golden Circle', which focuses not so much on the *what* a company does, or *how* they do it, but much more on *why* they do it. For him this core question of *why* explains how some people and organizations are more inventive, pioneering and successful than others and why they are able to repeat their success again and again. In addition Marc Gobé (2010) acknowledged the focus for brands should be on people instead of products. In latest edition of his book *Emotional Branding* he argues for a value and emotional driven approach, which is comparable to the imagineering process.

Imagineering: towards a definition

Imagineering is clearly overlapping with marketing more and more and is now becoming a business philosophy for many organizations. However, as more uses have been found for imagineering, different interpretations of the concept have also emerged.

For example, Kuiper and Smit (2011: 20) define imagineering as 'the strategic use of innovation and experiences for solving management issues. Imagineers develop instruments for suppliers to connect users (subjects) on an emotional, rational and social level aimed at creating a lasting effect and the mutual communication as such.' For them, imagineering is characterized by its application in multidisciplinary teams, combining various professional fields and stimulating innovation.

From a more practice-based perspective, Tinker Imagineers, an agency based in Utrecht (NL) define imagineering as 'The art to speak to the imagination' (Tinker Imagineers 2014). For them, not only the creative and imaginative part is crucial in this process, but very much so the *effective realization* of these ideas. After all, ideas only become successful if implemented in the right way.

The way in which experience concepts are co-created by producers and consumers is another important theme in imagineering. As Crowther and Orefice explain in Chapter 10, imagineering event experiences require consideration of the views of different stakeholder groups, and the facilitation of co-creation between them.

Having reviewed the history, evolution and current interpretations of imagineering, several findings are striking. Although different definitions exist, there are various key terms that appear, including imagination, experiences and co-creation. Therefore in the context of this chapter, we will define imagineering as the value-driven, co-creative and imaginative value creation process aimed at creating meaningful experiences, solutions and processes for stakeholders on an operational, tactical and strategic level.

Now that we have established a clear interpretation of imagineering, it is important to determine the status of contemporary event design and its connection to imagineering.

Event design

Design can be interpreted in many ways (see also Chapter 2). It is mostly referred to the planning of visual and physical objects, where the design process includes conceptualizing, directing as well as realizing new ideas. These are mostly related to the physical and tangible aspects of events.

However, (social) processes and (intangible) services can also be designed and planned. This is also referred to as service design, and this is closely related to event design (see Chapter 3). But how does service design differ from event design? According to Stickdorn and Schneider (2011), there are five core characteristics that define service design, which is user-centred, co-creative, sequencing (a sequence of interrelated actions), evidencing (visualizing intangible services through physical artefacts) and holistic.

Reviewing event design one could argue that sequencing and evidencing characteristics are especially recognizable in most event design theories, whereas its holistic approach, focus on the customer and co-creative methodology seem to be more related to imagineering. Does this mean event design and imagineering represent two different approaches?

Reviewing event design, one could argue that until recently most literature focused on the perspective of the *producer* and their *outputs* as the key elements in event design. Authors such as Watt (1998), Grit and Gerritsma (2008), Kaarsgaren (2010) and organizations such as the VVEM (2004) take this perspective as the starting point of event design. A design, from this perspective, is based on the key phases of project management such as initialization, preparation, execution and evaluation, and event design can be applied to key event areas such as communication, facilities, funding, planning, staffing and programming. Altogether a (producer knows best) traditional and output driven approach, based on fixed phases and components.

However, in recent years, new event design philosophies have emerged. Rippen and Bos (2010) for instance introduced the '5 Wheel Drive' concept. This event design model recognizes the existence of two 'realities' in the event design process: a 'first' reality, focusing on the producer's reality during which he/she creates the event. In addition, however, they mention a 'second' reality, referring to the intended temporary event experience of the visitors. This model not only distinguishes the producers' perspective, but recognizes the visitor and his or her experience as a crucial part of event design.

More and more authors include the visitor's perspective in event design models. Event design, at least as a corporate marketing communication tool, has evolved from being a solitary discipline to become an integrated part of the communication strategy of brand and organizations alike, which increasingly include the visitor's perspective. Ambassadors for this approach are Wiegerink and Peelen (2010) who, despite their focus on describing events as a strategic tool with clear intentions and goals from the producer's perspective and as an integrated part of the marketing policy of organizations, *do* recognize the visitor's actual event experience as crucial in the design process. They take key elements such as motives, drives, sensory perception, emotions and meaning into consideration in creating the optimal event experience.

In line with the previous authors, Gerritsen and van Olderen (2014; see also Chapter 5) mention in this context the 'touchpoint model' for the design of events. This approach is driven by all moments of contact between the producer and the visitor and the recognition that these touch points should be central to event design. They realize that actual added value is not so much a producer's initiative, but the choice and activity of the visitor. Although the 'staged experience' provided by the producer has a vast impact, it is the 'consumer-created experience' which determines its true value.

Reviewing these various theoretical approaches, it becomes evident that imagineering is gaining interest and support in a business context. Its value-based approach, focus on emotions and experiences and transformational potential are recognizable in many contemporary business models. However, how can imagineering be practically applied to the challenges faced by the corporate events industry today?

The corporate events industry in the Netherlands – an insight

According to Kuiper (2008) business events are initiated by an organization and they have a specific (organizational) purpose that distinguishes them from public events, and their funding is also different from public events (Wiegerink and Peelen 2010). Gerritsen and van Olderen (2014) further add that corporate events are often (but not always) exclusive, and they distinguish three specific categories of corporate events:

1   Business-to-Business events (B to B), where the target group is invited for business reasons and where the attendees participate for business reasons;
2   Business-to-Consumer events (B to C), where the target group is invited for business reasons but where the attendees participate out of a private leisure motivation;
3   Business-to-Employee events (B to E), where the target group (employees) is invited for business reasons and the employees participate due to their relationship to the employer. These events are also referred to as staff events.

In addition to the type of corporate events mentioned above, this chapter additionally focuses on a specific *type* of organization, within the corporate events industry. Overall, like any industry, the corporate event industry can be divided into various types of organizations, which vary in terms of product and position in the value chain. The main parties involved are event locations, caterers, technical suppliers, audio-visual suppliers, decorators and external event agencies. This chapter focuses on event agencies, which support companies/commissioners in the organization and coordination of their events. It could be argued that they play a central role within the industry, as they function more as advisers and event consultants, rather than mere suppliers. Developments within this specific type of company therefore present us with interesting indications about the state of the industry. It could also be argued that event agencies are a representation of the state of professionalism within the industry. Are separate specialists needed in the first place? What is their added value? And if they have added value; what is their role and how has it developed over the years? Therefore this chapter will examine mainly these 'generalist' event agencies, and how they have evolved in a changing business context.

Before we look into the quantitative and qualitative changes of the corporate events industry in the Netherlands, one other important characteristic of this industry should not be overlooked, as it provides an explanation for the current changes. Events in general, but also corporate events in particular, are to a large extent dependent on societal prosperity. In the Netherlands this development is as recognizable as in any other country (Wiegerink and Peelen 2010). In times of economic growth, the industry grew, just as it declined in times of recession, suggesting a high degree of elasticity. More recently, the decline became clearly evident both in terms of the number of events organized as well as the average turnover per event. In the Netherlands this became particularly clear after the events of 11 September 2001, when a flourishing period for the corporate event industry ended. Until that point bigger was really better, the experience and wow-factor were central in the event set-up and status and exclusive exposure played a major role in event design. After 9/11, however, things changed. For the industry, the 'golden years' finally came to an end. An ever-increasing number of event agencies that until then profited from this prosperous growth, now faced new challenges and needed to reconsider their product portfolio. Corporate clients became more aware of questions regarding the ethical, efficiency and effectiveness aspects of corporate events, and so the corporate event industry needed to follow. Although to some key players argued this would only be a temporary development, and things would soon get 'back to normal', it could be considered, in retrospect, that this was a sign of how the market would develop in future.

The development of the corporate events industry in the Netherlands

Although the corporate events market recovered after 2001, the recession of 2008 again showed the vulnerability of the industry. Research by the market research company NIDAP confirms this development. For staff/employee events annual expenditure fell from €262 million in 2007 to €179 million in 2010, a drop of almost 32 per cent. In addition business events exhibited a similar trend with turnover falling from €577 million in 2007 to €389 million in 2010, a decline of almost 33 per cent (NIDAP 2011). The prognoses for the events market in 2012 did not show any improvement (NIDAP 2012).

The decline in demand in turn led to a lowering of prices by event companies. Almost 50 per cent of the suppliers within the corporate events industry dropped their prices by 10–25 per cent (EventBranche 2013b). For 2013 most corporate event managers expected the number of events to be stable, but with the possibility of more price cuts. In spite of the price cuts, however, there was a decline in the use of event agencies, and the proportion of the average event budget going to external agencies fell from 31 per cent to only 23 per cent in 2010. In general companies choose to organize *fewer* events, and to take up the organization *themselves*, instead of hiring external expert agencies (NIDAP 2011). This means that event agencies need to be increasingly creative in finding ways to generate business, and imagineering can play an important role in this.

Qualitative development of the corporate events industry in the Netherlands

The changed financial reality of the events industry had serious consequences. Some prestigious event agencies went bankrupt, unable to cope with the trend towards decreasing event budgets (Anonymous 2011; Weikamp 2011). Additionally, it became evident that commissioners were increasingly selective in the choice of events within the marketing mix. Due to lower budgets, accountability became an increasingly important motive in the choice for events and event services (NIDAP 2012).

Additionally, the trade association for event agencies in the Netherlands, the Independent Dutch Event Association (IDEA) indicated that there was a growing need for more 'content related' events, where 'bonding' and creating connections with target groups was mentioned by 68 per cent of respondents as most important reason for organizing their event (NIDAP 2012). Commissioners have increasingly become selective with the events marketing tool. This is not only reflected in the actual lower overall costs for events. Moreover, commissioners focus on events that are more content driven and *perceived* to be cheaper and more functional than more luxurious entertainment-related events. This is reflected in more transparent return on investment (ROI) and an increasing focus on the educational aspect of events rather than entertainment aspects, which also seems to be an international development (Hosea 2009).

More recent research conducted by the Dutch event, conference and trade-fair industry organization CLC-Vecta (2012) into the live communication industry confirms these findings. But this study also suggests that live communication success will only come to those event agencies who can deliver content-driven events as part of the overall marketing mix of commissioners. Content and communication instead of entertainment, creativity instead of project management, return on investment instead of a sheer experience focus, have become the new reality. According to this research successful corporate events in the future need to be: relevant, measurable (ROI/added value), part of the marketing mix, small scale, part of communication strategy, co-creative, meaningful and sustainable in order to be commissioned (EventBranche 2013a). Event agencies that cannot provide in these types of events will not be viable in the long term. However, some event specialists argue that the event industry will never lose its relevance due to the unique live contact characteristic of events (Bakhuys Roozeboom 2013).

So many argue that live communication or event marketing is here to stay. Wiegerink and Peelen (2010) support this conclusion and refer to various international studies that all predict a growing interest in this industry. Characteristics of an event such as live contact, experience context and the possibility to create experience worlds around brands and products remain interesting tools for corporate commissioners.

Event marketing, live communication; an evolving industry

If event agencies manage to adapt to the rapidly changing context of the corporate event industry, growth is possible. Whereas in the 1990s event agencies provided mostly organizational, technical and logistical expertise regarding event organization, the industry has changed. Event agencies that positioned themselves before as 'full service event organization agencies' are now an almost extinct breed. The market has simply changed, and is increasingly looking for expertise beyond the basic organizational, technical and logistical domains.

A review of event trade magazines over the last decade shows that live communication, event marketing, experiential communication and emotional marketing are now key themes that event agencies use to position themselves with organizers. The very fact that there are so many labels used for a similar industry indicates the evolving landscape. Event agencies are adapting to this change by focusing on content and message instead of sheer experience, on ROI instead of intuitive effect judgement and on communication instead of entertainment. This change requires a new generation of event specialists, who are able to integrate their event portfolio within the broader context of marketing and both internal and external (brand) communication. Those suppliers who *can* adapt to this change are currently evolving into a new breed of event agencies: hybrid event agencies that are part communication companies, able to integrate their product within the bigger communication mix of organizations, and part event specialists, able to integrate the specific event tool within the communication strategy.

This new breed of content- and result-orientated agencies directly reflects the changes in the market place. Event agencies are currently in transition; searching the outskirts of their product portfolio, looking for the overlap with communication and branding. Production experts and project managers are becoming more and more interchangeable and are now hired on a freelance basis by event agencies. This development has been strengthened by the economic crisis, as event agencies laid off production staff, leading to an increasing number of freelance event production/project management professionals. Whereas the creative and account team has become more and more important for event agencies, former production staff are now hired via the freelance network. This development supports the claim that there is a shift happening from a production to a conceptual and communicational expertise within event agencies. In combination with the trend that more and more commissioners organize their own events, this also requires a co-creative approach from event agencies, in which they determine their role and added value in the process of event realization. This process is characterized by a more integrated collaboration between commissioner, event agency, freelance independent professionals and other preferred suppliers of the commissioner, working in the field of strategy, communication, audio-visual production, marketing and PR. So the corporate event industry has changed, but how far does imagineering provide a context and explanation for this change?

Imagineering solutions for the corporate events industry

If we interpret imagineering as defined by Disney as imagineering 1.0, and its renewed European interpretation at the beginning of this century as imagineering 2.0, we could refer to the current broader definition of imagineering as imagineering 3.0. In this new definition imagineering has evolved into much more than just an experience focused (1.0) or an additional value-based approach (2.0). In imagineering 3.0, co-creation and the focus on the process of imaginative value creation (so not only on the output), are additional crucial components. Moreover, this method can be applied not only on an operational or tactical (experience design) level, but even on a strategic level. These new components have become indispensable parts of the overall imagineering domain. Imagineering has reached maturity, providing a methodology for multiple processes on a variety of levels.

Event agencies therefore need to redesign and evaluate their role and the added value they can bring to event design. With the increased demand for meaningful experiences, effective results and co-creative processes, something needs to change. We already pointed out that corporate event solutions need to be an integrated part of the overall brand, communication and marketing strategy. But in the imagineering 3.0 phase, corporate events need to do even more. They need to match the societal context, reflecting the values of the very target groups the events are organized for. Imagineering provides the right tools for this; a method that reflects the values of those involved, using their imaginative power to create meaningful experiences.

Also in the Netherlands the corporate event industry is changing. A number of developments and changes are taking place, which have a direct effect on the positioning and daily execution of event agencies. Providing a sound and effective solution for this change, three main developments are crucial for future survival:

1   Knowledge shift
    The needed expertise is changing. The focus on message, content, communication, and the related integration of the event industry into communication and marketing strategies, requires different knowledge. Furthermore, sustainability, CSR, ROI, effectiveness and result measurement are becoming more and more important (Penseel 2013; Wiegerink and Peelen 2010). The shift from project management expertise towards effective (live) communication expertise creates a new breed of event specialists and new knowledge.

2   Business model review
    As mentioned, whereas in the past revenues were mostly generated through the production of an event, and the concept/creative idea was merely a 'pitch winner', the industry is evolving from 'organizers' to 'advisors' (Bakhuys Roozeboom 2013). Creative ideas and communication expertise are more important and commissioners are willing to pay for this expertise, because

(parts of) the events are organized by the corporation themselves. Event agencies therefore need to review their business and revenue models in order to remain financially viable. This change is already evident in the professional literature (EventBranche 2013a).

3   Co-creative approach

Full service delivery seems to be a thing of the past. Corporate commissioners increasingly look for an integrated application of events within their overall marketing and communication strategy. However, this approach can only be successful through a collaborative process between internal and external experts. Providing event services 'from the outside' will therefore become more and more difficult. Collaboration with other communication, marketing and PR agencies or even seconded employees is becoming more common, creating value together, using specific know-how of various experts. Co-creation, however, is not only increasingly important within the event production process, but the input of the audience and key stakeholders is also crucial. The growing societal need for influence, the desire for individual freedom and growing experience with and demands on event experiences, need to be addressed with actively including guests and stakeholders within the event value creation process. Cooperation and co-creation are the key components of successful event design.

How can event agencies take their activities into the realm of imagineering 3.0?

Kuiper and Smit (2011) already argued that the modern interpretation of imagineering not only makes it a viable *instrument* for concept creation, but that it can also be used on a process level to fuse multiple disciplines, talents and techniques to find innovative solutions. Event agencies are increasingly co-creating with clients. The integration of events in the brand and communication strategy requires this, as it is extremely difficult to create these connections in an isolated and external position.

   If event agencies used imagineering 3.0 to its full potential, however, it could provide them with a new role. Imagineering can also be used on a process level to facilitate co-creation for commissioners. Optimally, this would not only include working together with different departments within the organization, but even including other (competitive) specialist external agencies and relevant stakeholders. If event agencies embrace the imagineering methodology successfully, focused on co-creative- and experience-orientated value creation, they could use it on *both* an instrument and process level to create competitive advantage. This would include actively integrating other disciplines into the co-creative process and therefore redefining the role (and therefore the added value) of event agencies. They would become 'co-creative experience facilitators', who build on the joint imaginative power of all parties involved, including the guest, which will eventually lead to the ultimate successful event experience. Event agencies could re-invent themselves, focusing much more on the process than solely on the output of events, and create a unique position within the vast supply of similar service suppliers in areas such as branding, communication, marketing, PR and advertising.

Why should event agencies do this? Partly because it is already happening and the chances are there to be taken. The current technological possibilities have already bred 'hybrid events', in which live streaming and video conferencing are used to include a great number of people in a live experience (Rose and Steinbrink 2011). In addition, combined events are emerging, during which several happenings with completely different target groups and goals are merged into one single event. Furthermore, social media enable event marketeers to extend the live experience in a pre- and post-event experience (see also Chapter 5). Using event experience knowledge to create brand experience centres, shops and meeting places also create opportunities (Bakhuys Roozeboom 2013). But most of all, the very core strength of events as unique moments of live contact provides many opportunities for network development and marketing communications activities.

References

American Marketing Association (2007) 'Definition of marketing'. Online, available at: www.marketingpower.com/AboutAMA/Pages/DefinitionofMarketing.aspx (accessed 1 July 2013).

Anonymous (2011) 'Planet event failliet', *BN de Stem*, 28 October. Online, available at: www.bndestem.nl/regio/breda/planet-event-failliet-1.533819 (accessed 1 July 2013).

Bakhuys Roozeboom, F. (2013) 'Altijd behoefte aan live contact', *Adformatie – Vakblad over Marketing en Media*, 7: 24–27.

CLC-VECTA (2012) *Branchebarometer*, Breukelen: CLC-VECTA.

EventBranche (2013a) 'Gevraagd: nieuwe verdienmodellen!' *EventBranche.nl*, 4: 16–21.

EventBranche (2013b) 'Prijzenoorlog of budgetvrede?' *EventBranche.nl*, 2: 23–25.

Gerritsen, D. and van Olderen, R. (2014) *Events as a Strategic Marketing Tool*, Wallingford: CABI.

Gobé, M. (2010) *Emotional Branding 2.0: The New Paradigm for Connecting Brands to People*, New York: Allworth Press.

Grit, G. and Gerritsma, M. (2008) *Zo Organiseer je een Event*, Groningen: Noordhoff.

Hosea, M. (2009) 'Entertainment must deliver a good return', *Marketing Week*, 32: 16.

Kaarsgaren, L. (2010) *Zakelijke en Publieksevenementen*, Amsterdam: Pearson Education Benelux.

Kartajaya, H., Kotler, P. and Setiawan, I. (2010) *Marketing 3.0: From Products to Customers to the Human Spirit*, Hoboken, NJ: John Wiley & Sons.

Kuiper, G. and Smit, B. (2011) *De Imagineer: Ontwerp Beleving met Betekenis*, Bussum: Coutinho.

Kuiper, G. (2008) *Basisboek Eventmanagement: Van Concept naar Realisatie*, Bussum: Coutinho.

NHTV (2011) 'Kritische reflectie leisure management: imagineering adds value', unpublished accreditation report, NHTV Academy for Leisure, Breda.

NIDAP (2011) *Bedrijfsevenementenonderzoek 2011*, Amsterdam: NIDAP.

NIDAP (2012) *Bedrijfsevenementenonderzoek 2012*, Amsterdam: NIDAP.

NIDAP (2013) *Bedrijfsevenementenonderzoek 2013*, Amsterdam: NIDAP.

Nijs, D. and Peters, F. (2002) *Imagineering: Het Creëren van Belevingswerelden*, Amsterdam: Boom.

Penseel, H. (2013) *Basisboek Entertainment-Marketing*, 2nd edn, Bussum: Coutinho.

Pine, B.J. and Gilmore, J.H. (1999) *The Experience Economy: Work is Theatre and Every Business a Stage*, Boston, MA: Harvard Business School Publishing.

Pink, D.H. (2006) *A Whole New Mind: Why Right-Brainers will Rule the Future*, New York: Riverhead Trade.

Rippen, J. and Bos, M. (2010) *Events and Beleven: Het 5 Wheel Drive-Concept*, The Hague: Boom Lemma.

Rose, N. and Steinbrink S. (2011) 'Real and virtual meetings technology', *PhoCusWright Innovation Edition*, September: 1–14.

Schmitt, B. (1999) *Experiential Marketing: How to get Customers to Sense, Feel, Think, Act and Relate to your Company and Brands*, New York: Free Press.

Schulze, G. (1992) *Die Erlebnis Gesellschaft: Kultursoziologie der Gegenwart*, Frankfurt am Main: Campus.

Sinek, S. (2009) *Start with Why*, New York: Portfolio.

Stickdorn, M. and Schneider, J. (2011) *This is Service Design Thinking – Basics – Tools – Cases*, Amsterdam: Bis Publishers.

Tinker Imagineers (2014) Online, available at: www.tinker.nl/#/over-ons/Imagineering (accessed 3 January 2014).

Toffler, A. (1970) *Future Shock*, New York: Random House.

VVEM (2004) *Handboek Evenementen Maken: Richtlijn Voor het Organiseren van een Goed en Veilig Evenement*, Utrecht: VVEM.

Watt, D.C. (1998) *Event Management in Leisure and Tourism*, Harlow: Pearson Education Management.

Weikamp, S. (2011) 'La promesse failliet verklaard', *EventBranche.nl*. Online, available at: www.eventbranche.nl/nieuws/la-promesse-failliet-verklaard-6815.html (accessed 1 July 2013).

Wiegerink, K. and Peelen, E. (2010) *Eventmarketing*, Amsterdam: Pearson Education Benelux BV.

Wolf, M.J. (1999) *The Entertainment Economy: How Media Forces are Transforming our Lives*, New York: Times Books, Random House.

5 From visitor journey to event design

Dorothé Gerritsen and Ronald van Olderen

Introduction

Event visitors with their individual needs are becoming increasingly important and should be the primary point of departure in planning and organizing events. When somebody visits an event, they effectively embark on a journey, encountering services at specific 'touchpoints' that are instrumental in producing an optimal visitor experience. Each visitor will react to these touchpoints differently and therefore experience an event differently. Understanding the individual journey of a visitor from the event's conception until long after completion, is essential for organizing and designing events to increase involvement. Involvement makes the event a meaningful experience for visitors. In this chapter we outline the increased importance of the individual visitor journey and its implications for event design. Important questions that are addressed include: What is the connection between visitor journey, touchpoints, organizations and customer experience? What methodologies can be used to measure the effects of touchpoints and their influence on the visitor experience? How can you use this knowledge to redesign your event?

This chapter starts with a short introduction to visitor journeys and event design, followed by a methodology based on touchpoints models. Two case studies are then presented that illustrate a methodology for measuring visitor journeys and touchpoints. The first case study concerns the visitor journey of festival visitors to the Paaspop festival in Den Hout, the Netherlands. The second study is about the perception of touchpoints of three networking events of the *Genootschap voor eventmanagers* (the sector organization in the Netherlands for professional event managers). We then analyse the different case studies and make a comparison between them. Finally, we conclude with implications of using this methodology and techniques for (re)design of events.

The importance of the visitor journey in contemporary society

Some important trends and developments are increasing the consumer's focus on their event journey. First of all, consumers today are in control or, in other words, consumers are media-literate, well informed through communication media and pro-active. They expect nothing less than to be in control of the consumption process. Consumers decide what, where and when they want products, services and communication. The customer determines why, when and how they communicate, so events have to appeal to visitors on an emotional level. It is crucial to understand the drivers of this behaviour, but customer behaviour is very difficult to predict. In addition, consumer behaviour in relation to event visitation is highly fragmented. This means that it is very important to keep a close eye on the behaviour of your customers. Technological advances also increase the need to analyse the customer journey. Consumers have easy access to information as well as greater freedom of choice. They can make better choices and have plenty of comparison tools. All of these developments mean that studying the customer journey is increasingly important to predict behaviour (Crowther 2011; Boswijk *et al.* 2012).

Strategic use of events

More often than not, events are an informal adjunct to marketing activities, lacking both strategic integration and intent. Practitioners looking to the academic world for guidance and inspiration will be frustrated by the current lack of research and conceptual development connecting marketing and events (Crowther 2011). Research into customer journeys and touchpoints of events could be an answer to this, because if you make a connection between the values of visitors, their experience before, during and after the event, and finally the effects of events, then you have made the changeover to using events as a strategic tool. The EVENTS-model (Gerritsen and van Olderen 2014) shows the relationship between all these aspects of events. Although research into this field is being undertaken in other disciplines, such as service design, it is still in its infancy in the event sector. There are a few examples of studies of customer journeys and events, such as the study of the visitor journey of Rotterdam World Port Days (Rooijackers *et al.* 2013). Moreover, recent research into festival experiences (Van Vliet 2012) demonstrated that generic motivations such as escape, novelty, family togetherness, significance, learning and socialization are important in the visitor experience. Finally, there are specific types of events, such as trade shows and conferences, that have been subjected to research with a clear focus on values and value creation (Wiegerink and Peelen 2011). So, as it turns out, the motives and values of event visitors are important in their experiences (Boswijk *et al.* 2012; Geus *et al.* 2013).

Staged experience versus visitor experience

It is becoming increasingly difficult for businesses to distinguish themselves from their competitors by means of products and services alone. Consumers have access to unlimited information, and products are becoming increasingly alike. Competing successfully requires a different approach, with the perspective shifting from the supplier (organization) to the individual customer. After all, the value of the product or service is no longer the only thing that counts. What is at least equally important, is the meaning attached by the individual customer to the product or service (Pine and Gilmore 1999; Wiegerink and Peelen 2010). Does the product or service adequately reflect the customer's values or respond to the customer's needs? In this respect, individual customer experiences are extremely important. As a result, event marketing is gaining in importance, particularly as events have the capacity to add emotional value to a product or service.

Figure 5.1 shows a continuum of value addition which starts with the organization and ends with the visitor. If the focus of value addition occurs at the extreme left of the spectrum (with the organization in full control), the customer will get a staged experience, orchestrated by the organization. The organization takes the value of the product or service as a guiding principle and builds a perfectly staged experience around it. The focus of value addition may also be at the extreme right of the spectrum (with the customer in full control); in which case we speak of customer-created experiences. Value and meaning are created by the customers themselves, whereas the organization takes a supporting role.

Touchpoints models

We have already emphasized that organizations need to get inside the heads of their customers to find out what really matters to them in the customer experience. In terms of events, organizations need to address the question of what

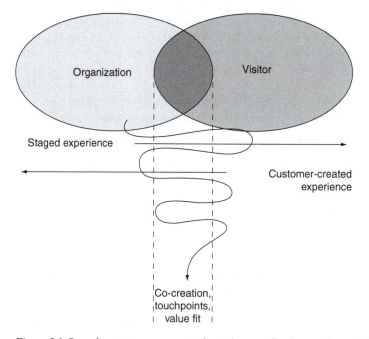

Figure 5.1 Staged versus customer experience (source: Gerritsen and van Olderen 2014).

visitors consider important and how the desired experience drives the customer proposition. Which phases does the event visitor go through at an event? In this respect, we are talking about the customer value chain or the aggregate (total) experience.

We argue that the focus of customer research at events should cover the visitor's total experience. Figure 5.2 shows that from a visitor's perspective, their values and motives constitute the point of departure, but that the successive phases before, during and after the event are critical to the visitor's total experience. The layer with the meaningful moments shows that the importance attached by the individual visitor to the touchpoints differs in each phase.

Organizations can use the layers in both models to check whether they are applying relevant touchpoints in the right phase and in the right manner, so as to build the optimal visitor experience. Figure 5.3 shows that both perspectives need to be connected with each other. The visitor perspective is becoming increasingly important (Boswijk *et al.* 2012).

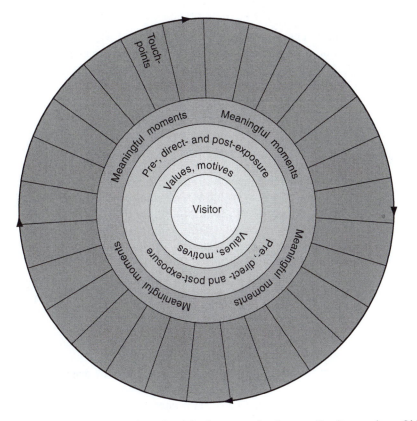

Figure 5.2 Touchpoints from the visitor's perspective (source: Gerritsen and van Olderen 2014).

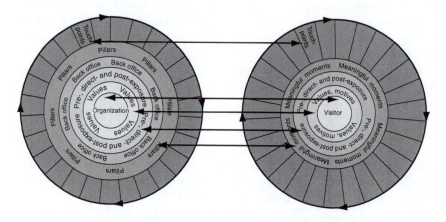

Figure 5.3 Value fit between organization and visitor (source: Gerritsen and van Olderen 2014).

It is very important to have an accurate understanding of which touchpoints have a high impact on the emotional experience. This knowledge can be used to make different choices for event design. If you know the impact of the different touchpoints for organizers and visitors then you will be able to consider the attention you give to touchpoints and make informed investment decisions.

Methodology

For both case studies, comparable methodologies were used. The objective was to test the suitability of methods to measure touchpoints and the influence of these touchpoints on the visitor experience. In the end the goal was to see if this knowledge leads to a better understanding of the (re)design of the event.

The methods used to study the visitor's journey and attendant touchpoints for both studies comprised the following elements:

1   Desk research and expert interviews on the customer journey and touchpoints
    Desk research and expert interviews focused on finding a connection between the motives, expectations and values of the visitors of all events, the customer journey (or perception of the customer journey) and the experience, as well as the degree of importance of the touchpoints from the visitors' perspective.
2   In-depth interviews with organizers (organizational perspective)
    To be able to get a better insight into the customer journey and the choices the organizers have made, in-depth interviews were held.

3 Mystery guest visits

Qualitative data from mystery guest visits were used as input to the questionnaire for the survey to give a deeper understanding of the emotional feelings and experiences of individual guests. As a point of departure, mystery guest visits were also used to draw up a complete list of touchpoints that was used for the visitor questionnaire.

4 Visitor survey

The visitor questionnaire contained questions to identify the customer journey and the visitor experience. The questions were based on a psychosocial framework which addressed the knowledge, values, expectations, experiences, motives and involvement of every visitor (Van Gool and Van Wijngaarden 2005). In addition, 'mood' was added to the psychosocial framework, because emotions influence people's physical and mental behaviour. They account for whether or not, for instance, they are interested, result driven, and/or open to stimuli and making decisions. Moreover, the questions were based on the input generated by the expert interviews, the in-depth interviews and the mystery guest visits. The bulk of the questions related to visitors' experiences with touchpoints and the importance they attached to each touchpoint. The questionnaire started with open questions supposed to uncover the 'meaningful moments' of the visit, such as 'What stands out in your memory as a positive aspect about the event and why?' In this way, touchpoint lists were produced for each event specifically. The final questions in the questionnaire were about the visitor experience. The purpose of these control questions was to clarify the level of the visitor experience: basic, memorable or transformational (Van Gool and Van Wijngaarden 2005). Table 5.1 shows the number of respondents at the different events.

Data for both case studies were compiled in the same period with the same starting point and the same commissioners. This chapter continues with a description of both studies and their outcomes.

Table 5.1 Overview of case study respondents

	Paaspop Den Hout	Genootschap voor event managers (Sector Organisation Event Managers)		
		Year of historic country houses 2012	Membership Meeting 'The lawsuit'	Study trip museum locations
Expert meetings	6	6		
In-depth interviews	2	1	1	1
Mystery visits	2	1	1	1
Visual material	Yes	Yes	Yes	Yes
Population	4,000	22	78	25
Survey sample (a-select)	351	22	78	25
Survey response	127	11	36	19

Case study 'Paaspop Den Hout'

Paaspop Den Hout is an annual two-day music festival held during Easter in Den Hout, a small village of 1,200 inhabitants in the province of Noord-Brabant in the Netherlands. The festival was organized for the first time in 1995. The study was carried out during the 2011 edition, which attracted 4,000 visitors. The line-up usually consists of a number of regional bands, an open stage for new bands and two or more performers of national stature. The festival's organization is in the hands of volunteers. With little attention being paid to the pre- and post-exposure phases of the festival, the event is primarily about the climax: the festival itself. Still, this festival is also facing the challenge of extending the experience in order build greater involvement as well as a more intense experience during the direct-exposure phase.

Findings

Organizers were asked about touchpoints in the pre-, direct- and post-exposure phase. The results are indicated in Table 5.2.

These results indicate that from an organizer perspective the most important touchpoints were the communication channels, the setting, atmosphere, programming and content of the event.

Examination of the visitor perspective began with two mystery guest visits to Paaspop festival in Den Hout to map the customer journey of the visitors. This resulted in a list of ten plus points and ten minus points (Table 5.3).

The mystery visit report was presented in a storytelling form, so as to create an expressive and true-to-life picture of the customer journey and visitor experience. Furthermore, visual material was gathered before, during and after the festival.

Visitors were asked via email, the festival website and the festival newsletter to fill in a questionnaire. The survey responses indicated that 70 per cent of visitors experienced 'meaningful moments'. These included experiences related to the line-up of artists, the atmosphere of the festival, the location, the company provided by others, food and beverage, overall organization and music and sound. Having identified the touchpoints related to these 'meaningful moments', it would be interesting to explore how the meaningful moments can be improved, so that unique and special memories will continue to exist long after the festival is over. Almost a third of the respondents from the survey indicated that they had had an ultimate experience (or 'flow'). A further 22 per cent of the respondents qualified this as neutral and 46 per cent as average. The ultimate experience, or the 'finished product', which was orchestrated by the organizer and the psychosocial framework of the visitor, was seen as a memorable experience by 70 per cent of the respondents. The visitor experience was rated at 8.2 out of 10 on average. The visitor questionnaire also demonstrated that the meaningful moments are determined by touchpoints such as line-up, ambiance, layout of the tents, enjoying the right people and

Table 5.2 Importance of touchpoints from the organizers' perspective

Touchpoint	Importance
Pre-exposure phase	
Website Paaspop Den Hout	Very important
Press releases	Very important
Social media	Important
Newsletter	Important
Printmedia	Important
YouTube	Neutral
Ticket sales	Important
Direct exposure	
Website Paaspop Den Hout	Very important
Camera team 'Brabant 10' (local news)	Important
Social media	Unimportant
Atmosphere	Very important
Location	Neutral
Decor	Unimportant
Technical aspects (light, image, sound)	Very important
Format/setting of the festival	Very important
Entertainment	Important
Logistics	Neutral
Parking	Neutral
Signage	Neutral
Safety and security	Neutral
Facilities and organization	
Toilets	Neutral
Cloakroom	Neutral
Personnel	Neutral
Information desk	Neutral
Ticket office	Neutral
Token sales	Neutral
First aid	Neutral
Event content	
Welcome	Neutral
Programming	Very important
Programme content	Very important
Catering	Neutral
Post-exposure phase	
Website Paaspop Den Hout	Very important
Press releases	Very important
Social media	Unimportant
Newsletter	Important
TV 'Brabant 10' (Local TV)	Important
YouTube	Neutral

Table 5.3 Plus and minus points of Paaspop identified by mystery guests

Plus points	Minus points
1 Parking close to the entrance	1 Poor directions to festival site
2 Attractive and large venue	2 Parking not well indicated
3 Friendly staff	3 Long queues to collect online tickets
4 Good light and sound	4 Loud music
5 Air conditioning	5 Little (healthy) food choice
6 Tasty hamburgers	6 Lax security controls
7 Good bar service	7 Separate programming for regional artists
8 Large stage	8 Aggressive atmosphere
9 Good entertainment	9 Rubbish on the ground
10 Sufficient toilets and toilet paper	10 Long wait for food

the right music, food and drinks, organization, music, sound and personnel. Respondents find all of these aspects crucial to experiencing meaningful moments. However a number of other touchpoints were not experienced positively, which indicates opportunities for improvement.

The customer journey and visitor experience of Paaspop Den Hout in 2011 began in the pre-exposure phase during which respondents had certain expectations and motives with regard to the festival. The expectations of the respondents of Paaspop Den Hout were mainly 'a fun night out' (82 per cent), 'good ambiance' (74 per cent) and 'some old-fashioned socialising' (51 per cent). The motive 'entertainment' (67 per cent) was the most important for visitors to the Paaspop festival, which is also connected with the value of 'fun'. The positive elements of the visitor experience and customer journey primarily occur in the direct-exposure phase, during the actual festival. Table 5.4 shows the touchpoints visitors have indicated as being important and which they experienced positively.

The organizers could do a lot more to extend the visitor experience before and after the festival. At the festival itself, the performance by a certain singer on the second day of the festival was the climax of the evening, with visitors 'unwinding and partying'.

The visitor questionnaire also showed that the mood of most respondents was very positive upon arrival (88 per cent), which makes for open-minded visitors. The vast majority of respondents had positive experiences with the festival in terms of its organization (84 per cent). The social environment also affects the visitor experience, as respondents at Paaspop Den Hout mostly visit the festival with friends (88 per cent). This, however, is not something that is sufficiently and consciously being addressed by the organization.

The most important parts of the customer journey of the visitors to Paaspop Den Hout tend to occur at the event itself. The experience during the event itself was rated very positive and of high importance by the visitors. Over 40 per cent of the respondents indicated experiencing an ultimate 'flow' moment, in which they forgot everything around them during the festival. The organizers pay little to no attention to the orchestration of the touchpoints in the pre- and

Table 5.4 Touchpoints that were positively rated and seen as important by visitors to Paaspop Den Hout 2011

Orientation phase	Ticket purchase	Preparation phase	Travel to festival	Participation in the event	Return journey	Post visit
Website Paaspop Den Hout	Website Paaspop Den Hout	Website Paaspop Den Hout	Own transport	Atmosphere	Own transport	Website Paaspop Den Hout
Posters/flyers	Ticket service	YouTube	Company of others	Location	Company of others	Friends/family
Friends/family	Ticketbox	Arrange transport	Signage	Sound, lighting	Afterparty/drinks	
Social media		Buying/listening to music	Parking	Entertainment		
Colleagues				Security Personnel Programming Acts		

Source: Wernsen 2011.

post-exposure phase. In the study, visitors were asked about their positive and negative experience with the various touchpoints, as well as the degree of importance they attach to each of these touchpoints. The touchpoints that are considered important are not all equally suited to being influenced by the organization. Table 5.5 shows touchpoints experienced as important by both the organization and the visitors.

Differences in the importance of touchpoints between organizers and visitors occur mainly in the pre-exposure phase. The organizers tend to emphasize touchpoints related to general event information, such as newspapers, social media and newsletters. Visitors on the other hand value more specific sources of information, such as friends and relatives and YouTube, and practical aspects of event orientation, such as parking facilities, signage and the ability to buy music. Differences also emerge between organizers and visitors in the direct-exposure phase, when organizers tend to emphasize the website and the physical setting of the event. Visitors, on the other hand, mentioned the location, entertainment, safety and festival staff.

In the post-exposure phase the organizers again reverted to local and regional media and their newsletter as the most important touchpoints, whereas visitors were most concerned about transport, the company of others, the after party and friends and relatives, and sharing the experience with friends and relatives. In general it seems that the organizers give more attention to the information content of touchpoints, whereas visitors are more concerned with the relational aspects of the touchpoints. This makes an important point about event design: the design elements that organizers consider to be most important related to the provision of information and the setting of the festival, whereas visitors find other touchpoints, such as festival staff or parking facilities important. Festival organizers may therefore be expending a lot of energy on the design of elements which are not so important to visitors.

Recommendations with regard to event design

Touchpoints that cause neutral or negative experiences, still present opportunities in terms of event design, because they are all perceived as important by visitors. These include, for example YouTube, signing and parking facilities. Other 'meaningful moments', such as the physical environment of the festival, the ambiance and festival staff are currently not being utilized to improve the visitor experience.

Table 5.5 Touchpoints experienced as important by both the organizers and the visitors

Pre-exposure	Direct exposure	Post-exposure
Website Paaspop Den Hout	Atmosphere	Website Paaspop Den Hout
Posters/flyers	Sound, lighting	
Hyves (social media)	Programming	
Ticket sales	Acts	

Better use should be made of the pre- and post-exposure phase in order to intensify and extend the experience. For example, the organizer could pay less attention to newsletters in the pre-exposure phase and more to YouTube as the visitors are more likely to value YouTube than newsletters. You will be able to extend the experience by using the pre- and post-exposure to put visitors in the right mood before the event, for instance. Just think of signage and logistics in the pre-exposure phase, and website use and after parties in the post-exposure phase. Another example is paying attention to the post-exposure phase by organizing after parties or trying to find creative ideas to end the festival by paying more attention to transport facilities or focusing more on togetherness after the event.

Case study 'networking events'

The networking events studied were small scale events organized by the *Genootschap voor eventmanagers* (the Dutch sector organization for professional event planners). Rather than being representative of all business networking events, the results and conclusions should obviously be taken as indicative only. Nevertheless, the survey did provide a couple of interesting new insights which justify further research. The following events were researched:

1 *Jaar van historische buitenplaatsen 2012* (Year of historic country houses 2012)
   The members of the association for event managers were invited for a meeting about the plans for the year of the historic country houses 2012 in Castle Groeneveld in Baarn (the Netherlands).
2 *Ledenbijeenkomst van het Genootschap voor Eventmanagers: 'De Rechtzaak'* (Membership meeting of the association for event managers 'The Lawsuit')
   This meeting was held in 2011 in 't Spant in Bussum (the Netherlands): members of the association of event managers, members of museums platform, event freelancers and event marketing agencies. The concept was that participants would work with legal cases dealing with responsibility issues.
3 *Studiereis Platform Museum Locaties* (Study trip of the platform of museum locations)
   The target group was a platform for museum locations.

The aim of this study was to investigate the customer journey in terms of the perception of touchpoints and meaningful moments of an event in the context of a relationship marketing strategy.

Findings

From the surveys held at these three networking events the most important findings are as follows. The most important motives to visit a business event were acquiring knowledge (92 per cent), obtaining information (91 per cent) and networking (75 per cent).

The touchpoints that were considered important turned out to be directly linked to these motives. One of the questions in the questionnaire was: 'Name three positive memorable moments (touchpoints) of this event and explain why these were memorable.' The analysis of the meaningful moments and the touchpoints demonstrates that they are closely related to visitor motives. For example in the case *Ledenbijeenkomst van het Genootschap voor Eventmanagers: 'De Rechtzaak'* (Membership meeting of the association for event managers 'The Lawsuit'), the top four mentioned by respondents are shown in Table 5.6.

The most important touchpoints are almost all in the direct-exposure phase. The touchpoints in the pre- and post-exposure phase were less important. This is not surprising, given that the actual knowledge gathering or networking occurs during the event itself. The meaningful moments that were mentioned are also directly connected with the motives that were considered as most important.

Another example of measuring the importance and touchpoints in the survey is from the event *Studiereis Platform Museum Locaties* (Study trip of the platform of museum locations). A total of 88 per cent wanted to gain knowledge and information (88 per cent as well) and networking (75 per cent). The top five touchpoints in the direct-exposure phase and the related experience ratings are shown in Table 5.7.

Implications for event design

The overall recommendation for event organizers is to focus especially on the direct-exposure phase of the event. In this process, it is important to make sure

Table 5.6 Top four touchpoints and related motivations

Touchpoint	Reason for importance
Enthusiastic lawyer and judge	Involvement
Customer care	Well organized
Networking	New contacts
Information	Knowledge development

Table 5.7 Top five touchpoints in the direct-exposure phase and related experience ratings for the study trip of the platform of museum locations

Touchpoint	Score experience touchpoint – scale: −2 to +2	Score importance touchpoint – scale: −2 to +2
Guiding trip	1.44	0.78
Walking distance between locations	1.44	0.72
Welcome Ludwig Museum	1.72	1.06
Content visit Ludwig Museum	1.44	0.94
Content visit Wallraf-Richartz-museum	1.17	0.94

that the motives of visitors to attend the event are reflected in the event pro-gramme. The role of the organizer in this process is a facilitating one. The moments at which you want to convey your message should coincide with the guests' touchpoints. Our research shows that although the most important touch-points are related to the direct-exposure phase of the event, all touchpoints con-tribute to the overall experience. This means that an event programme has to be dynamic, in order to capture and hold the visitor's attention from beginning to end of the experience.

Conclusion

From our research into visitor journeys and visitor experiences of events we can conclude that knowing your customer and the touchpoints they value will lead to greater customer involvement, more repeat visits and will allow you to create a truly transformational event experience. To this end, organizers have to ask themselves questions such as: What really touches visitors? What motivates visi-tors to come to an event? What are meaningful experiences to visitors? With which expectations do visitors come to your event? There is a strong connection between the visitor/customer journey, the touchpoints encountered and the experience of an event. It is also important to gain insights into the way event organizers look at touchpoints compared to the way visitors experience them. In this analysis it is useful to distinguish three phases: pre-, direct- and post-exposure (Gerritsen and van Olderen 2014) and measure the importance attached to the different touchpoints from the two different perspectives; organizer and visitor. This way it is possible to find similarities and gaps in perceptions between event organizers and visitors, and also to identify areas where organ-izers should concentrate their design efforts.

To analyse touchpoints effectively, it is important to combine qualitative and quantitative research. The case studies presented here demonstrate that every customer journey is unique and delivers useful knowledge about the visitor journey of one visitor. To describe the customer journey as fully as possible, qualitative research methods are required. Only then will you acquire a true-to-life picture of the emotional journey of a visitor. Subsequently, quantitative research should provide information on the generalizability of these results across the visitor population as a whole. The pre-, direct-, and post-exposure phases should be studied in particular, although the climax, the actual experi-ence, and the meaningful moments occur primarily in the direct-exposure phase. There also seems to be a connection between motives and expectations of visi-tors and the importance attached to different touchpoints by them. This is an effective method to get inside the skin of your visitors and to uncover the deeper reasons for the behaviour and emotional journey of your visitors. This was par-ticularly evident in the networking events studied.

All in all, event designers could use this knowledge about their visitors to (re) design their event to strive for more value fit with the visitor by making (other) choices for orchestrating touchpoints they are able to influence.

References

Boswijk, A., Peelen, E. and Olthof, S. (2012) *Economy of experiences*, Bilthoven: European Centre for the Experience Economy.

Crowther, P. (2011) 'Marketing event outcomes: from tactical to strategic', *International Journal of Event and Festival Management*, 2(1): 68–82.

Gerritsen, D. and van Olderen, R. (2014) *Events as a strategic marketing tool*, Wallingford: CABI.

Geus, S. de, Richards, G. and Toepoel, V. (2013) 'The Dutch Queen's Day event: how subjective experience mediates the relationship between motivation and satisfaction', *International Journal of Event and Festival Management*, 4(2): 156–172.

Pine, J. and Gilmore, J.H. (1999) *The experience economy: work is theatre and every business a stage*, Boston, MA: Harvard Business School Press.

Rooijackers, M.J.A.M., Remmers, G.J.M. and Weers, R. (2013) 'Rotterdam festivals: focus op festivalbeleving', in *Trendrapport toerisme, recreatie en vrije tijd*, Nieuwegein: NRIT Media, pp. 320–323.

Van Gool, W. and Van Wijngaarden, P. (2005) *Beleving op niveau, vrije tijd van vermaak tot transformatie*, Amsterdam: Pearson Prentice Hall.

Van Vliet, H. (ed.) (2012) *Festivalbeleving*, Utrecht: Hogeschool Utrecht.

Wernsen, I. (2011) 'Customer journey van de bezoeker van festival Paaspop Den Hout 2011', NHTV Breda: unpublished dissertation.

Wiegerink, K. and Peelen, E. (2010) *Eventmarketing*, Amsterdam: Pearson.

Wiegerink, K. and Peelen, E. (2011) *Een waardemodel voor beursdeelname: hoe waardedenken exposanten helpt succesvolle deelname zichtbaar te maken*, Breukelen: CLC-VECTA en Live Communication Research Center.

6 The discourse of design as an asset for the city

From business innovation to vernacular event

Marco Bevolo

Introduction

The competitive future of contemporary cities depends on their reputation, profiling and positioning within international networks. In Europe, this challenge has triggered cultural strategies that leverage urban identity. 'Design' has become an important part of such strategies because it has the power to mobilize people and networks by combining aesthetics, processes, ideas. Design can therefore be seen as a cultural strategy that transforms the physical fabric of the city into a 'place' that can be positioned in global markets. This chapter examines the role of design and in particular design events in the positioning of Eindhoven, a middle-sized city in the Netherlands.

The chapter reviews both 'branding' and 'design' as generic concepts, and how these have been applied to 'place' in the context of cities in the 'post-mass marketing' age. The analysis then shifts to the economic evolution of the city of Eindhoven through the twentieth century, with particular focus on the last two decades, when the local culture of family capitalism and corporate welfare was disrupted by the re-organization and departure of the Philips corporation. The empty industrial buildings and rising unemployment Philips left behind created a challenge for Eindhoven to ignite a new spirit of entrepreneurship. Design has been leveraged in this process as an economic innovation engine, as a socio-cultural discourse about the city and as a source of inspiration for events.

Place branding: the challenge of making cities immortal

'There is never any ending to Paris and the memory of each person who has lived in it differs from that of any other' (Hemingway 1964: 234). The ending of Hemingway's account of his Parisian years is just one of the countless testimonies of love for the French capital. Over the years the city of Paris has become much more than just a collection of buildings huddling around the Seine. Paris is now a 'place of the collective imagination' within global culture. The desire of cities to attain such cultural relevance and retain it over time, is the underlying theme of this chapter. Cities increasingly position themselves by creating and shaping their identity through storytelling and narrative. Events have a key role to play in this process in terms of creating visibility in globalized markets and cultures.

The origins of branding lie in the 'imprimatur' of quality and the unique signature 'that stands for' the name of the maker. This acts as a perfect semiotic device. For example, the fine books by typography and printing genius Aldo Manunzio set themselves apart from the rest of the bookshelf (Bevolo and Brand 2003) – except, of course, in the Venice of hundreds of years ago this was not called a 'logo'.

When it comes to city branding, even the design of a logo is an entirely different process from consumer branding or business-to-business branding. While the end result might look just like another graphic signifier, the ownership of the new icon is shared across multiple stakeholders, introducing a political dimension to the process (Lau and Leung 2011). While the positioning of consumer goods might be a relatively straightforward process, the branding of cities requires the combined skills of the strategist, the diplomat, the evangelist and of course of the designer. Together they must achieve the multilayered objective of closing the gap between urban reality and projected place image, and connecting perceptions and vicarious place experiences with information in digital and informal networks (Govers and Go 2009). For the purpose of 'branding' countries, cities or neighbourhoods universal models need to include a wide variety of constituencies to be managed: tourism, people, culture, investments, policy and brands (Anholt 2007). These can be organized under the brand management umbrella of 'competitive identities', the effects of which can be measured through indices and statistics (Anholt 2007). Place branding, however, requires more than quantitative measurement alone to achieve the desired positioning of a place in people's minds. The final outcome of place branding is a very fragile balance, influenced by external events, historical oddities and unforeseen circumstances. According to leading experts, this multilayered articulation of 'place branding' does not lend itself to conventional marketing approaches (Anholt 2010). This appears particularly true for the case of cities, where the human dimension of neighbourhoods is dissolved into anonymity and marketing budgets are limited.

On this restricted playing field everything counts, including for example the contribution of multiple sensorial dimensions to the experience of cities and neighbourhoods – primary senses like 'smell' can play a 'branding' role and ultimately make the difference (Barbara and Perliss 2006). The relevance of the 'senses' as a branding asset that can augment 'visual identity' was asserted at a deeper level of quantitative research (Bevolo *et al.* 2009), by measuring metropolitan preferences for sensorial design. The primary question that arises is: how can the 'design' of cultural themes for events help to position and profile a city internationally? The importance of branding in the positioning of cities then suggests a parallel question: how can the design of an event as an urban process enable the conversion of a physical place into a brand? 'Logos', brand management and 'sensorial experiences' all appear as mere collateral assets for urban branding, when compared to the vibrant dynamics of cultural networks in cities (Bevolo 2009) and the power of their local rituals. This is where urban events can best play a role in supporting and enabling place branding ambitions.

Design and the city: the ambiguities of a fine balance

The centrality of cities for our human futures (Sassen 2006) is the main assumption underpinning this chapter. Analysing the mechanisms of urban identity will help understand the potential for developing a better quality of life in the future.

Design could historically be defined as a converging 'grammar' where technology, aesthetics and talent give form to the 'language of things' (Sudjic 2008). In this respect, the interplay between cities and brands is evident when an established city positioning is used to support the launch of products by companies and brands: a luxury TV set will be designed in Northern Europe and launched with a fashion event in Paris, while an Italian lifestyle object will benefit most from the cultural aura that only being featured in New York's MoMA design collection guarantees (Bevolo *et al.* 2011). In other words, the design of events as triggers for memorable experiences traditionally requires a careful consideration of the nature and the culture of context, with the ultimate goal of leveraging and benefitting from the aura of a place, be it a building or a city. This is however an old paradigm, where a consumerist society 'consumes' not only products but cities as well, in terms of perceived positioning, and therefore 'marketing processes'. However, this established paradigm is no longer applicable.

A pivotal moment in the recent history of the creative industries was the shift of scope and ambition for designers, with the adoption of a socio-cultural approach and the inclusion within the design process of new competencies from anthropology, sociology and future studies (Marzano 1998). This important multidisciplinary extension towards understanding the future of people as the key originating factor of design has been paralleled by the rapid evolution of digital experiences, which constitute an opportunity to redefine the constituencies, processes and purposes of the design process (Andrews and Bevolo 2004). This happened first because of the evolution of digital design (Bevolo and Mol 2003), but also in a wider context of paradigm-changing strategic design practices (Bevolo and Brand 2003). In general terms, research in the US and UK shows that a redefinition of the purposes and directions of design is required, from 'marketing styling' to 'engine of meaning (through beauty)' in our everyday lives (Bevolo 2009). This means that the whole notion of design as static, visually driven discipline of 'just corporate logos on products' has been heavily challenged in the last decade. From these starting points, the role and the function of design within our culture has grown significantly in the last two decades: '(a) FROM: design as a simple business function anticipating customers' needs (Heskett 1989); (b) TO: design as a holistic force driving for change within any human context, applicable to any organization' (Brown 2009). In the second half of the last decade, therefore, 'design' increased its cultural relevance and ambition, taking centre stage in mainstream media, obtaining unique visibility as one of the thought-leading constituencies of globalized capitalism. Until the recent economic crisis, with its deep ideological implications, these achievements co-existed with blatant commercialism: in short, design was everything and everywhere. This position was deeply challenged by the events leading to the economic downturn first (Cannell 2009), and the general change of perceptions in public opinion that followed.

In recent decades, a number of 'ideologies of design' were a-critically adopted for cities as well. 'Design' itself became a ubiquitous cultural discourse within cities, with 'design districts' becoming a focus for tourism and shopping, and 'design' being applied as a cosmetic yet pervasive tool for consumption. The problem is that 'design' has been adopted by city administrators at a superficial level, as a reactionary discourse to normalize and re-position cities or neighbourhoods into the politically correct dialect of liberalist urban management. One example is the Red Light Fashion initiative in Amsterdam, where the world (in) famous red light district was linked with fashion. Fashion designers took over windows and displays from adult entertainment as a major step in sanitizing the area, hence contradicting at deeper political level the role of the red light district as a free space for unorthodox behaviours (Bevolo 2009). This subtle adoption of 'design' as a discourse of cosmetic marketing remains the most dangerous evolution that might affect design within cities and the design of urban events in the near future.

There is indeed more to the power of design in cities than rigid identity systems or vain marketing campaigns, however successful. A deeper approach can be found in the case history of Eindhoven, once an industrial centre of production, and at the moment of writing this chapter one of the three Dutch finalist candidate cities for the title of European Capital of Culture 2018, thanks to a unique strategic blueprint based on innovation and design.

From factory town to postmodern atelier: Eindhoven as a miracle?

The city of Eindhoven was not born as a city: until the end of the nineteenth century, it was one village in a network of surrounding settlements, some of which Eindhoven absorbed over time. In 1891, Gerard Philips, formerly associated with AEG of Germany, started up a 'high tech' company, producing light bulbs. After a couple of years, Gerard was joined by his more extrovert, commercially savvy brother Anton, who helped boost the company from a small regional factory to an industrial corporation with world-class research, multinational customers and a growing portfolio of innovative products (Kantelberg 2013). As pioneers of the industrial age, the Philips brothers and their management not only created one of the most prolific scientific R&D teams, but they also invested in the 'art of selling'. In the 1920s, this resulted in the birth of a 'Propaganda' department, where advertising activities were placed under the supervision of Louis Kalff, an architect and the first designer on the payroll of the corporation, who from there developed the ARTO, or 'Artistic Design

Group' (Various Authors 2005). From this starting point, the design practice at Philips matured over the following decades under the guidance of international directors like Knut Yran (Norway), Bob Blaich (US) and Stefano Marzano (Italy). In parallel, what would later become the Design Academy Eindhoven became a natural hiring playground for Philips and a key asset in the creative portfolio of Eindhoven (Schouwenberg *et al.* 2008). Until the late 1980s, Eindhoven worked efficiently and effectively as a 'company town', with a paternalistic yet benign culture of solidarity ensuring the redistribution of welfare and opportunities through company initiatives in housing, healthcare and leisure. The more avant-garde discourses in fine arts and popular culture were also represented in the city through the Van Abbemuseum, which blossomed during the 1960s and 1970s thanks to a sophisticated and daring policy by directors like Jean Leering (Debbaut and Verhulst 2002). There was also a lively alternative lifestyle scene, which saw legendary performances such as the 1977 Sex Pistols concert in De Effenaar, the local club of reference for this kind of sub-culture (Kantelberg 2013).

In 1991, however, this situation drastically changed when Philips launched 'Operation Centurion', a major restructuring effort engineered to save the company from bankruptcy. Centurion particularly impacted the local production facilities and workforce, leaving the Strijp-S complex of factories empty and nearly 90 per cent of technical staff and blue collar workers laid off (Kantelberg 2013). This was only the start of a major redesign for the Dutch corporation as well as a socio-cultural earthquake for the City of Eindhoven and its 'company town' networks of solidarity. This restructuring symbolically culminated at the end of the 1990s with the relocation of Philips' corporate headquarters to Amsterdam. This move symbolized the defeat of Eindhoven in the global 'war for talent', recognizing that the city was no longer an attractive location for the creative class essential to the digital era.

The reaction of Eindhoven as a local community went beyond the bitter surprise that could have easily turned into plain disbelief and paralysing despair. In the words of current Mayor Rob van Gijzel:

> The city was left orphaned, but the people who were left behind became enterprising. They gained more space to think, became more daring, were given the chance to exploit their knowledge, engineering skills and imagination to the full. Eindhoven has reinvented itself in the past 15 years. Government, business and knowledge institutions put their heads together and got to work, aided by a strong tradition of social networks in the region. This successful model of collaboration, which has come to be known as the Triple Helix, is now being copied in many other knowledge-rich areas, both in the Netherlands and beyond.
>
> (Various authors 2012)

The Triple Helix approach transformed 'design' in Eindhoven from 'artistic propaganda' into a fully fledged incubation process. Volatile yet elastic talent would connect to knowledge institutes, financial investors and diffused expertise, realizing a highly mobile, yet economically productive environment, recalling Andrea Branzi's (2006) urban idea of a 'weak and diffused modernity'.

Urban planning and architectural design have also crucially contributed to the re-thinking and re-making of Eindhoven as a 'place': a new place, geographically and infrastructure-wise re-qualified to absorb the new need for entrepreneurial elasticity and socio-cultural flexibility. Early ideas of planning intervention on the Strijp-S industrial area included a meta-project for a possible Master Plan drafted in 2000 by Andrea Branzi under the leadership of Stefano Marzano, for the Municipality in Eindhoven. In this vision of a different future that never happened, the industrial brown field site would be converted into an agriculturally planned area of green and nature, with micro-enterprises spread across the territory in harmonious rhythm (Branzi 2006). These visionary seeds helped stakeholders decide and define their priorities. The final choice for the fundamental change of destination for Strijp-S and its satellite area, Strijp-R, was instead one of preservation and restoration of the 'skins' of the majestic modernist buildings, to house highly affordable, 'start up-friendly' units, complemented by new tower buildings with a gentrifying purpose. 'Design' was the focal point in terms of commercial enterprises as well as leisure. This is exemplified by the use of future lighting design concepts created by Philips Design's Lorna Goulden (2008) and her experience design team on behalf of Park Strijp Beheer BV. The approach was to redesign the 'hardware' of the city to support its new ambitions in terms of profiling through knowledge, enterprise and leisure. This was not limited to Strijp-S, as proven by the creation of Piet Hein Eek's multifunctional 'factory', complete with a fashionable restaurant, galleries and production ateliers in the smaller, less central Strijp-R. This venue became centre of design-related events, both during the Dutch Design Week (DDW) and at other times of the year, with world class speakers like Paul Smith delivering lectures and a constant stream of shoppers. The same approach has been deployed in the even more geographically marginalized, economically under-privileged Sectie C, where student studios and start up firms by graduates of the Design Academy found their rough, yet functioning entrepreneurial nest. These industrial 'ghost towns' turned creative citadels have enabled the profiling of Eindhoven as Dutch design capital. Sectie-C became another focal point of the DDW, offering an alternative, cost-effective venue for a cutting edge programme of younger exhibitors and adding to the post-industrial character of this urban event.

Where renovation was not feasible, new interventions were initiated, including the Smalle Haven mixed programme of retail and residential dwellings, with the iconic Vesteda Tower (Ibelings 2007); the Piazza shopping mall and its two 'sister glass bubbles' by Massimiliano Fuksas. These were deigned to 'tie together' a square comprising a department store building by Gae Aulenti and the modernist 'Light Tower', formerly of Philips; and more. The quest for new 'hardware' icons is complemented by urban events and festivals that organically transform the hardware in terms of lighting design, pop-up stores or improvised catering outlets. While some of these new icons might be debatable in terms of their conformist aesthetics and their lack of authentic fit with the vernacular context, it should be observed how 'leisure' has become the 'urban lubricant', be it in the form of shopping or in the form of themed catering. Leisure, be it shopping, be it sports, be it live concerts, has played an increasingly transformative function not only in Strijp-S but across the entire city: no wonder that in order to amplify the echo of the 'Eindhoven miracle' storytelling of re-birth and new prosperity, an annual event with 'design' at the core of its discourse has been staged for the past decade.

Design and events: DDW as opportunity to brand the city beyond branding

Within any urban context, urban events help to generate an attractive aura of 'eventfulness' (Richards and Palmer 2010) around the cities for which they are designed. The specific challenges of city positioning require strong storytelling themes leading to powerful 'eventfulness'. This finds a resonance in the policies, curatorial decisions and development strategies of a city like Eindhoven, in the Netherlands. Here, 'design' has become in the last decade a carrier of meaning and a trigger of change at both local and international levels. The Dutch Design Week (DDW) is one of the key initiatives within the urban promotion portfolio of Eindhoven, hence it offers an excellent opportunity to apply theories and methodologies for city positioning beyond conventional place branding. Since its inception as a national event in 2002, the DDW has achieved a prime positioning in terms of international design events, with attendance of 180,000 over ten days for its 2012 edition (source: personal communication, DDW, December 2012). The event is organized to generate key legacies in creative education, scientific research and business innovation, with a peculiar mix of micro-enterprises (design studios benefitting from privileged rental conditions in re-qualifying industrial areas in town) and corporate sponsors (such as ABN AMRO bank and Philips). It is not the purpose of this chapter to present the DDW as a complete case history, but rather to relate how Eindhoven reached the status of 'Dutch Design Capital' through strategic event design.

The DDW has developed strategic design principles that have helped to support the positioning of the event and to generate the desired outcomes in terms of image, economic impact, networking and positioning.

It seems important to mention three specific design principles related to city positioning that are often lost in the cacophony of messages generated by and around the DDW.

1   Networking relevance: DDW was leveraged as a networking engine by connecting to sister design events in London, Belgrade, Helsinki and Istanbul. The latter two cities were protagonists of a joint effort in terms of shows in 2010 and 2012, and they were featured as full partners in the *Trend Book* catalogue edited by international trend analyst, Zuzanna Skalska. In

contemporary place branding a great deal of relevance is placed on networking and networks of opinion makers and influencers (Govers and Go 2009), including design professionals and media.

2   Self confidence: closer contacts with leading and emerging design cities led to the 2010 bid for World Design Capital of 2012, in which Eindhoven came second behind Helsinki. The failed World Design Capital 2012 bid might be seen as a stepping stone towards the later bid for the European Capital of Culture 2018, where a strong emphasis was once again placed on design and the creative industries, under the mission statement: 'To place art and culture structurally and lastingly at the heart of society' (2018Eindhoven 2012).

3   Vernacular authenticity: although the DDW is now an international event, the connection with informal networks and micro-enterprises at local level remains strong. This was symbolically represented by the cover image of the 2012 *Trend Book*, selected by Skalska to represent the production of bread by Eindhoven micro-bakery Broodt. This curatorial choice implicitly defined one of the key visual signifiers of that edition of the DDW, and it generated a powerful sign that will stand over time as a visual signifier of specific socio-cultural values, counter-balancing the high tech context of the regional economy with the high touch authenticity of the traditional farming way of life.

The *Trend Book* is just one example of the key carriers of the cultural discourse that Eindhoven channels through the DDW. It is already possible to identify a microcosm of dynamics and values, where the dialectic tension of the cultural discourse of 'design' visually projects a network of meanings, possibly leading to a 'schemata' in the mind of the experiential and vicarious audiences (Govers and Go 2009), which is the essence of place branding. One might conclude: 'All's well that ends well', in the Eindhoven fairytale of crisis and renaissance that transformed its physical skin (bricks and mortars, or better: buildings and icons) and its neurological systems (creative industry networks, or better: knowledge strategies and funding tactics). Eindhoven has become a 'darling' of glossy design magazines worldwide and international committees the world over.

In addition, the design principles applied to DDW have enabled the city to develop a positive relationship with the event in order to support broader urban regeneration aims. For example, van Winden *et al.* (2010) analyse the way in which DDW has helped to support the development of Strijp-S by engaging with bottom-up development with the design sector. Strijp-S, as a former industrial area in development offers a good backdrop for the event: 'Strijp-S offers roughness. There is also a possibility to party. Further development kills the unique atmosphere which makes it less attractive for our event' (Event Director, quoted in Van Winden *et al.* 2010).

In turn, DDW helps to project this rough area in the process of development on to the world design stage. The bottom-up nature of creative activities in this area also fits the ethos of DDW well, emphasizing creative freedom. In other words, the design of DDW as a relatively grass roots event fits with and is strengthened by the location of the event in the city of Eindhoven.

But before drawing the conclusion that Eindhoven's design strategy and strategy of event design is a success, a critical view should be cast on the possible challenges and risks that could emerge in the future.

Roadblocks towards a golden age: future challenges and risks

The dynamics of urban transformation in Eindhoven, although triggered by the changes in the globalized economy, are deep processes of socio-cultural change and adaptation that go well beyond the field of branding. In this respect, the achievements of urban transformation display a high level of fragility, as they are exposed to the (sometimes diverging) influences of multiple stakeholders. This is why it is necessary to identify the contours of three potential points of risk for the DDW, and for Eindhoven in general, in the forthcoming years:

1   From networking success to dilution by imitation
    The organizational model of Eindhoven – just like the aesthetic approach successfully exploited by the Design Academy Eindhoven – has become a 'formula': always admired, often analysed – sometimes successfully imitated. Eindhoven capitalized on a number of innovative models, from the aforementioned Triple Helix strategic management approach to the creation of events. For example, GLOW, the forum of light in art and architecture is a highly successful festival that constitutes a night-time counterpart to the Dutch Design Week (Various Authors 2010). Thanks to effective networking, this formula is now known and has begun to be adopted by other cities in Europe. For example, the Polish city of Lodz, itself protagonist of a 'comeback strategy' (Boom and Mommaas 2009) from its textile industry past, developed a leisure strategy by adopting at least two key modules of the Eindhoven footprint. First, Lodz did so in the form of a relatively small urban lighting design festival mostly located on its main artery, Piotrkowska Street, enriched by experimental installations by national architects facilitated by Philips Lighting Poland SA as part of their 'Architecture of Light' design programme. Second, a design festival was programmed in a disused industrial building, with a Polish programme but with a clear flavour recalling the DDW format. The presence of Skalska on the organizational board of this festival, as well as her crucial role as initiator of the School of Form in Poznan, yet another staple of contemporary Polish design, is a clear sign of an expansion of the 'Eindhoven model' to the design of events and the elaboration of city strategy throughout Europe. This transfer of expertise, knowledge and best practices across networks is very positive as it offers the opportunity to exchange and to mutually learn from each other, in the best spirit of cooperation. Nevertheless, the risk for Eindhoven is that the diffusion of its design practices (and its aesthetic look and feel) across more

and more urban events will inevitably result in the erosion of its leadership position through dilution of its uniqueness at visual impact level, ultimately endangering its relevance.

2   From self-confidence to nationalistic spiralling

In recent years, the aesthetic experimentalism and daring nature of Dutch designers, just like the effectiveness of the 'Eindhoven model' of micro-enterprise were publicly praised by the likes of creative 'guru', Alessandro Mendini and MoMA design curator, Paola Antonelli (Bevolo 2009). Few 'design schools' established a national signature as efficiently and memorably as the Dutch one did. Protagonists like OMA/AMO's architect Rem Koolhaas, perhaps the archetype of contemporary 'archistars' (La Cecla 2008) or Widdershoven as politically engaged post-modern art director (Bevolo 2009), established themselves and their work as a whole new notion of 'Dutchness', at least in the creative industries (Betsky 2004). When it comes to 'design', one can see the emergence of such 'Dutchness' as a process with its historical roots in the Heineken Pavillon by Karel Suyterman at the 1900 Universal Expo (Simon Thomas 2008), historically a reference event for the design of places and spaces alike. It is a remarkable journey of self-awareness, reflection and determination. The danger of such aesthetic exuberance is that it becomes just a cosmetic skin around the resurgent nationalism that has recently manifested itself in the Netherlands like in many other countries. While the 'Dutch Design Week' has so far enjoyed a strong accent on a notion of 'Dutchness' and 'Dutch' as synonym of social tolerance, creative openness and almost anarchist experimentalism, what would be the impact of xenophobic policies or simply restrictive law making on such meanings? Anholt clearly indicates how the driving force of place branding actually lies in political choices: it is therefore inevitable that if the essence of what is 'Dutch' swings to a different semantic field, whatever that might be, then 'Dutch Design' will inevitably follow.

3   From vernacular authenticity to city marketing gimmick

In the past, urban events were designed in a year-long process, leading to the staging of memorable experiences, where relevant investments were made at financial, cultural and symbolic levels: this is the power of vernacular authenticity. It is a common risk in fine arts and design that what was born as authentic, genuine creative DNA becomes, over time, nothing more than a styling cliché, a marketing gimmick to cash in on. Eindhoven is not exempt from this risk, *au contraire*. In this respect, the reduction of 'the real' to anesthetized aesthetic content – be it Koolhaas' research reports or over-priced design objects on display at architectural biennales (which represent a whole class of staged event about urban design) – represent a major danger for architectural thinking and city event practices (La Cecla 2008). Likewise, the exploitation of urban events for the purpose of conversion of authentic vernacular into media formats (La Cecla 2008) and marketing gimmicks (like the reactionary 'Palermo is Cool' based on art events designed to revitalize downgraded areas of town) represent an ineffective and inefficient degeneration of place branding (Anholt 2010). This is a high risk for the city of Eindhoven. The challenge here is to manage both the generative processes of a bottom-up event as well as the international exposure of Eindhoven, and of its flagships like the Dutch Design Week, without bastardizing the richness of its human texture into 'marketing postcards' for investors and selected target audiences. In this respect, place branding by its very nature should be a social, holistic, organic process, relying on the largest possible consensus and the deepest possible dialogue with citizens. Just as 'design' comes from a social innovation tradition, either place branding is truly inclusive, or it will be purely void of any relevance.

Eindhoven and the DDW are in a privileged position to represent a blueprint of how 'design' can be both a profitable business engine and a socially sustainable, culturally meaningful discourse for a popular, democratic event of international stature. The dangers dissected above represent a 'luxury problem' for a city and an event that has innovatively redefined the hierarchies, the relationships and the dynamics among urban stakeholders. The power of dialogue, the mastering of networks and the ultimate sense of belonging that the Dutch Design Week generated first and foremost amongst the citizens of Eindhoven represent the most notable evidence of why the future of this event seems bright. It should be regarded as a fundamental asset to support the further 'switching' of Eindhoven from its local dimension to those global flows of capital, communication and cultural relevance in which it aspires to operate. This relentless, restless, micro-enterprising work of profiling and positioning is what place branding is truly about in the contemporary context, as it will be in the years ahead.

Conclusions

By analysing the complexities of 'design' and 'place branding', this chapter aimed to reflect on the conventional wisdom about place branding, identity design and urban events, suggesting that in terms of event design there is much more at stake for the city than the simple cosmetic surface of logos, colours and shapes. The inadequacy of conventional marketing and traditional branding to generate and to manage the identity, image and reputation of nations, regions and cities has been reiterated by Anholt (2010). A city is simply too complex an organism, too contradictory a body, to be successfully communicated by a marketing slogan. As seen from the analysis of Eindhoven, a notion of 'branding' as rooted in culture and articulated through 'narratives' can be adopted, with 'storytelling' as the key focus (Vincent 2002). The 'power of the tale' should be investigated (Simmons 2003), with the aim of understanding how brands go beyond their marketing purposes, tapping into myth (Mark and Pearson 2001) and ultimately reaching the wider dimension of 'cultural icons' (Holt 2004). The challenge will be to connect the power of design to the authenticity of vernacular values and their aesthetic representations, to prevent the risk of superficial imitation and meaningless repetition of vernacular events, ultimately resulting in the neutralization of any 'cultural discourse' into void marketing gimmicks. The design of the Dutch Design Week will be key to ensure the respect of the participative, co-creative nature of the event. For example, it might inspire to a more open, less technocratic interpretation of the Triple Helix, for the ultimate benefit of the longer term design choices that will determine the nature and the appearance of the city of Eindhoven in the future. Leisure is the ideal field to search for these kinds of dynamics, especially in cities. Within the field of events, 'design' will remain an ideal theme to pursue such ambition, given its unique position at the crossroads of business, fine arts and creative industry (Bevolo 2009).

However, the use of design as a design strategy for events may also harbour potential dangers. The fact that design concepts are easily transferable between events and locations means that formats and programming can be relatively easily copied. There is a need to ensure that design is anchored into the cultural DNA of the city and/or location so that this essential element of event design is not so easy to copy. The fit between DDW and the developing creative cluster of Strijp-S is a good example of how events can be embedded in specific locations and can use the characteristics of the location to enhance the experience and feel of the event.

References

Andrews, A. and Bevolo, M. (2004) 'Understanding Digital Futures', *Design Management Review*, 15(1), 50–57.

Anholt, S. (2007) *Competitive Identity*, London: Palgrave.

Anholt, S. (2010) *Places: Identity, Image and Reputation*, London: Palgrave.

Barbara, A. and Perliss, A. (2006) *Invisible Architecture*, Turin: Skira.

Betsky, A. (2004) *False Flat: Why Dutch Design is so Good*, London: Phaidon.

Bevolo, M. (2009) *The Golden Crossroads*, London: Palgrave Macmillan.

Bevolo, M. and Brand, R. (2003) 'Brand Design for the Long Term', *Design Management Journal*, 14(1): 33–39.

Bevolo, M. and Mol, C.J. (2003) 'Marketing and Branding for Success', in E. Aarts and Marzano, S. (eds) *The New Everyday*, Rotterdam: 010, pp. 274–277.

Bevolo, M., Gofman, A. and Moskowitz, H. (2011) *Premium by Design*, London: Gower.

Bevolo, M., Shofu, R., Moskowitz, D. and Moskowitz, H. (2009) 'Putting Fragrance into Context', Conference Paper, presented at the Fragrance Conference, Cannes, June 2009.

Boom, N. van and Mommaas, H. (2009) *Comeback Cities: Transformational Strategies for Former Industrial Cities*, Rotterdam: NAI Publishers.

Branzi, A. (2006) *Modernita' debole e diffusa*, Milan-Geneva: Skira.

Brown, T. (2009) *Change by Design*, New York: Harper Business.

Cannell, M. (2009) 'Design Loves a Depression', *New York Times*, 3 January. Online, available at: www.nytimes.com/2009/01/04/weekinreview/04cannell.html?_r=0 (accessed 25 June 2014).

Debbaut, J. and Verhulst, M. (2002) *Van Abbemuseum: Het Collectieboek*, Eindhoven: Van Abbemuseum.

Goulden, L. (2008) 'STRIJP-S: Creating a Public Lighting Experience', Online, available at: www.light-s.nl/about/en (accessed 2 December 2013).

Govers, R. and Go, F. (2009) *Place Branding*, London: Palgrave.

Hemingway, E. (1964/2004) *A Moveable Feast*, London: Arrow Books.

Heskett, J. (1989) *Philips: A Study of the Corporate Management of Design*, New York: Rizzoli.

Holt, D.B. (2004) *How Brands become Icons*, Boston, MA: Harvard Business School Press.

Ibelings, H. (2007) *Smalle Haven Master Plan and Architecture*, Eindhoven: Municipality of Eindhoven.

Kantelberg, A. (2013) *Het Wonder van Eindhoven*, Amsterdam: Podium.

La Cecla, F. (2008) *Contro l'Architettura*, Turin: Bollati Boringhieri.

Lau, F. and Leung, A. (2011) 'Chongking's City Branding: The Role of Graphic Design', in K. Dinnie (ed.) *City Branding*, London: Palgrave, pp. 131–137.

Mark, M. and Pearson, C. (2001) *The Hero and the Outlaw*, New York: McGraw Hill.

Marzano, S. (1998) *Creating Value by Design: Thoughts*, Blaricum: V+K.

Richards, G. and Palmer, R. (2010) *Eventful Cities: Cultural Management and Urban Regeneration*, London: Routledge.

Sassen, S. (2006) 'Why Cities Matter', in *Cities: Architecture and Society*, exhibition catalogue of the Tenth Architecture Biennale Venice, Marsilio, Venice 2006, pp. 26–51.

Schouwenberg, L., Staal, G., Goedegebuure, M., van Hinte, E., Saam, H. and Tilborg, R. (2008) *House of Concepts: Design Academy Eindhoven*, Amsterdam: FRAME.

Simmons, J. (2003) *The Invisible Grail*, London: Texere.

Simon Thomas, N. (2008) *Dutch Design: A History*, London: Reaktion Books.

Skalska, Z. (ed.) (2012) *Trend Book*, Eindhoven: Dutch Design Week.

Skalska, Z. (ed.) (2013) *Trend Book*, Eindhoven: Dutch Design Week.

Sudjic, D. (2008) *The Language of Things*, London: Allen Lane.

Van Winden, W., De Carvalho, L., Van Tuijl, E., Van Haaren, J. and Van Den Berg, L. (2010) *Creating Knowledge Locations in Cities: Innovation and Integration Challenges*, Rotterdam: European Institute for Comparative Urban Research.

Various Authors (2005) *Past Tense, Future Sense*, Amsterdam: Bis.

Various Authors (2010) *Glow: Forum of Light and Architecture. Jubilee '06–'10*, Eindhoven City, Eindhoven: C-twee creatieve communicatie.

Various Authors (2012) *Imagination Designs Europe: 2018 Eindhoven/Brabant European Capital of Culture (Candidate)*, Eindhoven: 2018 Eindhoven/Brabant.

Vincent, L. (2002) *Legendary Brands*, Chicago, IL: Dearborn.

7 How to slay a dragon slowly

Applying slow principles to event design

Ilja Simons

Once upon a time there was a small village on the shores of the river Maas in the Netherlands. The village was called Beesel and it was definitely not an average village. In the water of the Maas, just below the surface, a dragon resided. Most of the time the beast was asleep and life in the village was almost normal. Although, when paying close attention, one could feel the presence of the dragon at all times.

But once every 7 years, the dragon wakes up and enters the village, spitting fire and making the blood of the villagers boil. A fever comes over the village, and only the slaying of the dragon can stop this.

(Verdonck 2012, adapted by author)

Welcome to Beesel, the dragon village...

Introduction

Getz (2012) describes an event as a planned experience. This suggests that the organizer can design and create experiences to suit the needs of all stakeholders. However, there are many different types of events that occur in different contexts (Shone and Parry 2004; Bowdin *et al.* 2010). Berridge (2012: 8) introduces the possibility that these 'differently classified events, may elicit different experiences'. This chapter focuses on a specific type of event: the traditional community event. It is argued that the specific features of such an event, like community involvement, the need to balance tradition and change, and the link to place identity, have implications for event design.

Recent literature on events shows a growing interest in the social impacts of events in addition to the economic impacts (Fredline *et al.* 2003; Kaplanidou *et al.* 2013; Richards *et al.* 2013). When focusing on social impacts, it is worth researching the design of events that are organized bottom-up, in close cooperation with the local community, because this is where much of the social impact occurs.

One of the concerns that traditional community events have is the balance between tradition and change. Although these events want to keep their historical elements, which are seen as authentic, they cannot rely solely on the original design.

As time passes, the demand of the visitors will change, as well as the technical possibilities to stage the event. Sewell (1996) defines a historical event as a gap between expectation and reality. In order to create such a gap, change needs to be incorporated in the event. Events that do not include change in the design, run the risk of being too obvious and in the end uninteresting for the public. In addition to this, there can be a tension between the preservation of a traditional community-based event, and the wish to attract tourists. Much has been written about commodi-fication and exploiting of cultural heritage (Saleh and Ryan 1993; Brewster *et al.* 2009). Traditional community events need to strike a balance between tradition and modernity. But as the case study in this chapter will show, modernization and authenticity do not necessarily have to be opposites, and cultural change does not necessarily mean loss of authenticity (Cohen 1988). Neither does change have to mean commodification. The Draaksteken event has seen many developments, and all of them are in line with the authenticity and the traditional values of the event, in the eyes of the participants. However, the change in the design is often an organic one, a change that grew into the design slowly, instead of a deliberate action to generate change. This is in contrast with existing models which focus on designing change in a more radical way, often used in mega-events (Fredline *et al.* 2003; Kaplanidou *et al.* 2013). These events are designed to generate many impacts in a short period of time. A more gradual change in design, as seen in traditional com-munity events, asks for a different, less radical approach (see Trono and Rizzello, Chapter 8). In order to gain more insights into a slower event design, this chapter explores the slow principles. The slow philosophy has successfully proposed a dif-ferent perspective in other areas such as slow food, slow tourism and so on (Gardner 2009; Lumsdon and McGrath 2011). The slow philosophy puts sustainability and social impacts at the core of the development, instead of economic gain. When applied to events, this could give a new perspective on event design. Consequently, the research question of this chapter is: What makes an event slow?

Methodology

This study adopts a qualitative approach. In order to apply slow principles to events, I studied the concepts of slow food, slow cities, slow tourism and slow travel, in order to extract characteristics that fit the concept of slow events. To illustrate this concept, the case of Draaksteken Beesel is described. This com-munity event is staged every seven years by the inhabitants of Beesel, a village in the south of the Netherlands. This case study was selected because it is a tra-ditional event, which has managed to remain successful for over 300 years, it is organized bottom-up by community members and it has seen many develop-ments. Besides that, the long time period between events gives the participants the opportunity to design it in a slow manner, and the long intervals make the developments in the design clearly visible.

The description of the event is based on desk research; internal documents and books about the event were studied. In addition to this, the author of a recent book about the event was interviewed and served as a key informant. Informal interviews were held with key stakeholders, such as the chairman and the former chairman of the board as well as inhabitants of the village, who are participants in the event. These informal interviews were conducted during two community meetings. The first meeting took place on 14 December 2012. It was a gathering during which it was announced that the event had been added to the Dutch UNESCO inventory of intangible heritage. During this meeting, I was able to observe and document the way the inhabitants of Beesel talked about the event. The second meeting took place on 18 June 2013. This was a community brainstorm session about the future of the event, and the impact of the event on the village. During this meeting I was asked to participate, and I joined several groups of inhabitants, who discussed the meaning of the event for the village. This meeting allowed me to observe and document more about the event, and I verified most of my earlier findings with community members. The framework of a slow event as described in this chapter served as a guideline in the interviews and observations. Questions were asked about the time element, the developments, the decision making process and the meaning of the event for the individual and the community. The documents, field notes and transcripts were analysed, and the outcomes used in describing the main themes: people, place, time and development. The outcomes were verified with the community and with the key informant in order to obtain an accurate description of the event as experienced by the participants.

Literature review

Timms and Conway (2011: 398) describe the slow movement as 'the antithesis to the fast and unsustainable life of modern industrial society through advocating a return to a more sustainable slow life based on savouring experience, rather than maximizing consumption.' The slow movement intends to reveal the possibilities that occur when life is experienced at a different, slower pace. The thought behind it is that rushing through life is causing mediocrity and that these days people need to be reminded of the alternative to a fast way of living. The slow perspective has been successful in other areas such as slow food, slow cities, slow travel and slow tourism.

Slow food

The slow food movement originates from Bra, Italy. It really started off in 1986 when in Piazza di Spagna in Rome, Italy, a protest took place against the opening of a McDonald's restaurant in this historic place. Carlo Petrini led a group of protesters, carrying bowls of fresh penne, to the opening of the fast food outlet (Petrini 2003, 2007, 2010; Dunlap 2012). This action marks the starting point of the slow food movement. The aim of the movement was simple: to protect local, fresh and seasonal food from the upcoming fast food trend and at the same time to promote sustainability and respect for the earth. The slow food movement promotes an awareness of eating habits and a mindful way of preparing food (Petrini 2003, 2007, 2010; Nilsson *et al.* 2011; Dunlap 2012; Warwick and Laing 2013). The movement was successful and expanded rapidly. Nowadays it is active in 150 countries around the world. The ideal meal of the slow food movement has three components: convivial, mindful and ethical (Heitmann *et al.* 2011; Dunlap 2012). A convivial is a group of people who host dinners and food tasting events and teach about food and taste. Conviviality entails engagement with participants as well as with the food prepared and consumed. Mindfulness refers to the sensual pleasures of home grown food, taste, texture and so on. Ethical refers to the engagement with the producers of the food (Dunlap 2012). When looking for a way to design community events, these three principles can form a resistance against commodification (Saleh and Ryan 1993; Brewster *et al.* 2009).

Slow cities

Slow cities (Cittaslow) is an extension of the slow food movement. The slow city movement was formed in 1999 in the town of Greve in Chianti, Italy. The mayor of this town created a new kind of development, based on improving quality of life. The main goal of Cittaslow was spreading the philosophy of slow food to local communities and to governments of towns. In their slogan, Cittaslow claims to be an international network of cities 'where the living is easy'. Nowadays there are more than 100 slow cities spread over 27 countries and four continents. The movement seeks a balance between modernity and tradition. Although modernity is not ruled out, the preservation of local and cultural heritage and the integration of local production and support of independent businesses are key elements of a slow city (Miele 2008; Heitmann *et al.* 2011; Nilsson *et al.* 2011). Achieving a balance between modernity and tradition is an important factor for community events that need to renew while remaining authentic.

Slow travel

Applying the slow principles to travelling, the time element plays an important role. The main idea is that the journey to and from a destination should not be seen as a waste of time and as something that should be done as fast as possible, but instead as a vital part of the tourist experience. The slow principles conviviality, mindfulness and ethics are clearly visible in the concept. Slow travel is about making time for the journey itself, for engagement with local people, for the environment, to minimize negative impacts and to relax (Dickinson 2009; Gardner 2009; Lumsdon and McGrath 2011). Planning the journey and taking the time that is needed to enjoy the city or the landscape, will lead to a better experience.

Slow tourism

Slow tourism is based on two principles: taking time and attachment to a particular place (Lumsdon and McGrath 2011; Yurtseven and Kaya 2011). Heitmann *et al.* (2011: 117) describe it as a 'shift from a focus on quantity and volume of experiences towards the quality of (generally fewer) experiences'. They state that the soul of the town and local heritage are important concepts (Heitmann *et al.* 2011). Attachment to a particular place is also something that can be applied to events, since especially traditional community events are often linked to the identity of a place (De Bres and Davies 2001). Furthermore, the slow tourism philosophy includes a specific view on development. The general idea is that development should suit the place and the people involved. Development is stimulated instead of physical growth (Daly 1990; Timms and Conway 2011).

Slow events

The previous literature review provides guidelines and ideas, which can serve as a foundation for the framework of slow events. When applying these ideas to events, a picture occurs of a slow event, which is convivial, mindful and ethical. The slow principles have implications for the design of a slow event. First of all, engagement with local people and the place in which the event is staged are important elements. One of the most important impacts of community events is place identity (De Bres and Davies 2001). Taking time is a second element which is emphasized in the slow movement and when applying this to event design, it has implications for the duration and the frequency of the event. And lastly, the development of an event can be slow, which means that the focus is on development instead of growth and quality is more important than quantity. Based on these ideas, the elements of a slow event are outlined in Box 7.1.

Box 7.1 A framework for slow events

Slow events

People
A slow event is organized bottom-up. The community is involved in decision-making processes. The benefits flow back to the community.

Place
A slow event is rooted in locality. It has a strong connection to the place where it is held, and it can make the visitor experience connect to this place through stories.

Time
A slow event takes the time that is necessary for the event to be experienced to the fullest by the people involved in the event as well as by the visitors. This means that the frequency as well as the duration is not based on maximizing profit, but on maximizing the experience. Additionally, time is taken for designing the event, involving the voices of different stakeholders.

Development
A slow event is focused on development instead of growth. The development will benefit the event itself as well as the people and the community involved. Decisions are made in close cooperation with or by the local community.

Based on the framework of slow events (Box 7.1), the case study of Draaksteken Beesel will be described as an example of a slow event. The emphasis in the case study will be on the four themes as stated in the framework: people, place, time and development.

The research question of this chapter, 'What makes an event slow?' has been answered from a theoretical point of view, but the case study will give more insights into how a slow event works in practice. It will show how a traditional community event can be rooted in locality, what the effect is of reducing the frequency of an event and how a traditional event can develop without losing its authenticity.

Case study Draaksteken Beesel

Draaksteken Beesel is an event that is staged only once every seven years by the inhabitants of Beesel, a small community in the south of the Netherlands. The event originates from 1736, when the legend of Saint George and the Dragon was first performed by the inhabitants of the village. The performance is based on the lyrics of the Song of the Poisonous Dragon. This is a local song, based on the story from the Legenda Aurea. It tells the story of a dragon that eats human flesh. To keep the dragon calm, every day a child is sacrificed, and one day this child happens to be the princess. When the princess is awaiting her destiny on a stone, a knight appears. In the name of Christ he challenges the dragon, and after a heroic fight the dragon is tamed, led through the village and finally slayed after all inhabitants have converted to Catholicism.

Saint George was patron saint of the civic guard of Beesel. In the nineteenth century, the play of Saint George and the Dragon would be performed during the annual fair. People gathered, and when there were enough people present, the dragon was slain and the Song of the Poisonous Dragon was sung. In the beginning the event only took place if the financial means of the civic guard were sufficient, but since 1902 the event has evolved steadily.

The Draaksteken event is of great significance to the community. Even though it is only staged once every seven years, it is a strong identity builder: the village is called, and calls itself 'the Dragon Village'. It is often seen that legends are claimed by a particular place or community. They are in fact local varieties of an international well known story (Hover 2013). The legend of Saint George and the Dragon is attached to different international places, which makes it a migratory legend (De Blécourt *et al.* 2010: 8).

In December 2012 Draaksteken Beesel was the fifth Dutch tradition to be added to the Dutch UNESCO inventory of intangible heritage. This was announced during a festive evening in Beesel. Many people attended the gathering and all age groups were present: families with babies as well as teenagers and elderly people. During that evening, the community's enthusiasm and love for the event became evident. The inhabitants speak proudly about their event. It is a vital part of their local identity and a great source of social cohesion and joy.

Draaksteken Beesel is an unusual event in the sense that it is only staged once every seven years. This fact, combined with the long tradition and the bottom-up organization, makes it a good illustration of all elements of a slow event: people and place, time and development.

Place

According to Richards and Palmer (2010: 23), 'events have taken on a new meaning in post-modern society, where they become not only an essential experience in themselves but also an important underpinning of individual and group identity'. De Bres and Davies (2001: 326) even call 'challenging the perception of local identity' one the most important outcomes of small festivals. As mentioned previously, the local identity of Beesel is closely linked to the story of Saint George and the Dragon. The village calls itself the Dragon Village. The event is staged near the local castle and it is performed in the local dialect. The dragon has become the symbol of the community and is ever present. The official logo of the municipality is a dragon, there is a statue of a dragon at the entrance of the village and the coat of arms portrays a dragon. Traces of the dragon are everywhere: the day-care centre is called Dragon's Nest, many houses carry shields of the dragon and local entrepreneurs are gathered in the Brotherhood of the Dragon. During the year of the event, many dragon-related products are produced: dragon bread, dragon chutney, dragon art, dragon coins and so on. In addition, more than 100 (painted) footsteps of the dragon can be found in and around the village.

However, although the identity of the people from Beesel is closely related to the event, many of the references to the dragon are invisible for outsiders, except during the months of the event. At the moment, efforts are made to make this dragon identity more visible, especially for tourists. This is created bottom-up, through brainstorm sessions with the community, together with the Draaksteken committee and the municipality. During the first brainstorm session ideas that were gathered ranged from dragon dishes at the local restaurant to dragon activities during other events in the region. Even though visitors will not always recognize it, the dragon is at the heart of the community and the event is of great importance to the inhabitants. Beesel makes Draaksteken and Draaksteken makes Beesel (Verdonck 2012).

People

The community of Beesel consists of 2,500 inhabitants of whom 1,000 are actively involved in the event. They perform in the play or they are part of one of the many committees, such as the Costume Committee, the Dragon Building Committee, the Stage Committee and so on. The rest of the community is more indirectly involved during the months of the event, for example by decorating their houses. The organization is completely bottom-up. All participants are volunteers, except for the director, who is hired by the steering committee.

To safeguard the event for the future, the children are involved in the event by performing with their parents, but they also learn how to stage the event in school, by organizing their own children's Draaksteken. This is a big school project in which the children can experience all the facets of the event. The Draaksteken director also directed the children's play and in 2009 the project won a regional prize for best cultural children's project.

The event is staged in the local dialect. This might seem obvious because it is the way people communicate on a daily basis, but most other plays are performed in Dutch. The dialect is an important part of the identity of the village, and speaking the dialect creates an immediate sense of belonging. The feeling of the event is described by one of the inhabitants as 'the Draaksteken bubble'. When Draaksteken is there, it creates a feeling of togetherness with a common goal. It mobilizes people to just go ahead and do things and make decisions that contribute to the Draaksteken feeling. The people of Beesel have no problem contributing their time, creativity, knowledge and materials to the Draaksteken event. According to the former chairperson of the organizing committee, 'Draaksteken helps to improve the sense of community, and at the same time one needs the community to organize something like this'.

The event can be seen as a successful interaction ritual which generates emotional energy and solidarity, amongst other effects (Collins 2004; Richards 2013). A successful interaction ritual has several crucial elements (Collins 2004). First, bodily presence is an essential element and obvious for most events. A mutual focus is a second element, which in this case is the performance and the dragon, which has become an emotionally charged symbol. Third, a distinction between insiders and outsiders is necessary, which is very clear in this case: only inhabitants of Beesel can participate and additionally the local dialect forms a barrier to outsiders. And, finally, a shared mood or emotional experience is essential, which is described in several ways: the Draaksteken bubble, the dragon fire and the Draaksteken virus. The time element, described below, seems to make this ritual even more intense and it allows for an interaction ritual chain (Collins 2004) to take place, as many smaller interaction rituals take place during the long preparation phase of the event.

Time

Time plays an important role in the slow philosophy. In the case of Draaksteken, we can see an interesting relationship between time and the intensity of the event. The event is only staged once every seven years, and, according to the participants, the effort in organizing the event is so big, that they cannot organize it more frequently. On the other hand, the intensity of the event also increases because of the time element. Because it only takes place once every seven years, everyone wants to be involved and people are willing to put in great effort.

The event absorbs the village completely. Auditions start a year prior to the event, the building of the dragon and the preparation of the costumes even two years before. Every committee starts on its own, and slowly they grow together.

During the year of the event, rehearsals take place every week, for the speaking roles. Participants do not go on holiday in the year of the event, instead they prepare for the event. The preparation phase actually consists of a range of smaller interaction rituals (Collins 2004; Richards 2013) leading up to the event. Examples are taking the costumes out of their storage place in the church tower, which marks the start of the costume committee. The male actors grow beards during the months before the event, and the day after the event they are all shaved by the local barber. Again we can see all the elements of successful inter-action rituals present in these smaller activities, leading to outcomes as solid-arity, emotional energy, collective symbols (the dragon) and sanctions (social exclusion) against violation of these symbols (Collins 2004; Richards 2013). This explains the strong impact the event has on the village and the participants and why the symbol of the dragon is so important to them.

Development

As described in the framework of slow events, a characteristic of a slow event is a focus on development instead of growth. The changes that occurred in the Draaksteken event were gradual and followed the signs of the times. It becomes clear that instead of being a (passive) object of change, the community is dealing with change (Richards 2007) and this is reflected in the event. Every edition of Draaksteken Beesel is different. And because of the low frequency of the event, changes that take place in the community as well as in society as a whole, are reflected and made visible by the event. Changes occur explicitly, by changing the storyline, and implicitly by the different people who are involved.

A first example of this is the role of the princess, which reflects the role of women in society. During the 1970s, the princess changed from a passive being into a powerful person, who supported her father in the fight against the dragon (Verdonck 2012).

A second example is the dragon, which has always been a symbol of evil, but the exact source of this evil has evolved. At the start of the event the dragon por-trayed the devil. After the Second World War, the event symbolized liberation and the dragon portrayed the enemy. The revenues of that event were used to rebuild the church tower, which was destroyed during the war. During the last editions, when the engagement of the visitors became more important, the dragon reflected the evil in ourselves.

A final development is seen in the role of the 'ordinary people' in the play. During the 1960s the ordinary citizen was introduced into the play. At first it was a play about royalty only, but now a common family runs from the dragon. In the play the ordinary people speak the local dialect, whereas the royals speak Dutch, although at emotional moments, they sometimes switch to dialect.

All these developments are watched and judged by the community, and when a change is made that is not in line with their sense of authenticity, they object. In 1960, a sound system was introduced. This caused some resistance, but it was accepted later and seen as a good decision. Seven years later the lyrics were changed into a modern version and more speaking roles were added. In 1981 an important change took place when Saint George was no longer the main character, but an ordinary village boy Michel. He fell in love with the princess and married her in the end. Moreover, the dragon was no longer the symbol of the devil, but was possessed by it. A much criticized act of exorcism was written in the play, until it disappeared again in 1995. Due to criticism from within the community, the 'Hollywood story' of Michel and the princess disappeared as well seven years later. 'Changes just happen. If it does not fit, it will be changed back' (Verdonck 2012). Very important in this sense is the original Song of the Poisonous Dragon, which is used to safeguard the storyline of the event. There is a consensus in the community that this song is the core of the event.

The 2009 edition of the event was more experience focused. A professional director, who was selected by the steering committee, took Draaksteken to a new level. Besides a more impressive dragon, due to technical possibilities, changes were made in the play itself: the storyteller was replaced by a group of troubadours and there were more visuals and less explanation. Hypothetically speaking, this design can be replaced by something else again, when the times change.

Finally, comparing the 2009 event with the original event as described by Verdonck (2012), one can see a change in purpose. And as Richards and Palmer (2010) state, the change in purpose also changes the design. Because event design is a strategy to generate stakeholder value, the design will change when the value is defined differently. Nowadays, Draaksteken is a community event and the design is focused on social cohesion. Many years ago, when the event belonged to the civil guard, it used to be much shorter, because a long play would keep people from drinking in the bar (Verdonck 2012), which illustrates it had a commercial function. Nowadays discussions are ongoing with the municipality, about how to make the event into an image builder and a tourist attraction. The municipality hopes that the event and the symbol of the dragon could lead to more jobs and income, which would prevent people from leaving the village. This could change the design as well, because it changes the purpose of the event (Richards and Palmer 2010). The framework of slow events could be beneficial here, arguing for a slow development which suits the event and the community. Community involvement is crucial, also for the perception of the event as authentic, both by the community as well as the visitors (Cohen 1988; Richards 2007; Brida *et al.* 2012). Furthermore, following Collins' theory on interaction ritual chains, the symbol of the dragon is a very strong symbol for insiders, but might be less strong for outsiders as it is symbolically charged during the ritual. This might be an obstacle to developing it as a tourist attraction.

Conclusions

In the first section of this chapter, the slow principles were applied to events, resulting in a framework for slow events. Moreover, the case study gave a clear picture on how the different themes of a slow event, people, place, time and development are dealt with in reality, and how they interact. This interaction demonstrates that a slow event, or a slow design for events, is more than a sum of separate elements. It is the interaction between the elements that is crucial for the concept. For example, the time element interacts with the experience of the participants: because the local community experiences the event as very intensive, they feel that the event cannot be organized more than once every seven years. At the same time, the rare occurrence of the event intensifies the local involvement and the experience. They cannot be seen separately. Another example is the development, which interacts with the people dimension. Often traditional events are seen as authentic as opposed to novel, experience driven, modern events. This case study shows that by combining a strong authentic base (the lyrics of the song) with a collective decision making process, many developments can take place without jeopardizing the sense of authenticity experienced by the participants. As stated before, it is important to incorporate change into an event, in order to keep it interesting. In this respect it is crucial to recognize the difference between growth and development. Although these two concepts sometimes go hand in hand, growth has a quantitative focus, whereas development has more potential to incorporate people and place elements like collective decision making and authenticity, which are essential for community events.

When we look at the research question 'What makes an event slow?' a definition can be given solely based on literature, but the case study shows that the different elements interact and that a slow event should been seen as a holistic concept. This has implications for the practical relevance for slow events. Looking at how to use the concept of slow events, two directions can be identified.

First of all, events can be slow by design. Designing a slow event can be done in close cooperation with a community. A new event could be developed according to the slow principles. The case study gives practical suggestions on how this can be done. The basis of the event has to be strong and supported by the community (in this case the Song of the Poisonous Dragon). An interaction can be sought between the event and community identity: the community defines the event and the event defines the community. In the case of Beesel, the community is very close, and the event strengthens this even more. The social impacts of the event reach far beyond the actual event.

Second, the concept of slow events can be used to identify existing community events as slow, and help maintain their slow identity in the next stages of their development. In practice, many traditional community events probably fit most of the characteristics of a slow event. What often happens is that community events want to attract more visitors which leads to a focus on growth. In Beesel this discussion is ongoing. The concept of slow events could contribute to this discussion and serve as a framework which allows developments to go hand in hand with community involvement and authenticity. In this way positive social impacts can be maintained, when opening up community events to a larger audience.

The holistic concept of slow events also implies that it would be difficult to make a fast event slower. Just adding more local elements to the design, or changing the time element, would not make it slow. The slowness needs to be integrated into the design. It is a combination of a strong connection to a place, a bottom-up organization, collective decision making, taking time and mindful development.

This case study is only approached from the perspective of the community; therefore it is not clear whether the visitors would also call the event slow. It might well be that Draaksteken Beesel is slow by design in the preparation phase and for the community, but not necessarily slow in the eyes of the visitor. Future research might take the visitor perspective into consideration.

The case study of Draaksteken Beesel is not just interesting when looking at slow events, but it is also an example of how an event contributes to the social identity of a community. These days identities are said to be a work in progress (Blackshaw 2010). The Draaksteken event illustrates how a traditional community event leads to solidarity, emotional energy and collective symbols (Collins 2004; Richards 2013). Future research might show how interaction rituals chains and social identities are linked, and how events contribute to one of the most basic functions of leisure: re-creation of both individuals and communities (Dunlap 2012).

Acknowledgements

Many thanks to Greg Richards, Lénia Marques and Karen Mein for supporting me in writing this chapter. Furthermore, thanks are due to Annet Ghering for her attentive reading. And especially thanks to Sanne Verdonck for sharing her valuable inside information and her enthusiasm about Draaksteken as well as to the steering committee of Draaksteken Beesel for welcoming me to their community meetings.

References

Berridge, G. (2012) 'Event Experience: A Case Study of Differences Between the Way in Which Organizers Plan an Event and the Way in Which Guests Receive the Experience', *Journal of Park and Recreation Administration*, 30(3): 7–23.

Blackshaw, T. (2010) *Leisure*, New York: Routledge.

Blécourt, W. de, Koman, R.A., van der Kooi, J. and Meder, T. (eds) (2010) *Verhalen van Stad en Streek: Sagen en Legenden in Nederland*, Amsterdam: Uitgeverij Bert Bakker.

Bowdin, G., Allen, J., O'Toole, W., Harris, R. and McDonnell, I. (2010) *Event Management*, 3rd edn, Oxford: Butterworth Heinemann.

Brewster, M., Connell, J. and Page, S.J. (2009) 'The Scottish Highland Games: Evolution, Development and Role as a Community Event', *Current Issues in Tourism*, 12(3): 271–293.

Brida, J.G., Disegna, M. and Osti, L. (2012) 'Perceptions of Authenticity of Cultural Events: A Host–Tourist Analysis', *Tourism, Culture and Communication*, 12(2): 85–96.

Cohen, E. (1988) 'Authenticity and Commoditization in Tourism', *Annals of Tourism Research*, 15(3): 371–386.

Collins, J. (2004) *Interaction Ritual Chains*, Princeton, NJ: Princeton University Press.

Daly, H.E. (1990) 'Sustainable Growth: An Impossible Theorem', *Development*, 3(4): 45–47.

De Bres, K. and Davis, J. (2001) 'Celebrating Group and Place Identity: A Case Study of a New Regional Festival', *Tourism Geographies*, 3(3): 326–337.

Dickinson, J. (2009) 'Slow Tourism Travel for a Lower Carbon Future'. Online, available at: www.bournemouth.ac.uk/icthr/PDFs/rgs_report.pdf (accessed 29 June 2013).

Dunlap, R. (2012) 'Recreating Culture: Slow Food as a Leisure Education Movement', *World Leisure Journal*, 54(1): 38–47.

Fredline, L., Jago, L. and Deery, M. (2003) 'Development of a Generic Scale to Measure the Social Impacts of Events', *Event Management*, 8(1): 23–37.

Gardner, N. (2009) 'A Manifesto for Slow Travel', *Hidden Europe Magazine*, 25: 10–14.

Getz, D. (2012) *Event Studies: Theory Research and Policy for Planned Events*, 2nd edn, London: Routledge.

Heitmann, S., Robinson, P. and Povey, G. (2011) 'Slow Food, Slow Cities and Slow Tourism', in P. Robinson, S. Heitmann and P. Dieke (eds) *Research Themes in Tourism*, Oxford: CABI, pp. 114–127.

Hover, M. (2013) 'De Efteling als Verteller van Sprookjes', Unpublished PHD thesis, Tilburg University.

Kaplanidou, K., Karadakis, K., Gibson, H., Thapa, B., Walker, M., Geldenhuys, S. and Coetzee, W. (2013) 'Quality of Life, Event Impacts and Mega Event Support among South African Residents before and after the 2010 FIFA World Cup', *Journal of Travel Research*, 52(5): 631–645.

Lumsdon, L.M. and McGrath, P. (2011) 'Developing a Conceptual Framework for Slow Travel: A Grounded Theory Approach', *Journal of Sustainable Tourism*, 19(3): 265–279.

Miele, M. (2008) 'Cittaslow: Producing Slowness against the Fast Life', *Space and Polity*, 12(1): 135–156.

Nilsson, J.H., Svard, A., Widarsson, A. and Wirrel, T. (2011) 'Cittáslow Eco-gastronomic Heritage as a Tool for Destination Development', *Current Issues in Tourism*, 14(4): 373–389.

Petrini, C. (2003) *Slow Food, the Case for Taste*, New York/Chichester, West Sussex: Columbia University Press.

Petrini, C. (2007) *Slow Food Nation: Why our Food should be Good, Clean, and Fair*, New York: Rizolli Ex Libris.

Petrini, C. (2010) *Terra Madre: Forging a New Global Network of Sustainable Food Communities*, Hartford, VT: Chelsea Green Publishing.

Richards, G. (2007) 'Culture and Authenticity in a Traditional Event: The Views of Producers, Residents and Visitors in Barcelona', *Event Management*, 11(1/2): 33–44.

Richards, G. (2013) 'Events and the Means of Attention', *Journal of Tourism Research and Hospitality*, 2(2): 1–5.

Richards, G. and Palmer, R. (2010) *Eventful Cities: Cultural Management and Urban Revitalisation*, London: Routledge.

Richards, G., de Brito, M.P. and Wilks, L. (eds) (2013) *Exploring the Social Impacts of Events*, London: Routledge.

Saleh, F. and Ryan, C. (1993) 'Jazz and Knitwear: Factors that Attract Tourists to Festivals', *Tourism Management*, 14(4): 289–297.

Sewell, W.H. (1996) 'Historical Events as Transformations of Structures: Inventing Revolution at the Bastille', *Theory and Society*, 25(6): 841–881.

Shone, A. and Parry, B. (2004) *Successful Event Management: A Practical Handbook*, 2nd edn, London: Thompson.

Timms, B.F. and Conway, D. (2011) 'Slow Tourism at the Caribbean's Geographical Margins', *Tourism Geographies, an International Journal of Tourism, Space, Place and Environment*, 14(3): 396–418.

Yurtseven, H.R. and Kaya, O. (2011) 'Slow Tourists: A Comparative Research based on the Cittaslow Principles', *American International Journal of Contemporary Research*, 1(2): 91–98.

Verdonck, S. (2012) *Draaksteken: St. Joris leeft voort in Beesel*, Schiedam: Pharos.

Warwick, F. and Laing, J. (2013) 'Communicating Persuasive Messages through Slow Food Festivals', *Journal of Vacation Marketing*, 19(1): 67–74.

8 Designing events for socio-cultural impacts

The Holy Week in Puglia (Italy)

Anna Trono and Katia Rizzello[1]

Introduction

In Italy, Spain, Portugal and Greece, Holy Week is characterized by intense expressions of devotion linked to the celebration of religious rites, popular customs and traditions, which attract a considerable number of worshippers, tourists and the simply curious. As well as local organizations, which recognize the event's strong tourist potential, the rites of Holy Week have been of interest to anthropologists (Marcovecchio 2005; Martini 2005; Zuppante 2005), geographers (Jorge 2009; Zammit 2009), psychologists (Noel and Johnson 2005; Pizzato 2005), historians (Caputo 1983, 1985; Caputo and Majorano 1998), photographers, television reporters and even film directors (Mel Gibson, producer, director and co-writer of *The Passion of the Christ* 2003).

In Puglia, Italy, the rites of Holy Week are celebrated in a manner that is deeply moving for the participants; they constitute an act of collective mourning, marked by the hushed involvement of the crowds. The rites of Holy Week are becoming increasingly popular not only within the local community and the faithful but also among tourists and the curious attracted by the mystical atmosphere of the event. The success and the distinctiveness of the rites also lie in the slow step of the hooded penitents, the costumes of the confraternities and above all in the musicality of *ritual chanting* (sung in the local dialect) used for the individual moments and symbolic stages of the rites.

The rites of Holy Week are an important form of intangible cultural heritage that produces a significant outcome not only in terms of the numbers of tourists attracted, but also in the socio-economic consequences for the areas involved.

After a brief general description of the rites of the Holy Week, this chapter presents the results of a direct investigation conducted in the city of Taranto in Puglia, where the event is one of the most important of the liturgical year in many small and large cities. The research focuses on the role of confraternities, parishes and local communities, with information drawn from direct sources. A total of 199 interviews were conducted with pilgrims, visitors and tourists (100) and about 20 special interviews with stakeholders, local authorities and persons involved in the planning and promotion of the event. The study made it possible to learn about the role of visitors, residents and stakeholders in the promotion of the event, their perception of the rites of Holy Week and the value they assign to them. This analysis considers the different aspects of the design of the event and their effect on event outcomes.

The specific character of events linked to religious celebrations

According to Janiskee, events include 'formal periods or programs of pleasurable activities, entertainment, or events having a festive character and publicly celebrating some concept, happening or fact' (1980: 97). The festive and celebratory characteristic brings together and involves the entire community and for this reason has direct effects on the cultural identity of regions. As Getz affirms, events 'give identity to places and individuals and bind communities together' (2012: 28). These events are even more important when the event is based on – and promotes – local culture (Archambault 2009). This is frequently seen in the festivities that celebrate the rhythms of agricultural societies (Rolfe 1992) and in rites and celebrations of a religious nature (Gotham 2005). On these occasions the event acts 'as an important means of collective identification for the communities' (Quinn 2009: 6).

Over time, religious celebrations have become not just an authentic expression of faith but also a chance for social interaction. The anthropological value of the rites and the shared participation in them lies not only in the forms of worship and expressions of penitence displayed by the participants, but also in their associative function. The presence of those who play roles in the rituals, together with the participation of the people present, strengthens the sense of belonging to a group (*communitas*) among its constituent elements.

From the organizational and management point of view, events of a religious nature are mainly staged by organizations or volunteer groups that actively involve the residents in all phases of organization, management and implementation of the event. The ability of people to work together towards a common purpose in groups and organizations (Coleman 1988; Cleaver 2005; Jones 2005; Saxena 2006) is at the basis of the formation of social capital. Indeed, the ability to cooperate voluntarily depends on the degree to which communities share norms and values and are able to subordinate individual interests to those of larger groups (Paldam and Svendsen 1998; Stewart-Weeks and Richardson 1998; Rudd 2000; Cattell 2001; Stone and Hughes 2002; Mattsson and Stenbacka 2003; Jones 2005; Saxena 2006).

In events, the mutual interaction and cooperation between different groups and stakeholders increases trust between members and their capacity for collective action. In addition, it gives people a greater sense of belonging and participation by facilitating social mobilization of residents and it increases communication among local residents. The basis of local events that involve the celebration of religious festivities is precisely these voluntary organizations and associations. Thus, if communities play a central role in the management and implementation of activities there will be a double result. On the one hand social capital will be enhanced and on the other hand there will be a deeper sense of belonging and a reinforcement of exclusive identities. The community becomes a protagonist in the festivities and shows itself in all its traditions and its folk knowledge. During these traditional religious events the community is clearly seen to 'play an important role in the production, safeguarding, maintenance and re-creation of the intangible cultural heritage' (UNESCO 2003). Indeed, the extensive involvement of the community in all phases of the event, from organization to implementation, ensures that each religious event has a unique atmosphere that distinguishes it from the others and guarantees its success. For the local community these events are so significant that they become emblematic of the locality and a showcase for the outside world. They acquire the same function that bell-towers and fortifications held during the Middle Ages: they are testimony to the development and cultural greatness of a community. Religious ceremonies also play an ethical role when understood as an opportunity for improving the image of the city, improving the socio-economic situation and promoting regional development (Brunet *et al.* 2001).

Events linked to religious celebrations have certain features that render them quite distinct from the broader panorama of cultural events in general and characterize their organization and management. Their main characteristics derive from their nature and meaning.

Religious events are closely linked to rites and celebrations that take place regularly in accordance with the calendar and change little over the centuries. For these reasons the programmes of religious celebrations remain broadly unchanged over time. Rich in symbols, these celebrations are charged with meaning for believers and are characterized by great emotional involvement, to the point that Getz (2007) describes them simply as 'religious experiences'.

Getz proposes a model of perception of the experience of the event which includes the concept of the *liminarity zone*, developed from the theories of van Gennep (1909) and Turner (1969). This denotes a zone, spatial and temporal, within which there is an interruption of the daily routine, or to use Falassi's term, a 'time out of time' (1987). In this zone the visitors perceive clearly that they are entering in a 'space/time that has been set aside for their special purposes' (Getz 2007: 178), a special and unrepeatable atmosphere, not only outside their normal routine but outside space and time. In the streets of the centre of Taranto, timeless scenes and atmospheres are reproduced, sending the spectators into a state of 'rapture, ecstasy, transcendence, revelation' (Getz 2007: 184), with an intense 'flow experience' (Csíkszentmihályi 1990) that causes deep involvement, intense concentration, lack of self-consciousness and transcendence of self.

The unique circumstances that take place during the events affect the visitors' emotions and feeling in terms of production of emotional energy. They become part of the representation, they share with the worshippers that carry the symbols of the Passion though the streets of the old town the same pathos and mood and they are for that reason part of the representation: they become the crowd of Jerusalem. In that way they mark a strong boundary both physically and psychologically with the external World, as they are a member of a cohesive group. That situation produces an intense emotional energy that, as Collins states, is 'a feeling of confidence, elation, strength, enthusiasm, and initiative in taking action' (2004: 49).

The capacity of the rites of Holy Week to create such a unique and special atmosphere has made this a hallmark event, enabling it to 'function like a monument, supporting and reinforcing the image of established power, whether religious or secular' (Bonnemaison 1990: 25). As Getz affirms, 'hallmark events are typically periodic and co-branded with the destination, yielding a positive image' (Getz 2012: 29). In this sense, ensuring this event fulfils its potential could be a strategic move for repositioning the image of the city of Taranto.

The Holy Week rites and the history of Taranto

The liturgical celebrations of Holy Week run from Jesus' arrival in Jerusalem to his resurrection and apparition to the disciples: the key moment is the sacred three-day period of Easter, which runs from the Thursday evening until sunset on resurrection Sunday. Holy Week is undoubtedly the richest of the celebrations during the year. It is a time when the liturgy is intertwined with manifestations of popular piety (Via Crucis, processions, holy representations). This dual aspect is the result of historical factors, and while the liturgical celebrations are clearly considered more important, a key role is also played by the other practices, in both historical and traditional terms. This is because they convey the same content as the liturgy by means of a language that is closer to popular sensibilities.

The latter adhere to an approach that is more theatrical and dramatic, consciously involving the emotional sphere, while the liturgical celebrations are characterized by a greater sobriety in their symbolic gestures and are founded on a broad adherence to the word of God. For example, the liturgy of Good Friday entails reading the passages in the Gospel relating to the Passion of the Lord, while in the popular piety the same story is enacted. A highly theatrical and scenic dimension is also evident in certain para-liturgical manifestations marking Holy Week in Puglia (Figure 8.1).

The events involve religious figures, local organizations and attract a considerable number of worshippers, tourists and the simply curious and confraternities, all custodians of deeply rooted cultural and religious traditions who play a key role: it is they who organize and bring to life the para-liturgical events in preparation for the most significant moments involving the visit to the sepulchres and the solemn processions. They are granted the ancient and exclusive privilege of carrying the effigies. The confraternities play an essential role in the execution of the evocative rites that each year draw numerous worshippers and tourists from all over Italy.

The presence of the local confraternities is evident in terms of both participation in the rites and their organization. There are 54 confraternities in Puglia with a total of about 15,000 members. Some of these are very

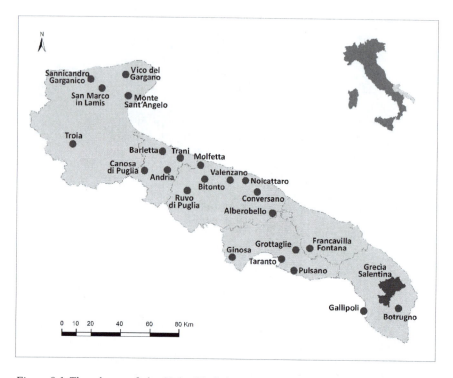

Figure 8.1 The places of the Holy Week in Puglia (sources: www.settimanasantain-puglia.it; www.viaggiareinpuglia.it/prov/BR/it; www.viaggiareinpuglia.it/prov/FG/it).

numerous, having up to 1,000 confrères, such as the 'Arciconfraternita del Carmine' or the 'Confraternita dell'Addolorata' in Taranto or the 'Arciconfraternita della Morte' in Molfetta in the province of Bari. They acquired their role during the Counter-Reformation when, following the Council of Trent (1545–1563), the 'holy representations', i.e. the manifestations of popular devotion in the form of plays, called 'Misteri' (i.e. mystery plays), were banned. The Misteri consisted of theatrical representations of texts from the Gospel, above all the Passion of Christ, performed in front of the churches. The 'holy representations' were replaced by processions organized by the confraternities, in which the 'Misteri' were no longer represented by actors but statues of Jesus Christ, the Madonna Addolorata (Our Lady of Sorrows) and the various characters of the Passion (Angelini 2005).

The confraternities are composed of lay members involved in liturgical activities or the defence of local religious traditions. The statutes of some of the confraternities envisage works of charity: the Arciconfraternita di S. Stefano in Molfetta provides assistance to the needy via an organization called the 'Bontà di Santo Stefano'.

The Holy Weeks in Taranto

The rites of Holy Week are very popular in Taranto, a city that in the last few years has suffered greatly in terms of environment, health and employment, but which continues to value its local religious traditions in spite of it all. Indeed, it is the respect for certain religious events, understood as cultural heritage, that guarantees the survival of the community. A social group (the organizing committee) plays a key role, in accordance with Collins' (2004) Interaction Ritual Chain model, via intense interactive rituals that bring the population together, thereby maintaining interest in the tradition (the Easter rites). By linking the secular and ecclesiastical worlds and constructing a sort of collective emotional excitement of Durkheimian memory (Collins 2004), the group is able to construct a network of interests, including tourism. This network can be the starting point for the social and economic recovery of a city that has been beaten down by powerful economic interests, amid the shameful indifference of the national, regional and local authorities.

The city of Taranto is situated in a strategic geographical location in the Mediterranean that has made it an important centre of migration, trade and cultural exchange since ancient times. It is also a thriving port: as well as traditional activities like fishing and fish-farming, until the late 1980s it was also a centre of shipbuilding (by the Cantieri Tosi and successor companies) and still hosts a large naval base (the Arsenale della Marina Militare). In 1960, it became the site of the fourth major steelworks in Italy, which is the largest but also the most polluting industrial plant in Europe. It is situated next to a settlement (Tamburi), near a housing estate that was not built illegally (as has been claimed) but by a state company, the social housing board. The building of the plant in this location shows the extreme indifference on the part of the authorities towards the potential social and environmental consequences for the community of Taranto. It was the result of a political decision by the new leadership of the Christian Democratic party after De Gasperi, which was justified by the claim that it would generate income and employment in the underdeveloped south of Italy. The industrialization of the backward Mezzogiorno involved the creation of areas of industrial development that would benefit from the integration of markets envisaged by the treaties of the European Economic Community. Above all, the new plant would increase the production of Italian steel in accordance with the overall logic of the Italian economic system (Celant and Morelli 1986: 115 and *passim*). The government desired an impressive industrial plant, designed mainly to produce cast iron, raw steel and laminates used for large scale metalworking,[2] which would give rise to economies of industrial agglomeration. Unfortunately, the creation of the Taranto industrial estate failed to create a pole of development, with the growth of small and medium sized local companies directly or indirectly dependent on this central industrial 'engine'. Not only this, it strangled local craft industries and agricultural activities linked to traditional modes of production (viticulture and olive groves) based on the fertility of the soil (Trono and Viterbo 1995).

Figure 8.2 The city of Taranto and pollution from the steel industry (source: Luigi Oliva).

Without doubt it has produced an environmental disaster that cannot be described as 'accidental'. There has been wilful negligence of all safeguards against accidents at work, contamination of foodstuffs, aggravated damage to public property, dumping of dangerous substances and atmospheric pollution (Figure 8.2), with dramatic effects on the health of the local population (including increased deaths from cancer) and their quality of life, which now ranks lowest in Italy.

The regional and local administrations responsible for the city over the last 50 years have made no effort whatsoever at urban renewal and have allowed its population to become brutalized by obliging them to choose between their health and employment. In this dramatic environmental and social situation, the community of Taranto manages to maintain an interest in its history and respect for its traditions and cultural, religious and social values. They have a deeply rooted attachment to popular forms of worship, local traditions and religious ceremonies, particularly the rites of Holy Week, managed by the parishes but conducted with the support of the confraternities, who are the real protagonists of the Easter rites (Caputo 1983: 30).

The confraternities of Taranto pay for the organization and management of the processions, the hiring of bands to play music, the setting up of the scenes of Christ's tomb known as the 'sepolcri', the restoration of the respective churches, the maintenance of the chapels in the cemetery and various charitable works (Figure 8.3). They provide assistance and are involved in philanthropic activities and promotion of self-help. An example is the Confraternity

Figure 8.3 Pairs of confrères from the Confraternity of Our Lady of Sorrows and of Our Lady of Mount Carmel (source: Laboratory of Political Economic Geography, University of Salento).

of the Addolorata in Taranto, which has set up an award called 'Cuore di Donna' (Woman's Heart), given annually to a woman from Taranto who has distinguished herself in terms of abnegation.

Numerous contributions from the confraternities, as emerges from direct research and interviews conducted with their members and leaders, have shown that the income from the events is offered to those members who require assistance, the poor of other parishes and certain prisoners' families.

To this may be added the annual study grants paid to student confrères and the recognition, by means of a diploma and a gold medal, of those confrères who each year mark 50 years of membership.

A significant source of income for the confraternities of Taranto is the *gare* (tenders): at these special assemblies, which take place on Palm Sunday, the symbols and statues to be carried in the processions are sold to worshippers. Members anxious to carry the symbols of the Passion make bids as in an auction. The *gare* are a system for awarding the right to carry the symbol in procession during the rite to the member who makes the highest bid in cash terms. They were introduced in the early decades of the nineteenth century to help the organizations bear the expenses, which were already high even then. In order to take an active part in the rites and carry in procession statues or individual symbols such as the *Troccola* (a characteristic musical instrument like a rattle) (Figure 8.4), Gonfalone (heraldic banner), Cross of the Mysteries, Christ in the Garden, etc., it is necessary to participate in the *gare*. The members of the confraternities

Figure 8.4 'Troccola' (source: www.settimanasantainpuglia.it).

are generally people without a high income (fishermen, manual workers, office workers, etc.), although the sums paid by them have always been substantial. In the last few years there has been an increase in the number of young members who save for a whole year in order to carry a 'symbol' in the procession.

The earnings of the confraternities are high, as shown by the accounts of the respective *gare*. The bids for symbols and statues have been and are still high, despite the economic slowdown and the city's serious environmental and social problems. In 2013 they ranged from a minimum of €2.55 for the *gonfalone* and €5,000 for the *troccola*[3] to €42,000 for the dead Jesus and €40,000 for the Addolorata.

Overall, sale of the symbols raised €78,000 for the procession of the Addolorata on the Thursday before Easter and €185,700 for the procession of the Misteri on Good Friday, making a total of €264,250. The Holy symbols, purchased for the rites of Holy Week, represent the individual devotion related to a more evident willingness to be part of the rite: 'sentiments can only be prolonged by symbols' (Durkheim cited in Collins 2004). The emotional energy that arises from the deep physical and emotional involvement 'makes the individual feel not only good, but exalted, with the sense of doing what is most important and most valuable' (Collins 2004: 39). Such strong experience fully justifies the important economic investment, and it activates a process that produces a widespread patronage. That means that the local community itself invests in and supports rites and traditions that constitute their own intangible cultural heritage.

The above-mentioned model of event design and management is sustainable both socially and economically, as it ensures reproducibility of the event without risk of commodification. Joy, disappointment, tears: these are the moods felt at the conclusion to the *gare*, which are known as the 'Markets of the Temple' and are part of the heritage of customs and habits of the people of Taranto.

The sound of the marching bands, the other protagonists of the rites in Taranto, also helps to characterize the event. Their strident notes mark the progress of all the processions, from the early afternoon of the Thursday before Good Friday until the morning of Easter Saturday.

The procession partially takes place in the ancient city. A high point in the religious celebrations, above all concerning their external manifestations, comes on the Friday before Palm Sunday, which was once known as Passion Sunday or the Sunday of the Sorrows, when almost every locality hosts a procession dedicated to the Addolorata or the Desolata (Our Lady of Sorrows) (see Figures 8.5 and 8.6).

Further processions are held over the following days, especially on Good Friday with the Procession of the Mysteries (see Figure 8.6).

The rites of Holy Week in Puglia are organized and managed by an organizing committee composed of lay and religious elements of the local community representing parishes, confraternities, cultural associations etc. The processions are the culmination of many other activities: concerts, photographic exhibitions and a series of events that are rich in atmosphere and have their own rituals and protagonists, who feel themselves to be the bearers of a tradition handed down from father to son.

The Holy Week Rites promote inclusive growth and social cohesion as well as raising awareness regarding the value of local cultural and religious heritage. They are an asset for the city and the region in terms of tourism. The result has been, in fact, an increase of about 20 per cent in tourist flows in the Easter period in the last ten years. The event has also paved the way for the structured and integrated provision of cultural tourism products and services in Taranto that were once considered 'off the beaten track' and has increased tourism outside the high season.

Socio-economic impact and ethical management

For the townsfolk of Taranto, Holy Week is a spectacle of faith which, seen from outside, is not easy to understand. It is not just religious fervour that animates the 'Tarantini', nor is it the charm of a fascinating and mysterious ritual. For the city it is a special occasion. During Holy Week the citizen of Taranto is proud to be such, because 'there are no rites more beautiful than these'. In addition, despite the passing of the centuries, they have maintained their fascination and

Figure 8.5 Procession dedicated to the Addolorata (source: Laboratory of Political Economic Geography, University of Salento).

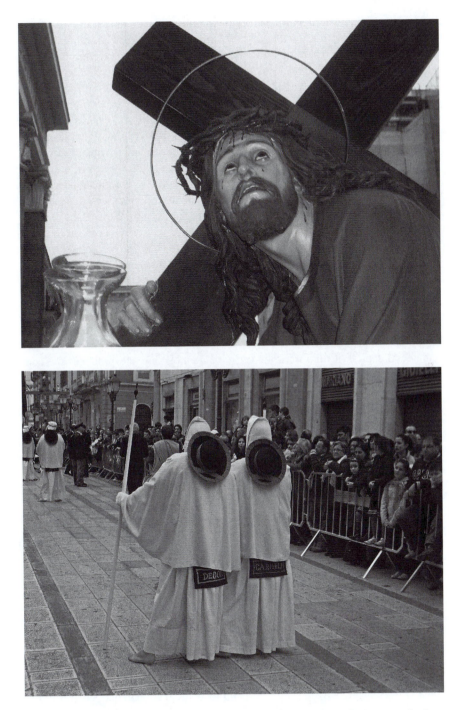

Figure 8.6 Procession of the Mysteries (source: Laboratory of Political Economic Geography, University of Salento).

have not lost their more spiritual meaning. In a city such as Taranto where so much has been lost due to neglect, the rites of Holy Week are an asset that nobody can destroy: traditions that are constantly renewed over the centuries. The city cherishes this great wealth of the past. What remains unchanged over time in Taranto is precisely the rites of Holy Week.

As well as the local community, an important role in the recognition and promotion of the rites of Holy Week is played by the local cultural associations, which work with the confraternities to promote the rites via photographic exhibitions, conferences, concerts and prizes (e.g. the 'Troccola D'Argento' awarded by Associazione Capital). The people who contribute to the success of the Easter rites become important symbols for the community, full of emotional energy and initiative, which enables them to participate in the religious ceremonies with enthusiasm and to attract new components to the group. We see the process described by Collins and Guillén: 'A network generates differential success, not merely by the information passed along in it, but by additional micro-interactional mechanisms that generate motivations and emotions, build reputations, form collective movements, and establish linkages both to the upstream and the downstream' (2012: 529).

The network, in terms of the large number of individuals who share the same objective and that work together for the accomplishment of the event, it becomes an important element in designing events. That network creates group solidarity and social capital, it reinforces the sense of membership and produces the conditions for the success of the event. The impact of the rites on *outside visitors* is highly positive from the emotional point of view, but is disappointing in ethical terms, due to the poor management of the flows they generate and the limited marketing of services and cultural goods – despite the city's rich potential in this regard – many of which are unknown even to residents.

Holy Week has been cited by many as the most important of the city's traditions. It is considered to be something that needs to be promoted at the highest levels in order to project a positive image of the city, whose identity appears to be lost and uncertain. What is missing, however, is the commitment of local and regional authorities to a suitable promotion of what represents an important event recognized by local television stations and the increasing numbers of tourists.

The city administration has proven to be ineffective in the organization, management and promotion of the event. Its services are limited to lighting, cleaning and the provision of safety measures for the streets along the Procession itinerary in the 'old town', the city's historic heart that now lies mostly abandoned, never having been redeemed from its decades-old state of environmental, social and economic decay.

Also inadequate has been the regional administration, although it does however promote and generously finance other cultural events in Puglia such as the folklore-inspired *Notte della Taranta*, a festival of popular Salento music known as 'pizzica' that takes place in various municipalities in the province of Lecce (especially those of the traditionally Greek-speaking area known as Grecìa

Salentina), and the *Focara* in Novoli, a small town in the Salento that hosts the winter cultural event held in honour of Sant'Antonio Abate (St Anthony Abbot) with a large bonfire and a magnificent fireworks display that light up the sky over the town.

The Puglia Regional Administration does not provide direct funding for the rites of Holy Week, limiting itself to simple 'promotion' of the events on tourist markets and at tourist trade fairs, organizing press trips and communication campaigns. It treats Holy Week in Taranto as a 'tourist product' (the rites and traditions of Puglia), an element of attraction and regional identity, seeing it as an element of great attractive value for the modern tourist, always on the hunt for 'authentic' places and for knowledge of communities and their anthropological characteristics.

The absence of suitable involvement and investment on the part of the public authorities has negative consequences for the city in ethical terms. Commercial activities (restaurants, hotels, etc.) benefit little, as shown by the low levels of business during the rites of Holy Week. In some villages affected by the rites of Holy Week, opportunities arise for the local economy, which sees greater entrepreneurship and self-reliance while business improves. Various stalls are set up around the main square, as well as along the streets through which the procession passes. Part of the tradition of Holy Week is the sale of locally made products, particularly food and sweets. This leads to the creation of new businesses in many cultural and economic sectors (local craft traditions such as papier-mâché, wood carving, embroidery, artistic jewellery, gastronomy and the musical bands accompanying the rites) and brings a degree of seasonal adjustment to an industry that is still largely tied to seaside tourism.

With the involvement of local operators, local government and civic organizations, promotion of the rites of Holy Week has followed a holistic approach, capitalizing on the cultural value of local heritage and fostering transversal cultural cooperation and cultural democracy. The poor management of the rites of Holy Week in Taranto is seen in almost all the towns and cities involved, despite the commitment of the 'Opera' cultural association, which takes care of the promotion of events linked to the rites of Holy Week in Puglia on a regional level. It provides tourist services in connection with tours of the main towns in which the rites take place, creating a network of partners composed of various players who can guide the initiatives and combine moments of devotion with the promotion of the region and the activities that take place there.

There is little involvement of the local community in development plans and programmes and the operators need better training and skills since they do not always work with the right expertise and are often guided purely by improvisation. Generally, the benefits of the rites of Holy Week for the local communities of Puglia are not so great. The rites of Holy Week do not play an ethical role. They are not an opportunity for improving the socio-economic situation and promoting regional development.

Conclusion

The religious event held every year in Taranto during Holy Week mirrors to a large extent Collins' (2004) model of Interaction Ritual Chains, which can be seen as a key design element for the event.

As we have shown, the Rites of the Holy Week have a very strong involvement of local residents and visitors in the implementation of the event. They are an active part of the representation and as Collins states 'the sense of collective solidarity and identity is stronger to just the extent that the crowd goes beyond being passive observers to actively taking part' (2004: 82). This causes the entire event, constituted by the historical city centre, the confraternity figurants and the crowds attending, to be identified as the Durkeniam 'sacred object' and to become consequently charged with a multilayered symbolic value. As Collins (2004: 161) notes: 'Individuals care about nothing but maximizing their Emotional Energy.' This explains why being at the centre of the Rites drives people to invest a large amount of money in the auction.

The *gare* system is at the base of the sustainability of the Rites both from an economic and cultural point of view. The amount of money collected every year during the auction allows the event to be implemented without any form of commodification or modification of tradition. At the same time in terms of design elements of the event, the *gare* system produces social integration, it strengthens local identity and increases social capital. The *gare*, in many ways, can be seen as a traditional value creation platform.

Notes

1 This chapter is the result of the concerted efforts of the authors. Sections two and three are by Anna Trono, section one by Katia Rizzello.
2 In 1975 the plant in Taranto produced 7,011 million tonnes of steel and employed 18,901 people, with a further 6,600 working for external companies supplying services such as maintenance (Celant and Morelli 1986: 118).
3 Musical instrument made of wood with a highly distinct sound, made by dragging it across the metal studs held by the master of ceremonies. The ritual playing of this instrument starts the procession.

References

Angelini, E. (2005) 'Le confraternite di Priverno', *La Ricerca Folklorica*, 52: 29–31.
Archambault, M. (2009) 'L'impact de la trame événementielle comme élément de notoriété: le cas du Québec', in J. Spindler and D. Huron (eds) *L'évaluation de l'événementiel touristique*, Paris: Harmattan, pp. 283–297.
Bonnemaison, S. (1990) 'City policies and cyclical events', *Design Quarterly*, 147: 24–32.
Brunet, S., Bauer, J., De Lacy, T. and Tshering, K. (2001) 'Tourism development in Bhutan: tensions between tradition and modernity', *Journal of Sustainable Tourism*, 9(3): 243–256.
Caputo, N. (1983) *L'Anima incappucciata*, Manduria: Editore Mandese.

Caputo, N. (1995) *I giorni del Perdono*, Taranto: Editrice Scorpione.

Caputo, N. and Majorano, A. (1998) *Le poste, l'addolorata, i misteri: processione, riti, tradizioni pasquali a Taranto*, Manduria: Editore Mandese.

Cattell, V. (2001) 'Poor people, poor places, and poor health: the mediating role of social networks and social capital', *Social Science and Medicine*, 52(10): 1501–1516.

Celant, A. and Morelli, P. (1986) *La geografia dei divari territoriali*, Firenze: Sansoni ed.

Cleaver, F. (2005) 'The inequality of social capital and reproduction of chronic poverty', *World Development*, 33(6): 893–906.

Coleman, J. (1988) 'social capital and the creation of human capital', *American Journal of Sociology*, 94(Supplement S95–S120): 95–119.

Collins, R. (2004) *Interaction ritual chains*, Princeton, NJ: Princeton University Press.

Collins, R. and Guillén, M.F. (2012) 'Mutual halo effects in cultural production: the case of modernist architecture', *Theory and Society*, 41(6): 527–556.

Csíkszentmihályi, M. (1990) *Flow: the psychology of optimal experience*, New York: Harper Perennial.

Falassi, A. (eds) (1987) *Time out of time: essay on the festival*, Albuquerque, NM: University of New Mexico Press.

Getz, D. (2007) *Events studies: theory, research and policy for planned events*, Oxford: Elsevier.

Getz, D. (2012) 'Event studies', in S.J. Page and J. Connell (eds) *The Routledge handbook of events*, London and New York: Routledge, pp. 27–46.

Gotham, K.F. (2005) 'Theorizing urban spectacles: festivals, tourism and transformation of urban space', *City*, 9(2): 225–245.

Janiskee, R. (1980) 'South Carolina's harvest festivals: rural delights for day tripping urbanities', *Journal of Cultural Geography*, 1(1): 96–104.

Jones, S. (2005) 'Community-based tourism: the significance of social capital', *Annals of Tourism Research*, 32: 303–324.

Jorge, J.P. (2009) 'Religious tourism and rites: the Holy Week of Óbidos (Portugal)', in F. Dallari, A. Trono and E. Zabbini (eds) *I viaggi dell'anima: cultura e territorio potenzialità e problemi dello sviluppo del turismo religioso*, Bologna: Patron, pp. 157–167.

Marcovecchio, A. (2005) 'Oggetti e ritualità confraternale in due comunità della Valle dell'Aniene', *La Ricerca Folklorica*, 52: 61–68.

Martini, A. (2005) 'Origine e sviluppo delle confraternite', *La Ricerca Folklorica*, 52: 5–13.

Mattsson, K. and Stenbacka, S. (2003) 'Gendered social capital: a case study of sport and music association in Leksand and Rattvik, Sweden', Paper presented at the European Regional Science Association (ERSA) conference, Jyvaskyla, August 2003.

Noel, J.A. and Johnson, M.V. (2005) 'Psychological trauma, Christ's passion, and the African American faith tradition', *Pastoral Psychology*, 53(4): 361–370.

Paldam, M. and Svendsen, G. (1998) 'An essay on social capital: reflection on a concept linking social sciences', Working Paper No. 8, Denmark: Department of Economics, University of Aarthus.

Pizzato, M. (2005) 'A post-9/11 *passion*: review of Mel Gibson's *The Passion of the Christ*', *Pastoral Psychology*, 53(4): 371–376.

Quinn, B. (2009) 'Festival, event and tourism', in T. Jamal and M. Robinson (eds) *The Sage handbook of tourism studies*, London: Sage, pp. 483–503.

Rolfe, M. (1992) *Arts festivals in the UK*, London: Policy Study Institute.

Rudd, M. (2000) 'Live long and prosper: collective action, social capital and social vision', *Ecological Economics*, 34(1): 131–144.

Saxena, G. (2006) 'Beyond mistrust and competition: the role of social and personal bonding processes in sustaining livelihoods of rural tourism businesses: a case of the Peak District National Park', *International Journal of Tourism Research*, 8(4): 263–277.

Stewart-Weeks, M. and Richardson, C. (eds) (1998) 'Social capitals: how 12 Australian households live their lives', Policy Monograph (Vol. 42), Sydney: Center for Independent Studies.

Stone, W. and Hughes, J. (2002) 'Measuring social capital: towards a standardised approach', Paper presented at the Australian Evaluation Society International Conference, Wollongong, September 2002.

Trono, A. and Viterbo, D. (1995) 'Nuove tendenze e strategie di sviluppo delle aziende industriali pugliesi', in F. Dini (ed.) *Geografia dell'industria: sistemi locali e processi globali*, Torino: Giappichelli, pp. 261–297.

Turner, V. (1969) *The ritual process: structure and anti-structure*, New York: Aldine de Gruyter.

UNESCO (2003) *Convention for the safeguarding of intangible cultural heritage*, Paris: UNESCO.

Van Gennep, A. (1909) *The rites of passage*, London: Routledge & Kegan Paul.

Zammit, V. (2009) 'Holy week at Zebbug (Malta): a cultural and religious experience', in A. Trono (ed.) *Proceedings of the international conference tourism, religion & culture: regional development through meaningful tourism experiences, Lecce, Poggiardo 27th-29th October 2009*, Galatina: Congedo Ed., pp. 147–158.

Zuppante, A. (2005) 'Le confraternite di orte e la processione del Cristo morto', *La Ricerca Folklorica*, 52: 33–37.

9   Design processes around dynamic marketing communications for event organizations

Anne-Marie Hede and Pamm Kellett

Introduction

New ways of delivering events are continually being explored and tested around the globe. In some cases, this means expanding the opportunities to participate in events beyond traditional physical spaces. For example, in the United States, sporting events are now being broadcast live to cinemas (Fairley and Tyler 2006) and big screens are being used in public spaces to overcome issues related to the accessibility of events (Hede and Alomes 2007). Other events are toured across regions rather than exclusively held in one destination. For the 2011 Rugby World Cup matches between competing teams were hosted in different cities throughout the tournament within the host nation of New Zealand. For larger events, such as the Commonwealth Games for example, different strategies have been employed yet again – when components of the event were dispersed across an entire region. That is, some events within the larger umbrella event, have been staged in both the primary host destination and in a number of satellite destinations simultaneously (Kellett *et al.* 2008).

These are some examples of new forms of event design and delivery, that aim to provide new and distinctive ways for people to experience events, challenge work practices, work systems and the ability of people who work to deliver events to achieve their desired event outcomes. A more recent innovation, and the focus of this chapter, is the way in which event organizers are using the second generation of the Internet (Web 2.0) to redesign event delivery and enhance the experience of events for consumers. With Web 2.0, event designers are extending the presence of their events into virtual worlds. For example, the FIFA World Cup Soccer, with its online Club House, invites members to join and create networks, fantasy teams and their own avatars to engage in soccer in a virtual space. As event organizers adopt these types of strategies more widely, Web 2.0 technologies (such as social media platforms including Facebook, Twitter, LinkedIn, wikis and blogs) will change the way consumers and other stakeholders participate in events. Web 2.0 is allowing events to be *imagineered* – or themed using creative imagination and technological engineering to enhance the experience of those who participate in them (Hover 2008; Salazar 2011). Indeed, through imagineering, events can be extended beyond any geographical and temporal boundaries when a Web 2.0-based approach to marketing communications is adopted.

This new horizon for event design and management has implications for the people who work in the event sector. It means that the way that they work, the skills they require and the systems that are designed to support them also require rethinking, or, more specifically, imagineering. In the context of events, imagineering 'concerns creating and managing worlds of experience, based in internal values (DNA) on the one hand and/or values of the target groups on the other, with the objective of creating the emotional involvement of all stakeholders' (Hover 2008: 43). Indeed, the core tenet of imagineering is that target groups (event attendees) will feel connected to the experience, *as well as* those who are internal to the organization (event managers and workers). Eventually there should be a level of engagement of both parties where the borders between attendees and managers are blurred.

In the event sector, where work is highly casualized, there is an increasing need to imagineer the management of human resources so that events can be delivered in such a way that they meet the demands of consumers. Thus, we argue that there is a need to consider how event organizations themselves can be imagineered to prepare for the impending challenges and major changes brought about by the use of Web 2.0 in these organizations and in the expectations consumers have of events.

This chapter aims to address this gap in knowledge. We propose a series of processes in design methodology for event organizations that focus on aligning event organization strategy with human resource management (HRM) practices. More specifically, we focus on imagineering *high performance work systems* (HPWS). HPWS are a suite of HRM practices, such as selective hiring, employee involvement and participation, transformational leadership, job security, extensive training and development, and contingent rewards, that can improve employee commitment and individual performance (Boxall and Macky 2007) and can assist to align employee attitudes and behaviours with the strategic goals of the organization (Zacharatos *et al.* 2005; Bartram *et al.* 2012) – the very purpose of imagineering (Hover 2008).

The chapter proceeds with background to event organizations using the 'pulsating' and 'iterative' paradigms. We provide the backdrop for work in event organizations in the digital world in order for us to understand that the advent of Web 2.0 is not something that event organizations can afford to leave to chance.

Event organizations: classically pulsating and iterative

Event organizations have been compared with holiday camps or retail pop-up stores as they are iterative and characterized by discontinuity (Foreman and Parent 2008). Following their activation (to launch and staging), they move into a phase of dormancy (post-event) thus requiring regeneration the next time they are activated, when the event organization must again focus on planning and preparation for a new iteration of the event (Hanlon and Cuskelly 2002) and therefore to create event experiences all over again. In this sense, event managers (and increasingly managers in the retail sector) grapple with the unique attribute of iteration. It is because iterative organizations are short lived, and often perennial, that there is a need for them to be rejuvenated periodically. This attribute has been shown to precipitate peculiar conditions for employees in the event sector. Figure 9.1 highlights the three stages of event regeneration, activation and dormancy, as conceptualized by Foreman and Parent (2008).

Recruitment and retention is impacted greatly by the iterative attribute that besets event organizations. Event employees very often operate on short-term projects and contracts, therefore leading them to have precarious work environments and employment insecurity (Hanlon and Cuskelly 2002). The intensity of the work in phases coupled with the short-term nature of work in event organizations exacerbates work intensification where workers are required to do more with less and in short periods of time. These types of workplace issues are compounded within event organizations (Halbwirth and Toohey 2013).

As a result, effective human resource management (HRM) is critical for the success of events. For example, in the context of sport events, Taylor *et al.* (2008: 7) note that

> the success of [...] organizations to cope with the challenges that they face in the future will depend on how well they manage their people and succeed in new ways of working and how successful [*sic*] they are at negotiating associated change.

Similarly, in the arts, organizations have tended to adopt a product-based approach and work in them has been characterized by short-term contracts, casualization and poor pay (Throsby and Hollister 2003; Hesmondhalgh and Baker 2010). Yet, with the shift to a co-creative environment in the arts context, managers have

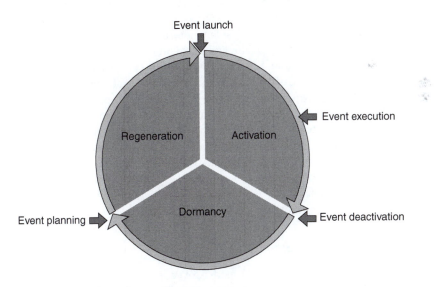

Figure 9.1 The three phases of iterative events.

started to recognize that effective HRM is imperative for sustainability (Fillis and Rentschler 2005), and perhaps more pertinent is the resulting need to imagineer HPWS in events.

Web 2.0 and the workplace

The advent of Web 2.0 has impacted workplaces and the people that work in them considerably. Indeed, Schultz (2011) suggests that social media is revolutionary. Schultz sees social media being far from a commercial aberration, but something that has impacted the 'world as we know it'. Lessons from a range of industry sectors can provide insights for the event sector as to how event managers might respond to the advent of this phenomenon in a strategic manner. The lessons around the impact of social media on HRM that the event sector must heed fall into three main categories where imagineering around HPWS is necessary. First, work and social lives are becoming increasingly blurred. Second, there is an increasing and almost insatiable demand for information exchange between consumers and organizations on a '24/7' basis. Third, there seems to be ambiguity within this increase of demand for information in the sense that there is often a lack of clarity of who does what with regard to social media communications in organizations. We now discuss each of these in turn in the proceeding section.

The blurring of boundaries of work life and social

While only a relatively recent phenomenon, some information is emerging about workplace behaviours associated with the advent of Web 2.0, and how Web 2.0 has facilitated the blurring of work and social lives. This blurring is two-way: workers are increasingly blending work into their personal time (Waller and Ragsdell 2012) and personal activities into their work time (Vitak *et al.* 2011). The catalyst for the development of this phenomenon was first through email. However, the use of Web 2.0 platforms such as Facebook, Twitter and LinkedIn further accentuate the interconnections between work life and social life and offers challenges for both employees and employers. Companies are taking advantage of, and are also concerned about, this issue across the employee lifecycle. Many companies are now checking the personal social networking sites to screen potential employees (Brown and Vaughn 2012) yet firing employees on the basis of their inappropriate use of social media in and often about the workplace (Ciochetti 2011). Web 2.0 and social media have changed the way in which people work and are expected to work. It has impacted many employees' work–life balance as they work to meet the demands to stay connected with their clients, customers and stakeholders, and to keep social media content on business sites relevant, timely and credible.

The need for information 24/7

The advent of the adoption of social media for marketing communications, or what we refer to as dynamic marketing communications, is set within the context of rapid changes in society and organizations. Major forces, such as globalization, workforce casualization and the increasing pace at which information is disseminated have all contributed to this phenomenon. We now observe an almost insatiable need for information to be disseminated as soon as it becomes available regardless of its veracity. In Australia where there is one of the highest adoption rates of the Internet and Web 2.0 around the globe, even the nation's politicians have been put under excessive demands to provide information to their constituents outside the traditional hours of work via social media platforms such as Facebook and Twitter. Lewis (2011) reported that the outcome of a Remuneration Tribunal that 'email, Facebook, Twitter and the like have increased community expectations on members as regards their availability to their constituents'. Consequently, Australia's politicians received a pay rise, in part to compensate them for the considerable impost that they were experiencing because of the impact of dynamic marketing communication on their work practices (Lewis 2011).

Role ambiguity: who does what when?

As Web 2.0 and its associated social media platforms continue to be anchored in the workplace, it is making work and design processes in organizations particularly turbulent. In their study of social media managers of 15 large German enterprises, Meske and Stieglitz (2013) found that social media managers faced a range of challenges related to role clarity. Social media managers are generally charged with the responsibility to lead the effective and appropriate use of social media throughout an organization, and to simultaneously develop the social media strategy for the organization. In large enterprises, multiple departments often have vastly different functions and target audiences, thus devising strategies that are independent of autonomous departments was found to be particularly challenging for many social media managers (Meske and Stieglitz 2013). In many cases, because the work of social media managers spanned across many parts of an organization, their position and power to make decisions was often lessened. They were essentially seen as masterminds of many things, but the master of none.

Despite the growing body of literature that explores the way in which social media impacts work and workers in many sectors of business, there has been little research that understands how social media has impacted work, and the management of HPWS in the event sector. The proceeding section provides an exploration of this issue.

Web 2.0 and dynamic marketing communications: preliminary evidence from the event sector's experience

Hede and Kellett (2011, 2012) and Kellett and Hede's (2013) qualitative inquiries into the use of Web 2.0 technologies and social media in Australian event organizations, identified that event organizations used a variety of social media tools to enhance the brand community for their events – and ultimately the experience of their event consumers. They found that event organizations are becoming selective about the dynamic marketing communications that they use in each iterative phase (regeneration, activation and dormancy). Hede and Kellett (2012) found some event managers adopt an active approach to marketing communications for their events. Indeed, when event organizations adopted dynamic marketing communications for their events early in their lifecycle, they were more comfortable with using social media platforms in their organizations, and, not surprisingly, were more strategic about how they used them. Early adopters were proactive in using different platforms for different purposes in different phases of their events, and had a clear sense of why they used certain platforms over others. In particular, event managers were cognizant of the fact that social media could assist them to continue conversations about their events well before and after the events themselves were staged. In this way, event managers were using dynamic marketing communications to reduce the amount of time that their organizations spent in a dormant stage between the end of the event and the next iteration of the event (as referred to by Foreman and Parent 2008).

While Hede and Kellett's research work did not set out to investigate HPWS, it revealed some interesting insights into the three core areas that HPWS can help us to understand – what work systems prevail, in which contexts and why. In this way, we can also better understand how HPWS can be imagineered in the event sector. The strategic use of dynamic marketing communications was found to have a profound impact on the nature of the work that individuals in positions that implemented social media did, and hence the kinds of work systems that prevailed. Some of the organizations who were early adopters of social media expected their employees to respond to social media activities with immediacy and little strategy. These organizations were spontaneous and reactive in their strategic use of social media. Other event organizations were highly strategic and structured in that they planned which social media platforms would be used to communicate with their different target audiences, and were comfortable with allowing consumers to converse through their social media platforms without expecting their employees to be constantly monitoring and responding to social media activities.

Kellett and Hede (2013) highlighted that the adoption of social media was not consistent across the event sector, which supports previous research such as (López *et al.* 2010) who examined this in the arts sector. Furthermore, Kellett and Hede (2013) showed that there did not seem to be any conventions as to how dynamic marketing communications may best be managed from an HRM perspective or which specific work systems should prevail in this context. What this work highlights is that event managers are experiencing some common challenges with regard to managing the adoption and implementation of social media and dynamic marketing communications in their organizations. Event managers reported that they and their employees were often over-extended technically and physically by trying to adopt social media. Not only did they report that the advent of new Web 2.0 technologies was difficult to keep up with from a technical perspective, but the demands of resourcing this aspect of marketing communications beyond traditional working hours and beyond the normal pulsating cycle of events was becoming a challenge. This was evident in situations where both paid employees and volunteers were being asked to take on the roles of dynamic marketing communications.

Moreover, making decisions about who was responsible for social media activities (beyond traditional marketing responsibilities) was an emerging area of concern for managers as most event organizations recognized that they needed to adopt an integrated approach to marketing communications simultaneously implementing traditional marketing communications alongside their dynamic marketing communications. This was a problem in terms of finding the right personnel and expertise, as well as structuring the organization accordingly, but was a particular problem for strategic alliances. Event managers grappled with the strategic intent and integration of dynamic marketing communications with traditional marketing communications for their event organizations.

In summary, many of the event managers reported that they grappled with Web 2.0's advent, social media and a dynamic approach to marketing communications and how it was impacting HRM policy development and practice. This situation indicates that there may not yet be a clear understanding of the challenges, risks and opportunities associated with dynamic marketing communications in the event sector. Such a situation limits the event sector's potential to cope with the shift in value creation away from a transactional economic value paradigm towards a social or relational value paradigm. We suggest therefore that there is a need to consider HPWS and dynamic marketing communications in the design methodology for events.

Event design methodology: using HPWS to respond to dynamic marketing communications

Designing effective processes for the management of work and people, or HRM, is an essential function in any organization. HRM provides the information, strategies and tools to offer a better place for work and workers. How it links to organizational performance is embedded in understanding *high performance work systems*. HPWS can improve employee commitment and individual performance (Boxall and Macky 2007) leading to organizational performance (Zacharatos *et al.* 2005; Bartram *et al.* 2012). The value of HPWS is that they can assist us to understand *what* work systems prevail in *which* contexts, and *why* (Boxall 2012). HPWS therefore can potentially align employee attitudes and behaviours with the strategic goals of the organization.

There is a growing body of literature that identifies the unique elements of work in the context of events. What makes the event sector unique is that the ways that people work form an integral part of the events themselves. The event context has traditionally necessitated a particular pattern of work; known for its high work demands – in particular the pulsating nature of events and the different work demands during pre-, in-situ and post-event have been examined previously (Hanlon and Jago 2004). The way in which event organizations begin with few employees, then expand with more full-time, casual and volunteer staff at the time of an event, then shrink back to their original size (or disband completely) post-event renders HRM difficult.

Indeed, recruitment and retention of quality employees is problematic in the events sector so much so that Hanlon and Stewart (2006) concluded that standard HRM practices are less than effective in the events sector. HRM practices must then be revised in the light of the recent developments and be included in the event design in a way that will be part of new practices and adjusted ways of working.

In an effort to gain insights into how events can be better managed from a human resource perspective, considerable time has been spent on understanding the unique elements of HRM in this context with a number of strategies for management to adopt in this situation proposed (see for example Baum *et al.* 2009 for an overview). Exploring how the impact of dynamic marketing communications can best be managed using an HPWS paradigm extends this research as it takes a more comprehensive view of HRM across the lifecycle of the event employee. Furthermore, mapping HPWS across the stages of events means that strategies can be developed to enhance long-term sustainability.

Designing HPWS around dynamic marketing communications: an agenda for knowledge discovery

Understanding event organizations from a perspective that takes into account the context (iterations) as well as the HPWS that need to underpin the nature of the work undertaken assists us to imagineer new ways that people can and do work, the skills they require, and the resulting systems that are required to support them. Work in this area is embryonic and an agenda for building our knowledge is required.

Foreman and Parent (2008: 226) note that in iterative organizations 'as the level of discontinuity rises, the particular event or episode or iteration becomes increasingly disconnected from their priors'. However, Kellett and Hede (2013) have found that social media has helped event organizations mitigate the pulsating or iterative nature of events. That is, social media allows the organization to continue connections with their consumers and associate stakeholders throughout the calendar year hence providing evidence that perhaps dormancy as described by Foreman and Parent (2008) is different for organizations and individual workers due to the way in which they use social media. Therefore, this also implies that changes are occurring in the event sector. What has been described as dormancy in such work contexts may indeed be very different under the guise of social media. This leads us to the questions that need to be asked by scholars in order to better understand what work systems prevail in events, in which contexts and why.

First what is needed is an understanding of how dynamic marketing communications are impacting HPWS and the way they are being imagineered currently in event organizations during the individual stages of an iteration of an event (regeneration, activation and dormancy); and then how dynamic marketing communications and HPWS are imagineered for subsequent iterations of events. Second, it is necessary to explore how event managers and workers in the event sector respond to imagineering as a result of the adoption of dynamic marketing communications during the individual stages on an iteration of an event and then subsequent iterations of events and their organizations. Third, there is a need to better understand how organizations can be imagineered to use HPWS effectively to achieve their organizational objectives.

Although the current chapter has pointed to research that provides some insights into the problems event organizations face, it has highlighted that as yet, we do not know enough about the impact of dynamic marketing communications on HPWS in the unique context of events. Further, we are not aware if these might be different depending on the type or size of an event or event organization.

It is possible to make observations of HPWS (e.g. selective hiring, employee involvement and participation, transformational leadership, job security, extensive training and development, and contingent rewards) in various settings with various actors and material artefacts (Yanow *et al.* 2012). Although there has been little research thus far that specifically examines HPWS in events, the work of Hede and Kellett (2011, 2012) and Kellett and Hede (2013) has been instructive to begin to unpack elements of HPWS in the three stages of event regeneration, activation and dormancy as noted previously. The main insights of this research have been summarized in Table 9.1, which links HPWS with regeneration, activation and dormancy and provides key points for consideration towards the design process.

Key implications for event design come from careful consideration of the unique elements of events. As noted throughout this chapter, and in Table 9.1, an important consideration for design is in the iterative nature of events and in particular the event phases of regeneration, activation and dormancy. The three stages of event ask for different elements to be considered in the design process. The imagineering of these elements should be developed and adjusted according to the different type of events. More importantly, upstream of the event design process, it becomes clear that there is a need for creating and improving structures and processes that can contribute to the effectiveness and appropriateness of HPRW in the context of dynamic marketing communications. The importance of the latter in the context of event design, throughout the three phases is essential. Paying attention to these factors particularly in the third phase (dormancy) is becoming essential in a more competitive eventscape but also in a world where Web 2.0 is shaping new challenges and new ways of working. This also means that the concept of 'dormancy' itself might be reconsidered in a nearby future. Post-event involvement is getting increasingly connected to the regeneration phase and the role of HPRW in making this link through the optimal use of the resources related to dynamic marketing communications is then fundamental within event design.

Table 9.1 Dynamic marketing communications, HPWS, event stage and key points for consideration

HPWS/event stage	Regeneration	Activation	Dormancy
Selective hiring	Imagineering hiring processes that match applicant experience and skill set with strategies for dynamic marketing communications	Imagineering skill sets that match with strategic choice of dynamic marketing communications used	Imagineering HRM practices that match strategy for dynamic marketing communications post-event
Employee involvement and participation	Imagineering induction processes for volunteers and employees that match event activation strategies	Imagineering structures that allow for simultaneous dynamic and traditional marketing communications	Imagineering how post-event involvement can be fostered through dynamic marketing communications for volunteers and potential employees in preparation for re-engaging for the next iteration of an event
Extensive training and development	Imagineering planning for resources allocated to training in dynamic marketing communications	Imagineering new workplace structures to deliver dynamic marketing communications throughout the 24/7 demands of event activation	Imagineering how post-event involvement can be fostered for volunteers and potential employees for regeneration phase
Job security	Imagineering new ways of working with Web 2.0 in planning for events, and supportive workplace conditions	Imagineering new ways of working with Web 2.0 to deliver events, and workplace conditions that support this	Imagineering new ways of harnessing dynamic marketing communications for work post-events to mitigate casualization in event sector workforce
Contingent rewards	Imagineering employment contracts and remuneration packages that support work and workers to relaunch events in the planning phase	Imagineering a remuneration package that supports the demands of work and workers in dynamic marketing communications during event activation	Imagineering employment contracts and remuneration packages that support work and workers to continue conversations about events in what might traditionally have been phases of dormancy

By imagineering the crucial HRM elements that are specific to each of the event phases in relation to the unique work context of events will mean event managers can create better event businesses, and offer the event workforce a more stable and predictable working environment.

Conclusion

Surprisingly, little is known about how event organizations can effectively use HRM practices to respond to the advent of dynamic marketing communications. Gaining this knowledge is critical for developing effective strategies around *dynamic marketing communications*, and understanding this phenomenon's broader effects on organizational sustainability and for the potential to build high performing work systems that are both beneficial for organizations and their employees.

Further research is needed to better understand how event organizations can take advantage of Web 2.0 to effectively imagineer or design events beyond the temporal and geographical boundaries that they currently experience and through the various stages of iteration. The next steps are to explore which HPWS might best be utilized across the iterations of events, and how they might be designed in each of the event phases. The settings around the execution of dynamic marketing communications might be designed in ways that include formal meetings, workshops, casual meetings at the photocopier and social events. Actors might involve both management and staff, including volunteers. Material artefacts might include official documents, HPWS policies and procedures, internal communications such as emails or other Web 2.0 internal and external communications on, for example, social media platforms such as Facebook, Twitter and LinkedIn. Additionally, more informal material artefacts, such as cartoons, jokes or photos on office doors and bulletin boards, blogs, wikis and webpages might also provide useful signposts to the HPWS employed in event organizations. An approach that encompasses many of these design elements will enable triangulation. As seen throughout this chapter, relevant research in event organizations points to the need for developing HPWS in a variety of aspects and phases in order to face the challenges associated with the advent of Web 2.0 for event organizations.

References

Bartram, T., Casimir, G., Djurkovic, N., Leggat, S. and Stanton, P. (2012) 'Do high performance work systems influence the relationship between emotional labour, burnout and intention to leave? A study of Australian nurses', *Journal of Advanced Nursing*, 68(7): 1567–1578.

Baum, T., Deery, M. and Lockstone, L. (2009) *People and Work in Events and Conventions: A Research Perspective*, Wallingford: CABI Publishing.

Boxall, P. (2012) 'High-performance work systems: what, why, how and for whom?' *Asia Pacific Journal of Human Resources*, 50(2): 169–186.

Boxall, P. and Macky, K. (2007) 'High-performance work systems and organisational performance: bridging theory and practice', *Asia Pacific Journal of Human Resources,* 45(3): 261–270.

Brown, V.R. and Vaughn, E.D. (2012) 'The writing on the (Facebook) wall: the use of social network sites in hiring decisions', *Journal of Business and Psychology,* 26(2): 219–225.

Ciochetti, C.A. (2011) 'The eavesdropping employer: a twenty-first century framework for employee monitoring', *American Business Law Journal,* 48(2): 285–369.

Fairley, S. and Tyler, B.D. (2006) 'Bringing baseball to the big screen: building sense of community outside of the ballpark', Paper presented at the North American Society for Sport Management conference in Kansas City, Missouri (USA), June 2006.

Fillis, I. and Rentschler, R. (2005) 'Using creativity to achieve an entrepreneurial future for arts marketing', *International Journal of Nonprofit and Voluntary Sector Marketing,* 10(4): 1–13.

Foreman, P. and Parent, M. (2008) 'The process of organizational identity construction in iterative organizations', *Corporate Reputation Review,* 11(3): 222–244.

Halbwirth, S. and Toohey, K. (2013) 'Information, knowledge and the organisation of the Olympics', in S. Frawley and D. Adair (eds) *Managing the Olympics,* London: Palgrave Macmillan, pp. 33–49.

Hanlon, C. and Cuskelly, G. (2002) 'Pulsating major sport event organisations: a framework for inducting managerial personnel', *Event Management: An International Journal,* 7(4): 231–244.

Hanlon, C. and Jago, L. (2004) 'The challenge of retaining personnel in major sport event organizations', *Event Management,* 9(1–2): 39–49.

Hanlon, C. and Stewart, B. (2006) 'Managing personnel in major sport event organisations: what strategies are required?' *Event Management,* 10(1): 77–88.

Hede, A. and Alomes, S. (2007) 'Big screens: exploring their future for the special event sector', Paper presented at the Fourth International Event Research Conference Melbourne, Australia, July 2007.

Hede, A.M. and Kellett, P. (2011) 'Marketing communications for special events: analysing managerial practice, consumer perceptions and preferences', *European Journal of Marketing,* 45(6): 987–1004.

Hede, A.M. and Kellett, P. (2012) 'Building online brand communities: exploring the benefits, challenges and risks in the Australian event sector', *Journal of Vacation Marketing,* 18(3): 239–250.

Hesmondhalgh, D. and Baker, S. (2010) *Creative Labour: Media Work in Three Cultural Industries,* London: Routledge.

Hover, M. (2008) 'Imagine your event: imagineering for the event industry', in U. Wünsch (ed.) *Facets of Contemporary Event Management: Theory and Practice for Event Success,* Bad Honnef: K.H. Bock, pp. 37–62.

Kellett, P. and Hede, A.M. (2013) 'Web 2.0 innovations in events: human resource management issues', in A.M. Munar, S. Gyimóthy and L. Cai (eds) *Tourism Social Media* (Tourism Social Science Series, Volume 18), Bingley: Emerald Group Publishing Limited, pp. 193–205.

Kellett, P., Hede, A.M. and Chalip, L. (2008) 'Social policy for sport events: leveraging (relationships with) teams from other nations for community benefit', *European Sport Management Quarterly,* 8(2): 101–121.

Lewis, S. (2011) 'Tweet deal: social media blamed for politicians' huge pay rise', *Daily Telegraph,* 16 December.

López, X., Margapoti, I., Maragliano, R. and Bove, G. (2010) 'The presence of Web 2.0 tools on museum websites: a comparative study between England, France, Spain, Italy, and the USA', *Museum Management and Curatorship*, 25(2): 235–249.

Meske, C. and Stieglitz, S. (2013) 'Responsibilities and challenges of social media managers', in S. Yamamoto (ed.) *Human Interface and the Management of Information: Information and Interaction for Learning, Culture, Collaboration and Business*, Berlin-Heidelberg: Springer Verlag, pp. 342–351.

Salazar, N.B. (2011) 'Imagineering cultural heritage for local-to-global audiences', in A. van Stipriaan, P. van Ulzen and M. Halbertsma (eds) *The Heritage Theatre*, Newcastle upon Tyne: Cambridge Scholars Publishing, pp. 49–72.

Schultz, J. (2011) 'Storytelling, sense-making: past, present and future', *Griffith Review*, 33: [1]–[3]. Online, available at: http://search.informit.com.au/documentSummary;dn=306582204506309;res=IELLCC (accessed 10 February 2014).

Taylor, T., Doherty, A. and McGraw, P. (2008) *Managing People in Sport Organizations: A Strategic Human Resource Management Perspective*, London: Elsevier/Butterworth Heinemann.

Throsby, D. and Hollister, V. (2003) 'Don't give up your day job: an economic study of professional artists in Australia', Division of Economic and Financial Studies, Sydney Macquarie University and Australia Council for the Arts.

Vitak, J., Crouse, J. and LaRose, R. (2011) 'Personal internet use at work: understanding cyberslacking', *Computers in Human Behavior*, 27(5): 1751–1759.

Waller, A.D. and Ragsdell, G. (2012) 'The impact of e-mail on work-life balance', *Aslib Proceedings*, 64(2): 154–177.

Yanow, D., Ybema, S. and van Hulst, M. (2012) 'Practicing organizational ethnography', in G. Symon and C. Cassell (eds) *The Practice of Qualitative Organizational Research: Core Methods and Current Challenge*, London: Sage, pp. 331–350.

Zacharatos, A., Barling, J. and Iverson, R. (2005) 'High-performance work systems and occupational safety', *Journal of Applied Psychology*, 90(1): 77–93.

10 Co-creative events

Analysis and illustrations

Phil Crowther and Chiara Orefice

Introduction

The storyline to this chapter is of events as an increasingly enticing and sophisticated approach that organizations employ to achieve strategic outcomes. Renowned writers, such as Wood (2009) and Berridge (2012) endorse this view, commenting upon the increased appeal of events as an instrument to achieve many and varied outcomes, hence the event inflation referred to by Richards (2013). This is consistent with the commentary of other writers who reflect upon the increased number, size, scope and significance of events (Bowdin *et al.* 2011; Getz 2012). Organizations, in many different settings, select events as their preferred approach to achieve outcomes that could ostensibly be achieved in many other ways, and as indicated below this is a growing tendency. The following discussion evaluates this, and through analysis of the co-creative possibilities of events, provides a context from which to interpret this trend.

Framed within the context of the growing primacy of experience (Pine and Gilmore 1998) we increasingly see observers, such as Gupta (2003) and Wood (2009), commentate on the widening range of outcomes that organizations can pursue through the adoption of enlightened event-based approaches. Other analysts, such as Hamso (2012) and Vanneste (2008) focus upon the return on investment of events and how this can be realized through participant-centred event design. Pioneers in the commercial world such as Red Bull, Vodaphone and Microsoft, invest 10 per cent of their entire marketing communications spend on events-led activity (Heasley 2010). The appeal of events is not restricted to the commercial world, but is equally apparent in the public sector, for example in cities (Richards and Palmer 2010), and also in charitable organizations where events, such as Cancer Research UK's 'Race for Life', are at the forefront of fundraising strategies. Further evidence of the robust appeal of events is that the business event sector is generally heralded as having survived the recent economic difficulties in the world economy reasonably well, although at the cost of significant changes in organizational structures and of radical innovations in the way in which event organization is approached (Davidson 2012).

A recurring dilemma of the networked society that we live in is the mass of information that is produced and the considerable challenge this presents senders as they struggle to engage recipients. It is within this broad context that we can begin to interpret the preliminary discussion above and the perceived charm of events. As Collins (2004) indicates, events can generate emotional energy by creating a mutual focus of attention. They also epitomize what Ramaswamy (2009), in his work around value creation, labels an 'engagement platform' given their capacity to unite organizations with their desired stakeholders. Given the challenging environment of preoccupied employees, customers, clients, tourists and benefactors, events represent a refreshingly intimate, and crucially participative, space. This is characterized as the co-creative ability of events, which is the recurring theme that is explored and illustrated in this chapter.

An inevitable consequence of their growing appeal is the delivery of more events and therefore a maturing of the event management field. McCole (2004), for example, talked about experience being the new battleground for marketers, as more and more organizations seek to purposefully create events, and refashion existing ones. As business people and consumers become acclimatized to this glut of experiences, expectations and behaviours evolve, so what was once a rousing experience for a participant can quickly become rather ordinary. Consequently there arises an impetus to refresh, and indeed 'imagineer', the event creation and delivery process. As participant antecedents and expectations change and the competitive event marketplace intensifies, event creators must respond with insightful experience design. Accomplishing this demands consideration of many factors. At the heart of these is the co-creative makeup of events, which is discussed below and illustrated by the two events-based case studies.

Fertile landscape for events

The network society creates a landscape where the experiential, interactive, relational and targeted qualities of events provide a refreshing antidote to more traditional marketing channels, and also new media (Crowther 2010a). This is endorsed by the thinking of Roy and Cornwall (2004) who refer to the existence of 'marketing clutter', and similarly by Parsons and Maclaren (2009) who identify the hyper competition that characterizes the marketplace. Therefore, from the perspective of an organization there is an imperative to have 'an obsessive focus on individualized interactions between the individual and the company' (Prahalad and Ramaswamy 2004: 7). As a result we observe a shift in recent literature towards the priority of notions of participation, engagement and experience. Equally we see a raft of research charting the character of Generation Y and their thirst for experience, preferably individualized, and also a democratization of marketing whereby more control swings away from the organization and towards the individual (Parsons and Maclaren 2009).

Traditionally, the literature portrayed organizations as using events with a fairly narrow focus, for example 'events are occurrences designed to communicate particular messages to target audiences' (Kotler 2003: 576). Such depictions are accurate but unnecessarily limiting, given the wider possibilities of events. Prompted by the advent and development of experiential marketing thinking, portrayals evolved towards phrases such as 'special stages' (Yuan 2008), and 'brand hyperreality' (Whelan and Wholfeil 2006), which emphasized the opportunity for organizations to stage experiences and performances consistent with notions of brand entertainment. This language is more expansive, reflective of the wider possibilities of events, but nonetheless the emphasis remains upon doing things to attendees, perceiving them, more typically, as a passive audience rather than much more active participants.

In more recent research, a need for a renewed perspective has been identified, which recognizes the mutuality of the event space as a setting where, in addition to the above, organizations coalesce and interact with participants, hence such depictions as 'value creation spaces' (Crowther and Donlan 2011). Such phraseology implies a value creation potential of events which is also reciprocal and extends beyond the communication of messages and the production of experiences. This evolution in the way in which events are conceived is not specific to marketing, but also extends to business events in the corporate and also the not-for-profit sectors (see Ouwens, Chapter 4). The challenging economic environment, the advent of new generations in the workforce and the development of Web 2.0 technologies have all forced event professionals to reassess the function of meetings and events and their contribution to business success. In particular, the primacy of event legacy, perceiving events as longer-term investments, and also the importance of demonstrating their value, is leading to a shift to a more participant-centric approach in event creation. This logic underpins the emergence of a more holistic approach to event creation which extends beyond singular stakeholder groups and also moves beyond a more exclusive focus upon the time and space parameter of the physical event and involves a heightened concentration on the pre- and post-event phases. The event creator's role is consequently elevated as they design an elongated and multifaceted eventscape.

The emphasis indicated above is now at the centre of industry-led research and there are campaigns to raise awareness amongst event professionals and clients. Meeting Professionals International (2012) is an example of an industry association that is more active in this respect. Indeed it can be suggested that the industry and the practitioner community are leading in this shift, with the discussion still insufficiently covered in the academic event management literature. Academic perspectives and conceptualizations need to more fully evolve to interpret this evolution in the positioning of events as an organizational strategy. To achieve this it is helpful to examine the overlapping logic of various protagonists; the primacy of experience (Pine and Gilmore 1998), experiential marketing (Schmitt 1999), structural change from 'value in exchange' to 'value in use' (Vargo and Lusch 2004) and the swing from promise making to promise keeping marketing (Grönroos and Ravald 2011). These perspectives combine to provide a unifying lens through which we can interpret the context that underpins the new accord between events and strategy.

A co-creative space

Events can be considered a distinctly co-creative setting. Event scholars, along-side practitioners, are challenged to suitably articulate and interpret co-creation within an event context. Ramaswamy is a foremost writer in this area and it is useful to reflect on his overarching definition: 'Co-creation is the process by which products, services, and experiences are developed jointly by companies and their stakeholders, opening up a whole new world of value' (2009: 6). Expanding Ramaswamy's depiction, Grönroos and Ravald (2011) express the view that co-creation occurs when supplier and customer are involved in the same process of value creation. Both of these portrayals would suggest, some-what unsatisfactorily, that any event, given the requisite congregation of people, would, to some degree, be labelled co-creative. Equally, inept design and facil-itation can render events ineffectual, indeed more in keeping with a co-destruction, rather than co-creation, of value (Crowther and Donlan 2011). As a starting point it is therefore useful to concede that although all events are akin to co-creation, the starting point is a base level of co-creation by default, which is an indifferent position and one with limited impact in a competitive event landscape.

Therefore a more nuanced understanding is required, which is incited by a further sentiment offered by Ramaswamy (2009: 12): 'true co-creation enables consumers to engage with the company at whatever stage of the process, and whatever level of involvement, they desire'.

This provides a refined interpretation that moves beyond co-creation by default, towards what, at the other end of the continuum, would be classed as co-creation by ambition. In this case the event creation process would be purpose-fully designed to be infused with co-creative possibilities from the pre-event phase through until the post-event stage, with co-creative opportunities purpose-fully generated to maximize the longevity and intensity of experience. The event consequently morphs into what Grönroos and Ravald (2011) characterize as one of an organization's value facilitation process, interlinked with others. Hence the more recent lexicon of Crowther and Donlan (2011) who adopt the term 'value facilitation space' to adequately capture the present day possibilities, and utility, of events for organizations.

The essence of this discussion is that although events represent a guaranteed co-creative platform, inadequate design and delivery diminishes the co-creative impression, and therefore the value creation potential, conceivably to a point where the outcome for one or more stakeholders is actually indifferent or, even worse, destructive. The challenge towards co-creation by ambition is usefully articulated by Payne *et al.*'s (2008) framework of co-creation which comprises emotional, cognitive and behavioural components. This conception indicates a requirement that experience creation through events is multifaceted, and there-fore, what Kale *et al.* (2010) refers to as 'empathising' becomes a key factor. The implicit lesson in Payne *et al.*'s framework is that co-creation transcends the passive participation of listening or watching. More befittingly event design must be concerned with generating a sense of shared experience, or what Getz (2007) refers to as 'communitas', and also inciting an active and participative disposition.

This discussion concurs with the argument of Ramaswamy (2011) who places emphasis on mutuality, which he articulates as stakeholder centricity. It can thus be inferred that event imagineering should balance the aspirations of all stakeholders and seek to envision and activate event spaces to facilitate value creation for, but also between, the many participant groups. This interpretation advances conventional expressions of the event management role indicating that organizers have a duality of purpose. The first function being event managers as choreographers of the event setting seeking to generate the conditions where participants can journey through the event benefitting from opportunities to derive, or extract, their own value (Nelson 2009). They design the eventscape, and in so doing purposefully craft a unique blend of setting, programme, theme and so forth, that best lends itself to the profile of stakeholders and *raison d'être* of the event. The second aspect is the event manager as an enabler of co-creative exchanges, seeking to promote, or provoke, interaction between participants.

Therefore as the discussion so far indicates, for events to realize their co-creative potential informed consideration of all participant groups must underpin the event creation process. If organizers proceed without clarity of purpose and appreciation of what participant groups would perceive as valuable from the event, then the imagineering process exists in somewhat of a void. As indicated by Hamso (2012), clear objectives therefore need to be agreed and be representative of the participants. In this case an equitable purposefulness informs the event which provides a robust foundation from which the design process can flourish.

Before moving to the next section which explores how co-creation by ambition can be achieved, it is appropriate to highlight a discussion that directly follows from the above but is inadequately addressed in the existing research. Commentary on the strategic value of events, event evaluation and Return on Investment (ROI) has progressed significantly in the last few years (see for instance the contributions by Hamso (2012) and the study carried out by Meeting Professionals International (2012)). However, this discussion typically focuses on the process and challenges of defining measurable event objectives from the event planner and budget holder perspectives. Much more attention should be given to interpreting and acting upon wider stakeholder objectives, ensuring that the voice of all participant groups is adequately captured early in the event creation process, through, for example, working groups that encourage a transparency of objectives and that allow stakeholders to co-produce the event by being involved in the design process from an early stage. If participants are an essential component of the co-creative process then event creators must find approaches to, as Ramaswamy indicated, co-create at any stage of the process, preferably starting at the very beginning so that the event design can be mutually shaped. Activating participants at the earliest stages of the imagineering process enables a multiplicity of voices to shape the formation of the event, an occurrence that is strongly aligned with co-creation by ambition.

Activating co-creative possibilities

Underpinning the above is the imperative for a strategic, inclusive and freethinking event creator who can 'extract' critical information for all stakeholder groups and as Ravn (2007) suggests, to then use this understanding purposefully to frame the event context and therefore to assist participants in realizing their own aspirations and co-creating their individual output which will be valuable to them in their own way. A 'space' thus needs to be built where participants can connect with others. To this end a recent review by Wood (2009) identified 14 different event platforms, under the canopy of experiential marketing events, each with their own strengths and limitations. This gives a flavour of the diversity of possibilities open to the event imagineer seeking to create an apposite setting given the specific configuration of outcomes required. The malleability of events offers the creator considerable scope to craft imaginative event settings and programmes that are tightly designed around the required stakeholder outcomes. Beyond decisions about the particular event platform that is adopted, the more extensive experience design literature (but also event design thinking with key writers such as Berridge (2007)) signposts many further considerations towards achieving a gainful event space. In accomplishing the challenge of co-creation by ambition the creator has many approaches they can engage with, and some are introduced below.

According to Fuson (2012) the event programme should be designed following a pace similar to a movie plot, with moments of action and moments for reflection. Speaking in a conference context, Tinnish and Ramsborg (2008) suggest that a safe environment should be created, which challenges participants intellectually and at the same time encourages experimentation and creativity. An element of surprise or unexpectedness can be interjected to capture or maintain attention, and different session formats should be included to match the attendee's level of experience and personal preferences. Moreover, time away from formal activities should be included to allow participants to informally co-construct solutions but also to reflect and plan for their own daily activities and then share action plans.

Fuson (2012) goes on to emphasize how music, lighting and stage sets must support the development of the event story. Facilities such as the setting, furniture, equipment and ambient conditions have an impact on group cohesion and can facilitate the creation of personal relationships and of the emotional connections that are conducive to co-creation (Nelson 2009; De Groot and Van der Vijver 2013). Food and music in particular can be used to increase attention and performance levels and facilitate social interaction (Braley 2011).

The ideas introduced here are aligned with some very useful literature in the area of experience design. Pine and Gilmore (1998) advocate five experience design principles of theming the experience, harmonizing impressions with positive cues, eliminating negative cues, mixing in memorabilia and engaging all five senses. The different dimensions of customer experience, such as sensorial, emotional, cognitive and relational, regulate attendee experience and can be impelled through the designing of a range of attributes which are posited to enhance the event experience, including innovation, integrity (Wood and

Masterman 2007), personal relevance, surprise, engagement (Poulsson and Kale 2004), interactivity and dialogue (Wohlfeil and Whelan 2006). Although conceived around physical events, these experience design principles are equally as relevant and important for virtual experiences, such as webinars.

Technology boost

If event design is approached in the way advocated above, co-creation transcends the event itself and instead is elongated both pre- and post-event, which widens the possibilities, particularly using technology to enhance the co-creative impact of the event. Indeed pioneering approaches such as the 'unconference' (Segar 2010) increasingly challenge the status quo of traditional tightly planned, and pre-defined, event programmes that strictly dictate content, format and timing of the event. Instead, participants should be given the opportunity of contributing to the 'imagineering' of the event before the event date, for instance by recommending topics to be discussed, session formats and possible speakers. This way the programme can become closely relevant to the audience and engage them at a deeper level (Ravn and Elsborg 2011). Technology advances and the advent of Web 2.0 in particular can help event designers in achieving this.

Technology has substantially bolstered the opportunities that event creators have to generate co-creative events. As mentioned above, technology provides diverse opportunities to generate meaningful content and enable interaction, starting well before the event, continuing during and extending the life of the event after the on-site delivery is over. Kale *et al.* (2010) for instance discuss the use of blogs and a YouTube competition to expand the experience and boost engagement. A more sophisticated application consists in combining the virtual and the live audience to deliver a hybrid event, a strategy that more and more organizations are engaging in, due to budget constraints and the requirements of Corporate Social Responsibility (Pearlman and Gates 2010). However, delivering an event that keeps the online audience as engaged as the live one is a major challenge, since not all content is suitable for the virtual audience and remote attendees can become easily distracted. Therefore the content of the live event must be adapted to suit the needs of the remote audience. This can be achieved, for instance, with shorter sessions, respecting the schedule and not running late, training the speakers and including a dedicated presenter/moderator to look after the virtual audience, transmitting their questions to the floor and in general keeping the event engaging to overcome the lack of personal and emotional involvement and create a sense of belonging (Fryatt *et al.* 2012). This theoretical discussion leads us to two illustrations providing real examples of co-creative inventiveness within events.

Co-creative illustration 1: the FRESH Conference

The FRESH Conference provides an illustration of an event whose design is consistent with the aspiration of co-creation by ambition, as reasoned above. It is coincidentally a conference targeted at event creators but its relevance lies in how the event is designed so as to maximize the co-creative possibilities. FRESH defines itself as a 'forum to learn from experts and other participants, both inside and outside the (*meetings*) industry'. There have been two FRESH conferences so far (in January 2012 and January 2013) with the events designed to create a community that goes beyond the conference itself (FRESH 2013). An underpinning tenet of the event is that members share knowledge in innovative ways, and therefore the event is designed to imagineer a setting to facilitate this co-creative possibility (Ravn 2007). The participants are bound together by the common interest to increase the effectiveness of meetings and they are part of an informal, self-organized community that exists to identify examples of good practice and to share them across the members through dedicated websites and social media. The conference is the culmination of this relationship that is nurtured year-round (Fuson 2012). FRESH 13 was designed to allow participants to experience as many formats as possible, or as the organizers say 'to be totally immersed in different formats' (FRESH 2013). The different session formats were designed with clear link to the specified objectives to promote engagement and encourage varied forms of interaction where the participants' contribution is not only valued but necessary. This emphasis on purposefully provoking participation and interaction through creative event design is emphasized by Berridge (2012).

When planning for FRESH 13 the event creators did not have a pre-defined agenda, instead they looked for input from potential participants on the topics to be discussed, session formats and possible speakers (Ravn and Elsborg 2011). This was partly achieved through an online event, a few months before, using Synthetron (a real-time web-based application) where each participant can anonymously contribute. These contributions were then peer reviewed with the objective of co-creating the programme (Synthetron 2013) and through this process the programme could become wholly relevant to their aspirations. This provides a good illustration of how events can be co-created, rather than exclusively produced by the event creator, and is consistent with the argument of commentators such as Vargo and Lusch (2004) who advocate the engagement of customer, client and attendees in the development of products, services and experiences.

Storytelling, practical activities and case examples were used during the FRESH conferences to analyse the components of a meeting experience. Within the event programme, a combination of (live and virtual) speakers and facilitators provided different ways of encouraging interaction and taking advantage of participants' experience so that activities were related to their own projects/problems and time for active interpretation was included, with support from peers (Ravn 2007; Nelson 2009). This quest to trigger individualization is introduced by Masterman and Wood (2007) in their advocacy of the '7I's' in the design of experiential events. These writers also emphasize the importance of embedding interaction where break-out sessions and informal activities are included where participants can network, discuss projects, develop joint solutions, plan for their own daily activities and then share action plans (Ravn and Elsborg 2011). One of the '7I's' is also innovation, and this was captured in the FRESH Conference in 2013 where a bogus 'corpse' was hidden under a white sheet, which added an element of unexpectedness and allowed participants to collectively immerse themselves in the process of 'dissecting' meeting owners and understanding what their expectations are (Tinnish and Ramsborg 2008; FRESH 2013).

Movable furniture and changing room layouts are an integral part of the design of the FRESH conferences and delegates are asked to reflect and identify how, as Vanneste (2008) argues, they are used to enhance motivation, learning and networking. Food and music in particular were discussed, and used, to increase attention and performance levels and to facilitate a more co-creative setting (Nelson 2009; Braley 2011). Some pieces of music were especially composed by an 'experience creation designer' for the event, with one piece, for instance, aimed at encouraging brainstorming (FRESH 2013). These examples of creative events design, employed to trigger heightened engagement and co-creation, are captured in the discussion of 'creative set-up', in the fascinating work of Visit Denmark with their 'meetovation' concept (Visit Denmark 2013).

Technology plays an important role during the event, and organizers make sure that it is used with the clear and specific purpose to enhance engagement and interaction. To extend the event beyond the physical audience, a virtual component was embedded in the programme, where online delegates could view sessions on the conference website. To facilitate co-creation they were assisted by dedicated moderators to communicate amongst themselves and with the live audience through an App, and also via Twitter and a dedicated online platform with embedded video/audio and text chat. Virtual MCs and facilitators were looking after the online community and made sure that they were kept involved and engaged providing them with exclusive content (Fryatt *et al.* 2012). Social media, particularly, is used to extend the life of the FRESH conference with organizers continuing the conversation with participants with follow-up news and articles from speakers and other conference contributors including the posting of pictures and videos (Kale *et al.* 2010).

The main objective of the FRESH conferences is to promote discussion on the value of meeting design and advance the knowledge of meeting designers on the tools available to create effective meetings that achieve stakeholders' objectives. These objectives are achieved by facilitating a setting where participants can co-create their own programme, actively contribute with their own personal and professional experience and engage easily with fellow attendees and organizers pre-, during, and post-event. This case study shows how meaningful and long-term results can be achieved when an attendee is embedded in the context in which he/she is co-participating.

Co-creative illustration 2: MADE Entrepreneurs Festival

MADE describes itself as a 'festival of entrepreneurship', which has occurred annually in Sheffield UK, for the past three years. The emphasis on festival, as opposed to conference, is noteworthy and underpins the vision of the event to become a more co-creative setting. In an interview Brendan Moffet (Festival

Director) suggested that conferences can too often be 'dull very dry, very dusty', and that the vision for MADE is 'indoors, outdoors, there is corporate, there is cultural, so the mix makes it feel like a festival rather than a business conference'. In doing so they take a theme (entrepreneurship) that would typically be housed in a conference setting and inject all of the notions of entertainment, space and freedom that is more familiar with a festival setting. This intentionality of design is important in triggering the experiences that the event designer foresees (Darmer and Sunbo 2008).

The event is underpinned by a variety of objectives from different stakeholders and consequently there is also a disparate range of attendee groupings at the event, and in order to facilitate an eventscape that provides a mutuality of outcomes there is a design need to create different spaces and a more wide-ranging engagement (Fuson 2012). Michael Hayman, MADE Chair, refers to it as 'Glastonbury for Entrepreneurs', after the renowned UK music festival (SevenHills 2013). Brendan reflects upon the success of MADE in year one, particularly in terms of media coverage and corporate sponsorship, but bemoans that the event became primarily a 'promotional vehicle' and that 'felt like a hollow victory' as it only hit the narrow external promotion oriented objectives, primarily though PR generated activity. The inference being that it neglected to provide a rich and co-creative experience for core stakeholders, and attendee groupings, such as regional businesses people and the student audience. It was therefore reflected that year one of the event was too heavily stage managed with the event participants much more passive and detached.

Responding to a question about the stage-managed approach Brendan argued that their role needs to evolve; 'we need to just be a facilitator, we need to just let it [the event] breathe'. He went on to reflect how there is a need for them to 'devolve ownership' to broaden the base of the event and actively engage the stakeholder groups in content development (Whelan and Wholfeil 2006). Brendan's view is that

> the mistake we made in the first year of this event was that we went to stakeholders for support and sponsorship and we didn't have them fully engaged, so they weren't contributing and co creating. So I think the step forward in 2011 was this co creation thing. Because actually the truth for us is to be a facilitator instead of doing everything ourselves.

He went on to discuss how the first year's event missed the opportunity to trigger a more holistic event design approach and focus upon greater legacy. Hence, as he expresses, they shifted to a more stakeholder centric approach in year two to purposefully generate more 'residue after the event'. In year one the post-event debrief exposed some strong views from somewhat disenfranchised stakeholders, therefore 'we have been much more involving with some of those stakeholder groups which gives it [the event] more depth'. This revised outlook is notably consistent with the spirit of the discussion in Richards and Palmer (2010). One specific development of the event from the first to second year was the closer involvement, in the 'imagineering', of the council's enterprise team; Brendan reflects how their participation 'undoubtedly adds value in its fusion of disciplines'. As an example the council team were free within the event programme to create many different opportunities and spaces to connect the local and regional entrepreneurs with the high calibre business leaders and politicians in discussion-based sessions. A further example of the progression is the following:

> when Peter Jones [celebrity entrepreneur] comes to Sheffield and he talks about British dreams, the future of enterprise and inspirations, the key thing is to have the young people of the next generation on the front listening to him and being inspired, that was the big difference.

This, and other similar design decisions, inspired much stronger engagement with local educators and students which increased their involvement with the event. Another good example of this progression, in year two, was the fuller involvement of the University of Sheffield who used the event to collaborate with participants to plan a new MSc in Entrepreneurship. They engaged in direct research and other activities with attendees, the idea being that the degree was created by entrepreneurs for entrepreneurs. A key aspect of co-creation is creating engagement and involvement between participants who would not ordinarily unite; in many respects this is an underlying charm of events in that they can, when adeptly curated, trigger these opportunities.

The organizers express the notion that MADE is a canopy under which a rich mix of event spaces, and impromptu meeting spaces, coexist. Along with more traditional platforms such as the main conference hall, sponsored dinners, exhibition spaces, speaker's corners, they facilitate a fringe programme. Approximately 30 organizations host fringe gatherings in assorted venues, of different shapes and sizes, throughout the city, the event therefore boasts unlikely meeting places such as city centre pubs and community centres, with such venues making the event more inclusive to the many and varied participant groups, which includes school children, students, young entrepreneurs and media, in addition to the more traditional business and political audience. A guiding principle for the event, according to Brendan, is that they provide attendees with the opportunity to forge their own bespoke journey through the event, with participants pursuing whichever route fits with their motivations and expectations. The challenge is therefore to facilitate many and varied 'stages' (settings) where participants can derive their own value and also co-create with other participants in both formal, informal, typical and atypical settings.

As a final reflection on the MADE festival, and in line with earlier discussion, the co-creation extends beyond the parameters of the three days and the venues, with a growing number of sponsors and partners are keen to be involved. Brendan reveals how in year one the criteria to accept a sponsor was purely based around the monies they could put in and the prestige they would bring. However as the festival has grown the opportunity has arisen to insist on the sponsor bringing content to, and beyond, the event. Therefore the organizers can shape the activation approaches that sponsors use to cohere with the essence of the event. So for example Intuit, a US accounting software business, 'did a boot camp, outside of the event, as part of their sponsorship'. Without this their involvement would not have made sense as they had no previous brand recognition among the audience.

Concluding thoughts

These two illustrations signpost an imagineering process which is driven by a fixation with outcomes, which become highly transparent and direct the event design process. The outcomes emerge from appreciation of all key stakeholders whose interests combine to determine the recipe for the event. In forging co-creative spaces, the approach advocated in this chapter doesn't subscribe to traditional conventions of how things are done, but it embraces a steadfast commitment to reinventing the inputs, processes and structures to best achieve the aspired outcomes. This *raison d'être* has far reaching implications for the profession, placing emphasis on the strategic imperative, with the event imagineer being outcome obsessed and stakeholder centric.

Recognizing that an event is a mutual space that is populated by stakeholders with many and varied desired outcomes is fundamental to a proficient imagineering and facilitation process. The pursuit of what this chapter refers to as 'co-creation by ambition' impinges upon the activation of participants within and also beyond the time and space limits of the event. One of the implications of this approach is that for stakeholders to be actively engaged in the co-creative process their social and emotional involvement should be purposefully embedded all the way through. For example, within the event programme there should be no distinction between 'formal' activities, where cognitive development takes place (i.e. attendees 'learn' something) and 'informal' moments, where networking or social activities take place. To achieve a rich experience that enhances value beyond the time of the event itself, the programme should be a continuum of activities that involve participants on a rational, emotional and social level (Payne *et al.* 2008; Ravn and Elsborg 2011; Fuson 2012).

As the events landscape matures, along with people's consumption of experiences, a much more purposeful and sophisticated approach to event creation must prevail, certainly for the frontrunners. This chapter, and the illustrations presented, suggest that this progressive approach must supersede the more outmoded input-oriented psyche, and also the tactical, and managerial, event manager that has been unearthed in recent studies (Pugh and Wood 2004; Crowther 2010b). The label of event organizer, planner and managers should be discarded, along with their associated stereotypes, and replaced by more befitting characterizations such as experience designer, facilitator or perhaps imagineer.

To end, and inspired by the illustrations, here are five precepts for event imagineers seeking to foster an event setting that embodies co-creation by ambition, rather than, the less inspiring, co-creation by default.

1   Identify and interpret the value aspirations of the participant groups and place these at the heart of the event imagineering process.
2   Using precept 1, envision the outcomes and resolutely manipulate the inputs to imagineer an event setting that maximizes the opportunities for actors to realize their outcomes.
3   Compulsively engage the participants in the context as well as the content of the event. Democratize the event by involving the participants in the imagineering process.
4   Recognize the rich unpredictability of co-creation and provide space and time with the event setting, and beyond, for participants to co-discover and co-innovate. Perhaps realizing outcomes neither they, nor you, anticipated.
5   Share, with all stakeholders, the purpose and value of the co-creation process that you are trying to stimulate so as to arouse a higher level of engagement and participation.

References

Berridge, G. (2007) *Event design and experience*, Oxford: Butterworth Heinemann.
Berridge, G. (2012) 'Designing event experiences', in S.J. Page and J. Connel (eds) *The Routledge handbook of events*, London: Routledge, pp. 273–288.
Bowdin, G., Allen, J., Harris, R., McDonnell, I. and O'Toole, W. (2011) *Events management*, 3rd edn, Oxford: Butterworth Heinemann.
Braley, S.J.F. (2011) 'Brain food comes to meetings', Meeting and Conventions, 1 June. Online, available at: www.meetings-conventions.com/News/Features/Brain-Food-Comes-to-Meetings/ (accessed 31 January 2014).
Collins, J. (2004) *Interaction ritual chains*, Princeton, NJ: Princeton University Press.
Crowther, P. (2010a) 'Marketing space: a conceptual framework for marketing events', *Marketing Review*, 10(4): 369–383.
Crowther, P. (2010b) 'Strategic application of events', *International Journal of Hospitality Management*, 29(2): 227–235.
Crowther, P. and Donlan, L. (2011) 'Value-creation space: the role of events in a service-dominant marketing paradigm', *Journal of Marketing Management*, 27(13–14): 1444–1463.
Darmer, P. and Sunbo, J. (2008) 'Introduction to experience creation', in J. Sunbo and P. Darmer (eds) *Creating experiences in the experience economy*, Cheltenham, UK: Edward Elgar, pp. 1–12.
Davidson, R. (2012) 'EIBTM 2012 trends watch report'. Online, available at: www.eibtm.com/Media-Centre/ (accessed 15 June 2013).
De Groot, E. and Van der Vijver, M. (2013) *Into the heart of meetings: basic principles of meeting design*, MindMeeting BV: Amazon Digital Services.
FRESH (2013) 'Fresh story'. Online, available at: www.thefreshconference.com/ (accessed 6 February 2013).
Fryatt, J., Janssen, R.W., John, R., Garriga Mora, R. and Smith, S. (2012) 'Hybrid meetings and events: meeting professional international'. Online, available at: www.mpiweb.org/Libraries/Research_and_Reports/HYBRID-Executive_Summary.pdf (accessed 16 May 2013).
Fuson, G. (2012) 'Emotionally engaging events by design: MPI perspective'. Online, available at: www.naylornetwork.com/mpi-nxt/ (accessed 12 June 2013).

Getz, D. (2007) *Event studies*, Oxford: Elsevier.

Getz, D. (2012) 'Event studies: discourses and future directions', *Event Management*, 16(2): 171–187.

Grönroos, C. and Ravald, A. (2011) 'Service as business logic: implications for value creation and marketing', *Journal of Service Management*, 22(1): 5–22.

Gupta, S. (2003) 'Event marketing: issues and challenges', *IIMB Management Review*, June: 87–96.

Hamso, H. (2012) 'Event ROI institute'. Online, available at: www.eventroi.org/articles/ (accessed 10 June 2013).

Heasley, J. (2010). 'Inside Microsoft: a tour of one of the industries veteran event departments'. Online, available at: www.eventmarketer.com/article/inside-microsoft (accessed 14 February 2013).

Kale, S.H., Pentecost, R.D. and Zlatevska, N. (2010) 'Designing and delivering compelling experiences; insights from the 2008 Democratic National Convention', *International Journal of Event and Festival Management*, 1(2): 148–159.

Kotler, P. (2003) *Marketing management*, 11th edn, London: Pearson Education International.

McCole, P. (2004) 'Refocusing marketing to reflect practice: the changing role of marketing for business', *Marketing Intelligence and Planning*, 22(5): 531–539.

Masterman, G. and Wood, E. (2007) 'Event marketing: measuring an experience?' Paper presented at the 7th International Marketing Trends Congress, Venice.

Meeting Professionals International (2012) 'The business value of meetings: meeting professional international'. Online, available at: www.mpiweb.org/Portal/Business/BusinessValueofMeetings (accessed 10 June 2013).

Nelson, K.B. (2009) 'Enhancing the attendee's experience through creative design of the event environment: applying Goffman's dramaturgical perspective', *Journal of Convention and Event Tourism*, 10(2): 120–133.

Parsons, E. and Maclaran, P. (2009) *Contemporary issues in marketing and consumer behaviour*, Oxford: Butterworth Heinemann.

Payne, A.F., Storbacka, K. and Frow, P. (2008) 'Managing the co-creation of value', *Journal of the Academy of Marketing Science*, 36(1): 83–96.

Pearlman, D.M. and Gates, N.A. (2010) 'Hosting business meetings and special events in virtual worlds: a fad or the future?' *Journal of Convention and Event Tourism*, 11(4): 247–265.

Pine, B.J. and Gilmore, J.H. (1998) 'Welcome to the experience economy', *Harvard Business Review*, 76(4): 97–105.

Poulsson, H.G. and Kale, S.H. (2004) 'The experience economy and commercial experiences', *Marketing Review*, 4(3): 267–277.

Prahalad, C.K. and Ramaswamy, V. (2004) 'Co-creation experiences: the next practice in value creation', *Journal of Interactive Marketing*, 18: 5–14.

Pugh, C. and Wood, E.H. (2004) 'The strategic use of events within local government: a study of London borough councils', *Events Management*, 9(1–2): 61–71.

Ramaswamy, V. (2009) 'Co-creation of value: toward an expanded paradigm of value creation', *Marketing Review St Gallen*, 26(6): 11–17.

Ramaswamy, V. (2011) 'It's about human experiences ... and beyond, to co-creation', *Industrial Marketing Management*, 40(2): 195–196.

Ravn, I. (2007) 'The learning conference', *Journal of European Industrial Training*, 31(3): 10.

Ravn, I. and Elsborg, S. (2011) 'Facilitating learning at conferences', *International Journal of Learning and Change*, 5(1): 84–98.

Richards, G. (2013) 'Events and the means of attention', *Journal of Tourism Research and Hospitality*, 2: 2. Online, available at: www.scitechnol.com/2324-8807/2324-8807-2-118.pdf (accessed 12 June 2013).

Richards, G. and Palmer, R. (2010) *Eventful cities: cultural management and urban revitalisation*, London: Routledge.

Roy, D.P. and Cornwell, T.B. (2004) 'The effects of consumer knowledge on responses to event sponsorships', *Psychology and Marketing*, 21(3): 185–207.

Schmitt, B.H. (1999) *Experiential marketing: how to get customers to sense, feel, think, act, and relate to your company and brands*, New York: Free Press.

Segar, A. (2010) *Conferences that work: creating events that people love*, Marlboro, VT: Booklocker.

SevenHills (2013) 'Seven Hills co-founder Michael Hayman profiled in the Yorkshire Post'. Online, available at: www.wearesevenhills.com/news/2012/06/26/seven-hills-co-founder-michael-hayman-profiled-in-the-yorkshire-post/ (accessed 15 February 2013).

Synthetron (2013) 'Proactive crowd-sourcing'. Online, available at: www.synthetron.com/ (accessed 6 February 2013).

Tinnish, S. and Ramsborg, G. (2008) 'How adults learn, now. Convene. PCMA'. Online, available at: www.pcma.org/convene-content/archives (accessed 20 March 2013).

Vanneste, M. (2008) 'Meeting architecture: a manifesto', Meeting Support Institute, Turnhout, Belgium.

Vargo, S.L. and Lusch, R.F. (2004) 'Evolving to a new dominant logic for marketing', *Journal of Marketing*, 68(January): 1–17.

Visit Denmark (2013) 'Meetovation=meeting design'. Online, available at: www.visit-denmark.com/denmark/meetovation-meeting-designs (accessed 29 October 2013).

Whelan, S. and Wholfeil, M. (2006) 'Communicating brands through engagement with "lived" experiences', *Brand Management*, 13(4/5): 313–329.

Wohlfeil, M. and Whelan, S. (2006) 'Consumer motivations to participate in event marketing strategies', *Journal of Marketing Management*, 22(5/6): 643–669.

Wood, E.H. (2009) 'Evaluating event marketing: experience or outcome?' *Journal of Promotion Management*, 15(1): 247–268.

Wood, E.H. and Masterman, G. (2007) 'Event marketing: experience and exploitation. Extraordinary Experiences Conference: managing the consumer experience in hospitality, leisure, sport, tourism, retail and events', Bournemouth University, Bournemouth, UK.

Yuan, Y. (2008) 'Relationships among experiential marketing, experiential value, and customer satisfaction', *Journal of Hospitality and Tourism Research*, 32(3): 387–410.

11 Classical music, liveness and digital technologies

Arthur Maria Steijn

Introduction

Recent research has made it clear that live performance of classical music, in its present form, is in trouble. Johan Idema states: 'the classical concert ritual somehow seems to scare people off' (2012: 9). Why classical music events scare people off, and how this might be dealt with, is one major area of discussion in this chapter. The other concerns the relationship between the live format of the music and its mediatization, as discussed by Phillip Auslander (2008).

Late in 2012 several institutions in the Øresund region, a transnational region, including the cities of Copenhagen, Denmark and Malmö, Sweden, decided to initiate an interregional collaboration project in order to develop new audience experiences. This project is exploring the possibility of increasing interest for live performed classical music through deployment of new technologies. The Øresund region has a high density of large cultural institutions on both shores of the Øresund strait. Both Copenhagen and Malmö have concert halls and internationally respected orchestras. In September 2012 the collaborating institutions received EU interregional funding for the two-year project 'Classical Composition Music and Experience Design'. The partners involved in the project are: Copenhagen Phil (SS), Malmö Symphony Orchestra (MSO), Malmö University (dept. MEDEA), the Øresund Committee, the Royal Danish Theatre (DKT) and the Royal Danish Academy of Fine Arts – School of Design (KADK). Due to my affiliation with the School of Design, I shall elaborate on the aspects of the project in which this institution is involved. Examples are derived from student projects as well as from ongoing research projects. All of the concepts in connection with the School of Design, described and discussed here deploy motion graphics (Manovich 2013) in spatial contexts that relate to the liveness of classical music in one way or another.

Rethinking the concert ritual

In this section I shall present statistics, which indicate a decrease in the worldwide audience for live classical concerts. Thereafter I will identify problems related to the *concert ritual* itself, followed by several case studies that experiment with different *concert rituals*.

A declining audience

According to an audience demographic research review published by the League of American Orchestras, the paid attendance to live performed classical music declined by 8 per cent between 2002 and 2007 (2009: 4). Similar tendencies can be seen occurring elsewhere. In Holland, for example, the audiences for classical music performances, expressed in proportion of the population, shrunk from 17 to 14 per cent between 1995 and 2007 (Netherlands Institute for Social Research 2009: 133). In Denmark, the Royal Danish Theatre has recently been inclined to reduce the number of classical concerts due to falling audience attendances (2011: 6). The worldwide financial crisis seems to have had a negative influence on these statistics. On the other hand, a decrease in the paying audience for live performed classical music was a noticeable trend even before the crisis.

The classical concert ritual

Recent studies have indicated that one of the main reasons for a continuous decline in interest for live performed classical music is connected to *how* the music is offered to the audiences (Idema 2012: 14). Even sublime performances are looked upon by many as 'formal and passive concert experience' (15). It seems as if the focus of the musicians is entirely on the music, as if there is only one way to perform when expressing musical virtuosity. The drama expressed and intended by the music is not reflected in the presentation of the live perform-ance. 'The contact between the classical performers and their audience is often minimal when compared to other musical forms' (15).

In a report from the United States, one can read that: 'the problems of orchestras stem not from the music they play but from the delivery systems they employ' (Wolf 2006: 6). This also identifies the problem as related to the classical concert ritual. The report sees the orchestra as being responsible for a loss of 'the magic in the music' (8), and lists several focus points described as *lessons for orchestras*. So if we presume, as noted by Wolf (49), that classical music itself is not the problem, we might take the following points in account. First, 'The mission of an orchestra needs to be clear, focused and achievable' (49), in other words, orchestras need to serve their audiences in the ways they promise them. Second, 'No single magic bullet will address the many serious problems that orchestras face' (49), so it turned out to be an illusion that only changes inside the concert hall would be sufficient to transform the orchestras. What actually could contribute to solutions, according the report include for example: 'more varied and interesting programming'; 'a revital-ized concert hall experience'; 'more involved music directors'; 'more innovative use of technology'; 'more education and outreach'. A final point is that 'Orchestras need to do more research on those who do *not* attend their concerts.' According to the report, therefore, there might be larger potential audiences outside the existing number of visitors for classical music than one would expect.

A number of points might be considered when *rethinking the concert ritual*. These are listed in Table 11.1.

Table 11.1 A selection of points, including some directions for possible solutions (noted in italics)

---

1 The mission of an orchestra needs to be clear, focused and achievable
2 No single magic bullet will address the many serious problems that orchestras face
   a more varied and interesting programming
   b a revitalized concert hall experience
   c more involved music directors
   d more innovative use of technology
   e more education and outreach
3 Orchestras need to do more research on those who do *not* attend their concerts

---

Source: derived from 'The Search for Shining Eyes' (Wolf 2006).

Cases that rethink the ritual

There are several cases that rethink the classical concert ritual. I shall describe three cases derived from Idema's writings: *Present! – Rethinking Live Classical Music*, and see in what way selected points taken from *Lessons for Orchestras*, might apply to these cases.

In 1998 Philip Glass was invited to compose a score for the film classic *Dracula* that was originally released in 1931 (directed by Tod Browning and starring Bela Lugosi). The original movie could be shown as a silent movie, but also as a movie with basic speech. The original basic speech version of the movie lacked a specific music score, which is where Philip Glass came in almost 70 years later. The score was performed as a live soundtrack for the film (Idema 2012: 105). The score was performed by Phillip Glass and the renowned Kronos Quartet in front of a live audience while the film was projected on a screen behind the musicians. As the case described in the writings from Idema (2012: 105) this piece 'at the same time provides a perfect chance to turn movie buffs into contemporary music lovers'. If we look at this case and take heed of the points in Table 11.1, derived from *Lessons for Orchestras*, it is clear that some of these points are applicable. At least point 2a, 2d and 3 and maybe 1 are being addressed to a certain degree.

In 2001 installation artist Janet Cardiff created the sound installation: *The Forty Part Motet*. It turned into an installation with 40 loudspeakers, placed at ear height, each representing the voice of a singer from a choir composed of eight groups of five singers. The installation consisting of 40 speakers, positioned in a large, enterable ellipse shape has been shown at different, often sacral locations. The piece does not have a starting time and can be visited at random. Cardiff wanted 'the audience to be able to experience a piece of music from the viewpoint of the singers' (2001). The audience was enabled to listen to the piece, a reworking of a sixteenth century composition, either as a whole, or as individual voices; depending on the position of the listener in relation to the speaker(s). If we view the indexed selection from the *Lessons for Orchestras* from Table 11.1 once more, we can say that the following points might apply Cardiff's *The Forty Part Motet*. Here points 2a, 2b, 2d and 3 and maybe also point 1 are respected.

In 2011, 99 years after the disaster, *T. 1912*, a conceptual reenactment of the sinking of the *Titanic* by the artist Dominique Gonzalez Foerster (Idema 2012: 123) was staged at Manhattan's Guggenheim museum. The evening began with dinner for the audience; the same dinner as served from the menu on the last evening on the *Titanic*. After the last course the audience was placed, divided over the several *decks* that shape the levels of the museum's *rotunda*. At the ground floor one could see and hear the orchestra playing a special composed piece of music. The orchestra was illuminated in ways that were reminiscent to experiences of the *Titanic*'s house band that continued playing as the ship sank. Light design caused the cloth draped on the floor to change character from water, to ice to underwater as the piece came to an end. When considering Table 11.1, I would say that at least points 1, 2a, 2b and maybe point 3 are being addressed in this case.

This selection of cases has in common that they '(re)design the concert experience as a whole' (183), as Idema notices. These, and other cases mentioned in Idema's *Present! – Rethinking Live Classical Music*, represent a (re) consideration of the ingredients that determine how audiences experience music. A number of these ingredients are listed in the Table 11.2.

Points and contents as indexed in Tables 11.2 and table 11.3 will be referred to when relevant in the next section: 'Classical Composition Music and Experience Design'.

Though the majority of the cases described by Idema are not actually measured or evaluated, they provide insight into how various cases rethink the classical concert ritual. In the following section I will describe what motivated the Classical Composition Music and Experience Design project.

Classical Composition Music and Experience Design

The main purpose of the EU Interreg funded Classical Composition Music and Experience Design project is to rethink audience experiences and develop knowledge of applied technologies connected to classical music and live concerts. Another goal is to strengthen relations between cultural institutions, creative businesses and educational institutions in the Øresund region.

The cultural institutions involved in the project; two symphonic orchestras from Copenhagen and one from Malmö, have been experiencing a growing need to

Table 11.2 A selection of guidelines that need consideration for how audiences experience music

1	The physical location
2	The setting (or general atmosphere)
3	The programme (its relevance and urgency)
4	(The communication of) the overarching message or theme
5	The performers, and their presentation
6	The audience's engagement and involvement

Source: from *Present! – Rethinking Live Classical Music* (Idema 2012).

renew and therefore rethink the dissemination of their competences. Competition within the field of cultural and culture related experiences is fierce, especially when it concerns reaching out to younger audiences. Many cultural institutions consider digital media and new technologies as appropriate ways to reach new audiences. However, in the field of classical composition music, new technologies have been applied mainly to online ticket sales, web-based marketing and social media. New technologies have seldom been used in connection with physical, spatial and aesthetic experiences in relation to live performances of classical music. According to the European Commission (2014) programme 'Creative Europe', the cultural sector needs to adjust to the impact of globalization and the transition to digital technologies. Therefore the project Classical Composition Music and Experience Design focuses on: 'developing new and meaningful audience experiences where live classical music meets new digital technologies – at the same time it seeks to strengthen and expand the level of knowledge as well as the creative businesses in the Øresund region'. Besides strengthening interregional, Øresund-oriented, cultural development through multi-institutional collaboration, the project aims at advancing the development from the regional to a yet to be explored international field. The partners in the project aim to explore and develop new experience design concepts, through understanding and exploiting each other's complementary expertise. During the first phase of the project it is planned to develop and test several concepts that involve two or more partners and that can result in multiple artistic and technological projects. These concepts are meant to contribute to rethinking the classical concerts' live ritual, with integration of digital technologies and understanding for the live aspect of the music. In relation to the activities in which spatial and interactive experience design connect to live classical music the expected results are described in the EU Interreg application (see Table 11.3).

In connection to the activity *Spatial and Interactive Experience Design around Classical Live Music* a focus in this chapter will, as noted earlier, be on concepts and projects that are created at the School of Design (KADK). In the following section I shall describe a model, the method, terminology and workshops that led to the first sequence of concepts and projects executed by students. These concepts and projects relate to points 1 and 2 and are prepared for point 4 and 5 as listed in Table 11.3. The section on 'Connecting windows'

Table 11.3 A selection of expected results from the activity *Spatial and Interactive Experience Design around Classical Live Music*, as described in the EU Interreg application

1 Numerous audio-visual concepts
2 Numerous audio-visual digital interaction concepts
3 Concepts and prototypes for Internet streaming of interactive music
4 Communication of concepts, visions and experiences through exhibitions and showcases
5 Communication of visions, experiences and knowledge through papers and articles
6 Knowledge-building and knowledge-sharing in the Øresund region (centred around the cities of Copenhagen and Malmö)

(see below) will deal with aspects that relate to point 6, knowledge-building and knowledge-sharing in the Øresund region.

Involving design students

While preparing the EU Interreg application, the author together with colleague, dramaturge and researcher, Jakob Ion Wille, sketched a simple mode, or navigation tool, designed for mapping the performance radius of the live concert (see Figure 11.1).

> The live concert is the centre of the model. Surrounding the actual concert one could imagine various mediatized or physical installations that relate to the actual live concert...
>
> In this way the model illustrates possible installations, mobile units and other devices in different spatial and temporal distances surrounding the actual concert. The model also suggests possible routes of the audience when attending (or possibly not attending) the live concert...

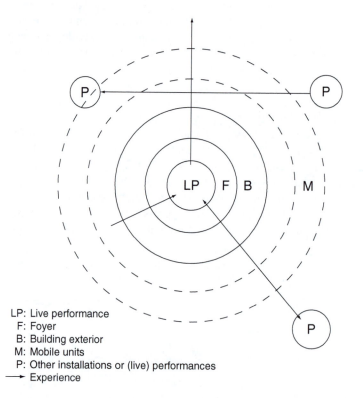

LP: Live performance
 F: Foyer
 B: Building exterior
 M: Mobile units
 P: Other installations or (live) performances
→ Experience

Figure 11.1 Illustration of the performance radius in relation to live concerts (© Illustration by Arthur Maria Steijn and Jakob Ion Wille 2013).

This path can be perceived as the individual dramaturgy of the event…

In short the idea of liveness, the possible media manifestations, and the architectural framework surrounding the actual musical content are suggested to take into consideration throughout the development of the student design concepts.

(Wille and Steijn 2013: 12)

Theory, terminology, method, tools and design-lab

'How can we create new and meaningful audience experiences in which classical music meets with new technology?' That was the question upon which we have based our project, which built upon a workshop that incorporated a selection of relevant theory, terminology, method and tools and resulted in the first range of design projects.

Live, liveness and mediatized performance

What is *live*? The word *live* in connection with music and performance was first published in the *Oxford English Dictionary* in 1934 after the invention of analogue sound recording in the 1890s and the advent of radio broadcasting in the 1920s. According to Auslander (2008) the word *live* first came to existence when the difference between *live* and the *recorded* became more obvious. This was not the case in the early days of radio, when all the sound and music broadcasted was *live*, as all the music transmitted by the radio stations was played *live* in the radio studios. In 1935 a BBC annual report noted that too much recorded music, played from gramophones, was used in the otherwise *live* radio transmissions. This undercut the clear distinction between the *live* and the *recorded*. Later, in 2008, Auslander argues 'that the relation between live and mediatized forms and the meaning of liveness (is to) be understood as historical and contingent rather than determined by immutable differences' (7). The word *mediatized*, in reference to *performance*, is explained by Auslander as follows: 'mediatized performance is performance that is circulated on television, as audio or video recordings, and in other forms based in technologies of reproduction' (4). One could argue that an event or a *live* performance is often being reinterpreted at the moment of *mediatizing*. The camera's point-of-view, framing, length of lens, camera movements, depth of focus or lack thereof, as well as the colour balance and contrast, are all aspects of *mediatizing*. We could also reflect on the similarities and differences between the time and place of the actual event or performance and the mediatized version. Auslander describes the changing relationship between *the live* and *the mediatized* by writing that 'Initially, mediatized events were modeled on live ones' (2008: 10) and he continues, 'The subsequent cultural dominance of mediatization has had the ironic result that live events now frequently are modeled on the very mediatized representations that once took the self-same live events as their models.' Auslander categorizes the historical development of the concept of *liveness* and indexes types of *liveness* in relation with their characteristics and their cultural forms (see Table 11.4).

Table 11.4 A selection of the historical development of the concept of *liveness*

Types	Characteristics	Forms
1 Classical liveness	Physical co-presence of performers and audience Experience in the moment	Theatre, concerts, dance, events, etc.
2 Live broadcast	Temporal simultaneity of production and reception: experience of event as it occurs	Radio, television, Internet, etc
3 Live recording	Temporal gab between production and reception; possibility of infinite repetition	LP, CD, film, DVD, etc.
4 Internet liveness	Sense of co-presence among users	Internet-based media

Source: derived from Auslander (2008).

Method: production design

As an overall method for the course, we mainly drew from a *production design method*, which has its roots in design for two-dimensional, pictorial experiences.

The *production design method* uses methods, theory and tools primarily, but not exclusively, linked to designing living images based on a dramaturgic, narrative content. The method is often used for creating the overall visual concept and design for film or TV series. Usually an analysis of the dramaturgic structure of the story is used. A story has three basic parts, as described by film producer Bruce Block (2008: 222).

1   exposition (ex), the beginning, which fundamentals were described by Aristotle;
2   conflict (co), the middle of the story, which will reach a climax (cx) and thereafter;
3   resolution (re), the end.

These three parts can be visualized as 'a story structure graph' (Block 2008: 226), as shown in Figure 11.2.

In their visualized concepts, depicted below, the graduate design students have used principles of this dramatic structure. In that section we will see examples of concepts in which the whole event around the classical music is considered as a narrative. An example can be read in *Case 2: the moon-concerts*. Here a student considers the time before, during and after the concert as parts of the narrative as a whole. This resulted in a contribution where the design of the experience, at least in length of time, exceeds the actual classical music performance.

This story structure graph can then be used as a starting point to conceptualize audio and visual means that might express the development and progression of the narrative over time. Five components as the main audio-visual parameters

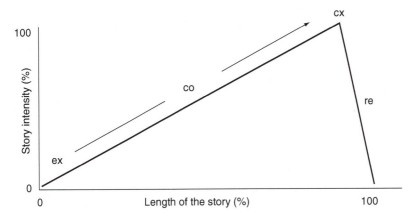

Figure 11.2 A generic story structure graph (source: based on descriptions and illustrations by Block 2008) (© illustration by Arthur Maria Steijn 2013).

are to be considered: (1) time, (2) movement, (3) space, (4) light and (5) sound. More parameters might be added if relevant. The expression or strength of these five main components can be varied in relation to the intensity of the narrative. The components are shown schematically in Figure 11.3.

Each of the five main audio-visual parameter components can have several sub-components. For example the component *time* has multiple sub-components, or variables, such as real time, historical time, experienced time. In Table 11.5, various sub-components are listed as part of their main component.

The sub-components/variables *before-during-after* of the component *time*, listed in Table 11.5 have been useful for the *moon-concerts* case.

Through exercises and analysis assignments the students became familiar with two-dimensional, pictorial sub-components as part of the component space. Block (2008) has defined the following four sub-components of the component space: 'deep, limited, flat and ambiguous space' (14).

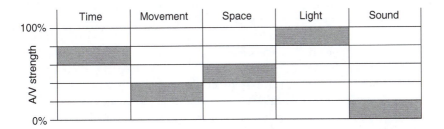

Figure 11.3 Illustration of the strength of various A/V parameter components at a given time in the story's narrative (© illustration by Arthur Maria Steijn 2013).

Table 11.5 The five main A/V parameter components listed including a preliminary index of relevant sub-components

Component	Sub-components/variables
1 Time	Real, historical, experienced, before-during-after
2 Movement	Realistic, acted, choreographed
3 Space	2-D, pictorial; *deep, limited, flat, ambiguous* 3-D, world: *inside, outside, wide, narrow, etc.*
4 Light	Daylight; *direct, indirect* Artificial; *projected, reflected*
5 Sound	Realistic; *live, recorded* Composed; *live, recorded*

In the project phase of the course, students often worked with audio-visual components and their sub-components, drawn from the production design method. The components are often depicted as sequences of images and/or as graphic representations on large sheets of paper in A2 format or larger. An example of creative use of the audio-visual parameters that visualize and communicate several audio-visual aspects of a design concept is seen in Figure 11.4.

The audio-visual parameters as depicted in Figure 11.4. are motivated by the students' interpretations of the meaning, development and progression of a modern music composition named *Stele*, composed by György Kurtág in 1994. On the x-axis we see the time passing in the reading direction. The y-axis represents several of the earlier mentioned audio-visual parameter components. The following components are illustrated (bottom to top): time, light (the height of the bar indicates intensity), colour, space, form, intensity (sound), movement and progression. The project to which these audio-visual parameters refer will be described in the last part of this section.

Tools and design-lab

Relevant tools for working on and experimenting with *motion graphics* in relation to music were introduced in the classroom, as well as in a design-lab. The design-lab is a place for considering, experimenting, trying out and testing certain aspects of potentially interesting projects related to the project Classical Music Experience Design. The design-lab will operate in several places, depending on the kind of project, the partners involved and their relevant expertise.

Motion graphics, formerly known mainly from title sequences for film and TV, now play an increasingly prominent visual, narrative and spatial role in, for example, dance and opera performance design. Often the motion graphics used are video projected on a large backdrop, and function as a visual element that changes over time as the music and/or the narrative proceeds.

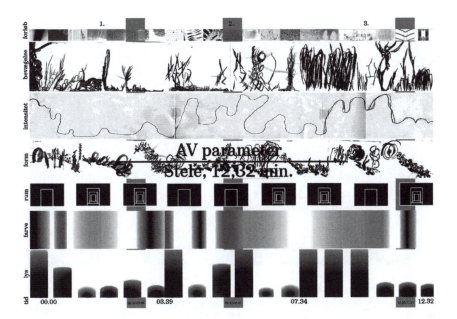

Figure 11.4 A fragment of A/V parameters illustrated and used as a working and communicating tool in practice (© illustration by Josephine Farsø Rasmussen and Joy Sun-ra Pawl Hoyle 2013).

The rapid development of motion graphics has been made possible due to more affordable computers as well as animation- and compositing software packages such as *After Effects*. Especially this software development initiated 'a new hybrid visual language of moving images during the period of 1993–1998'. Leading to what new media theorist Lev Manovich calls 'a 'Velvet Revolution' in moving image culture' (2006: 1). He describes motion graphics as 'moving image sequences, which are dominated by typography and/or design and embedded in larger forms' (8). While this definition is adequate for now, I will refer to an attempt to define motion graphics in more depth as described in the article 'Imagined Spaces: Motion Graphics in Performance Spaces' (Steijn forthcoming).

In addition to an introduction and hands-on exercises using the software package *After Effects*, analogue exercises and assignments based on music were offered. One assignment was to make a sketch of a continuous sound-inspired illustration based on a short piece of modern composition music (Figure 11.5). Interestingly, quite a few of the resulting illustrations were in the form of prolonged, horizontally oriented drawings, some presented on long pieces of paper, reminiscent of (part of) a scroll similar to the first artistic animations to music by artist Hans Richter (1888–1952) from the 1920s.

This sound-inspired illustration exercise led to an assignment that was conducted in the design-lab. The design-lab made it possible to test relationships

Figure 11.5 A continuous sound-inspired illustration based on a short piece of modern composition music (© illustration by Bogdan Stamatin 2013).

between images and sound, in which motion graphics were projected on a 175 cm by 95 cm sized back-projection PVC screen. The students were assigned to make a motion graphics sequence based on the same music used earlier for the sketching assignment. In order to accommodate testing of multiple relevant aspects, the design-lab was made scalable. Binder describes 'the laboratory metaphor as both suitable and useful, as it puts emphasis on a transparent, delimited process that is potentially scalable' (2007: 1). Various aspects of the relationship between sound and image (in this case moving images, motion graphics) were explored and discussed in the design-lab. While working on timing or synchronization between motion graphics and sound, experience in the lab seems to indicate that when only one or few visual elements in motion are visible the sound should be audible just after the image is visible, rather than at the exact same moment. When many moving objects are present synchronization seems less important.

Another focus of the work done in the design-lab was on the spatial qualities of the on-screen motion graphics. Here the sub-components, *deep, limited, flat and ambiguous space* from the main component space, mentioned earlier were discussed in relation to the spatial 'feeling' or 'atmosphere' of the music. A third aspect was the size of the back-projection PVC screen and its relationship to its surroundings. Here we discussed the difference in spatial perception between motion graphics that are mainly oriented within the borders of the two-dimensional screen space (see Figure 11.6.) and those that 'flow over' the edges of the screen.

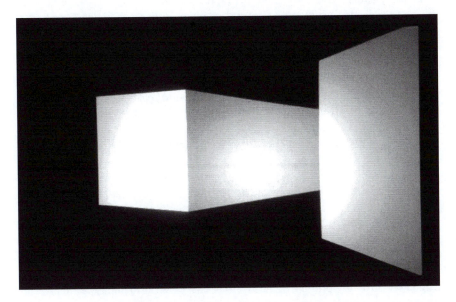

Figure 11.6 Motion graphics designed to stay within the borders of the 2-D screen space
(© photo: Arthur Maria Steijn, motion graphics: Sölvi Snæbjörnsson 2013).

Three visualized student concepts

In this sub-section I shall present three cases of visualized concepts materialized
by participating graduate students from the Royal Danish Academy of Fine Arts
– School of Design (KADK). These cases are chosen from work done during the
last part of the course, and are described in depth in the publication created for
the partners involved in the EU interregional funded project Classical Composition Music and Experience Design (Wille and Steijn 2013). The three projects
all use video projected motion graphics that relate to classical composition
music. Each case is supplemented with a table summarizing the main ingredients
that determine how audiences experience music (derived from Table 11.2),
related descriptions of *liveness* (see Table 11.4) and numerous relevant audio-
visual parameter components and sub-components (see Table 11.5).

Case 1. The orchestra conductor: the world's most underestimated painter

This concept acknowledges that a serious, well-educated audience is a prerequi-
site of appreciation of the art of live classical music events. Graduate design
student Bogdan Stamatin states that: 'A knowledgeable audience has been
exposed to classical music from a young age' (Wille and Steijn 2013: 33). He
considers it of great importance that one needs to train the ears of the young

audience. Bogdan writes in his project report: 'just like in sports where athletes are being trained since they are infants, a serious audience is grown into being, is formed by exposing the young to the classical music concert format'. He continues: 'the purpose of [this] concept is to bring a true, real-time visual dimension to the classical concert by adding a new function to the physical movements of the orchestra's conductor'. And 'besides conducting the flow of sound, the movements of the baton are put to use for drawing real-time motion triggered graphics, and thus recapturing any loose attention from the public's side'. This idea is inspired by the magic wand as used by wizards and magicians, seen in many movies that have been shown in cinemas and on television. The majority of Bogdan's main target audience, the five to 15 year olds, does not know of the magical power of the conductor's baton. But they do know the magic power that Harry Potter's magic wand possesses. And the shape and length of his magic wand and the way he controls it has a striking resemblance to the way a conductor swings his baton. Building on this idea Bogdan further conceptualized how the movements of the conductor's baton and the gestures of his right arm and hand might translate into live-generated motion graphics. These live-generated motion graphics can, for example, then be video projected on a large backdrop behind the live performing orchestra, but one could also imagine them elsewhere. These motion graphics might also function in the foyer, the outside of the concert hall or on mobile devices. I will introduce another possibility of showing these live-generated motion graphics in the next section entitled 'Connecting windows'.

A large variety of parameters are involved when conducting, and thereby controlling a large symphonic orchestra. Based on research, Bogdan put up a set of conditions defining which movements of the conductor shall be analysed in the 'correct' way when motion is captured by camera sensors (Figure 11.7). Bogdan defines these movement parameters as follows:

> the right hand – the one holding the baton – usually controls the *beat* and the *rhythm*. Both hands control the *quality* of the sound: sharp vs. soft; and the *amplitude* – general volume. The left hand, referred also as 'the hand of the heart', controls actions such as *start/stop* and also the way notes are played in a sequence: *legato, vibrato, crescendo, piano/forte, al niente/dal niente*.

The visualized concept *The Orchestra's conductor: the world's most underestimated painter* addresses some of the main focus points derived from the content and descriptions that are found in the tables in previous sections. The most relevant focus points are indexed in Table 11.6.

Case 2. The moon-concerts

This concept, defined and visualized by graduate student Sarah Gad Wøldike Sørensen, puts a visual and time-based framework around classical compositions

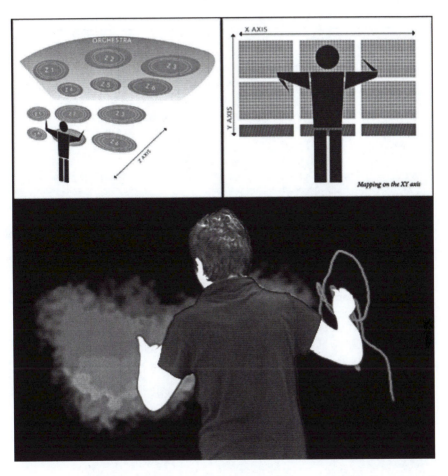

Figure 11.7 Principles and illustration of translating tracked movement into live-generated motion graphics (© Bogdan Stamatin 2013).

that in one way or another relate to our moon. The time-based structure was based on *before-during-after* periods of the live concert. Sarah, herself a musician, decided to keep the classical concert ritual in its original format during the period in which music is played. For example, there are no video-projected visuals during the live performance. She concentrated on creating matching atmospheres bracketing the themed live concerts, both in time and in place. The moon-concerts are to be announced by visual means that relate to the theme and the genre of the classical music compositions, like *baroque, classical, romantic* and *modernistic* (Figure 11.8).

These announcements can be visualized on printed posters, electronic media such as the Internet as well as on television. At the time of the event, at full moon, the building of concert venue, as well as the foyer shall be 'dressed up'

Table 11.6 Indexed focus points derived from previous tables complemented with descriptions from Case 1

Table	Description
11.2 Rethink!	1 Concert hall, foyer, concert building, etc. 5 The conductor as the performer
11.4 Liveness	1 Experienced in the moment 2 The live-generated motion graphics are a form of live broadcast
11.5 A/V parameters	1 Real, experienced time and a form of after time 2 Realistic movement of the conductor 3 3-D world, physical space combined with a 2-D pictorial 5 *deep* space Live performed classical music

and illuminated using video projected motion graphics that are inspired by the form and style of expression associated with the musical genre of the present moon-concert. Sarah carefully analysed properties belonging to the genres. Keywords used as inspiration and guidance for the baroque genre are for example: *heavy, rich, voluminous, gold, class distinctions, authoritarian and tactile.* The video projections will only be visible before, in the breaks and after the moon-concert, thereby creating a visual experience that conveys the mood of the music, without hearing the actual music.

Several qualities and focus points that were taken into consideration during conceptualization of Case 2: *The Moon-Concerts*, were derived from the previous tables. The supplemental aspects are indexed in Table 11.7.

Table 11.7 Indexed focus points derived from previous tables complemented with descriptions from Case 2

Table	Description
11.2 Rethink!	1 Concert hall, foyer and concert building 3 Alternative programme 4 Message/theme: the moon
11.4 Liveness	1 Experienced around the moment 3 The 'recorded' (motion graphics) relates to the genre
11.5 A/V parameters	1 Historical time, before-during-after 2 Speed of movement relates to 'speed' of music 3 3-D world, physical space combined with a 2-D pictorial 4 space 5 Moonlight Live performed classical music

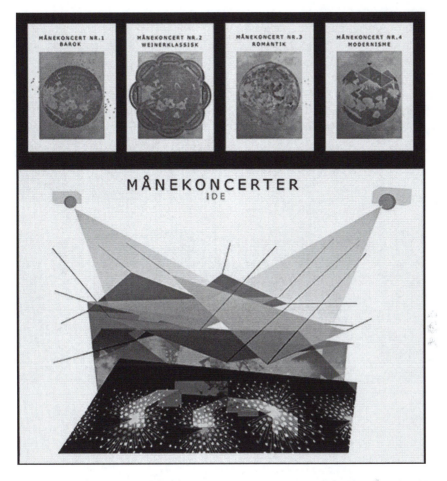

Figure 11.8 Poster proposals for the moon-concerts including a possible set-up for video projection through a semi-translucent screen in a foyer (© Sarah Gad Woldike Sørensen 2013).

Case 3. The beauty of the outskirts: a place specific music visualization

Graduate students Josephine Farsø Rasmussen and Joy Sun-Ra Pawl Hoyle collaborated on creating visuals for the so-called *sound portal*; a round, somewhat UFO-shaped construction built for experiencing high quality sound.

The outside of the portal measured approximately ten metres in diameter, around four meters high. The interior of the portal where high quality sound can be experienced, had a diameter of around six metres, with three entrances. Motion graphics will be projected to fill the walls inside the portal from top to bottom. The floor will be covered with a reflective material that will add a feeling of watery endlessness (see Figure 11.9).

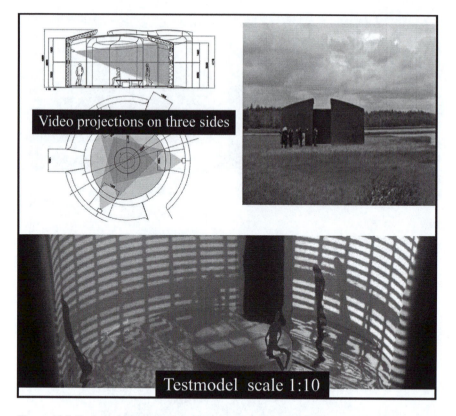

Figure 11.9 Technical drawing of the sound portal with three video projectors. The sound
portal placed in the outskirts and an impression of a video test in a scale model
(© Josephine Farsø Rasmussen and Joy Sun-ra Pawl Hoyle, 2013).

Since the sound quality proved to be of such a high standard, the DKT intends
to use the portal as an extension venue that would enable audiences in other,
sometimes remote locations to be able to experience the high quality classical
music concerts that the DKT can deliver. Initially the portal will broadcast a
selection of recorded concerts rather than direct broadcasts from live concerts.

The students were asked to develop concepts using the sound portal that
would aim at high quality experiences, which would enrich the audio experience.
Josephine and Joy developed a concept that takes the sound portal to remote
areas of Denmark. Through the integration of beautiful images and movies of
the local area within the motion graphics, the audience will get a sense of locality inside the sound portal. The concept includes a framework for a workflow to
use these local visual elements to be transformed into motion graphics for use in
the sound portal on that location. Their concept aims at using the portal to activate both audio and visual senses simultaneously; the visual senses through the
use of motion graphics projected by three video beamers on the inside walls.

Some of the main focus points and qualities that were taken into consideration during conceptualization of Case 3: *The beauty of the outskirts: a place specific music visualization*, derived from tables and their descriptions from previous tables. The supplemental aspects are indexed in Table 11.8.

Connecting windows

A new underground metro station in Copenhagen, located close to one of the main buildings of the Royal Danish Theatre (DKT) is projected to be inaugurated in 2018. The Design School, as one of the EU Interreg partners, was asked to draft a concept of how the public areas in the underground station might become *a window for the Danish Royal Theatre*.

The author of this chapter is one of the main designers of the project (still ongoing at the time of writing). There are two main reasons for developing this project under the EU Interreg umbrella. One is the fact that two of the music houses involved in the project will have underground metro stations close by. Both the DKT and the Malmö Symphony Orchestra (MSO) are interested in concepts that consider audio and visual connections between the nearest underground station and the concert house. The other reason is to fulfil the obligations regarding the EU Interreg project:

1 creating a number of audio-visual concepts;
2 exploring audio-visual digital interaction concepts, etc., derived from Table 11.3;
3 knowledge-building and knowledge-sharing in the Øresund region.

To accommodate these aims a laboratory, or design-lab, was created as a central, though not necessarily physical place for this form of 'constructive design

Table 11.8 Indexed focus points derived from previous tables complemented with descriptions from Case 3

Table		Description
11.2 Present!	1	Situated various places in the outskirts of the country
	5	Non-visible, only sound
	6	Locality and local artist are involved in visualization
11.4 Liveness	3	The music played in the sound portal is pre-recorded, and visualized with video projections of pre-made motion graphics
11.5 A/V parameters	1	Real time
	2	The movement and rhythm of the motion graphics relates to the 'narrative' and 'speed' of the music
	3	2-D worlds within a 3-D environment
	4	Video projector light
	5	Pre-recorded classical music

research' (Koskinen *et al.* 2011: 6), and seems like a workable metaphor for knowledge-building and -sharing.

Underground

The underground metro station near the DKT will have two street level exits/ entrances; both will be connected to a large central platform leading to the stairs and escalators down to the metro train platform. In this early concept phase of our project we are considering working with at least two audio-visual installations placed at the platform level and in the hallway between 'train station level' and 'earth level', see Figure 11.10. Both installations might refer to events taking place or future events, related to the DKT. In this section *installation 1* will be in focus.

For this project we plan to work with moving images on large screens as well as with audio that will be linking to the music and images from the nearby DKT. Since the project is in its initial phase, we have mainly been developing the principles to be considered for this project. First of all, for installation 1, we will be working with a curved LED screen, measuring around five metres wide and two metres high. This screen will have to be custom made.

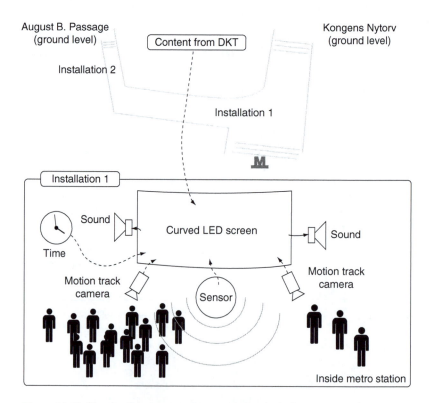

Figure 11.10 Sketch of underground metro station including several technical principles regarding installation 1 (© Arthur Maria Steijn 2013).

There are several concerns that will have to be addressed in order to create this installation. These will be presented in the next subsection, *laboratory*. The metro company has also requirements that must be met. First, it is important that passengers and commuters do not become so distracted by large illuminating moving images that the flow of pedestrian traffic becomes interrupted. Another concern was the audio aspect of the installations. It is necessary for everyone to be able to hear alarm signals, even when the space might be filled with music. And there is also the question of whether the music should be audible for everyone at all times?

Guidelines for resolving these concerns are being developed. Concerns about distraction might be addressed through the use of camera sensors connected to the screen installation, which could register the number and density of the passing passengers as well as the speed of their movements. These data could then be used to alter certain properties of the moving images on the large LED screen in real time. Concerns about the alarm signal can be addressed rather easily by connecting the alarm system to a switch that will disable the other electronic systems running at that time. Issues of general audibility can possibly be solved through the use of so-called *directional speakers* around the installation. *Directional speakers* have the advantage that the sound is only audible when standing underneath them.

Since it is only the initial phase of the project, the partners involved only have to investigate the possibilities of ways in which moving images on screens and sound could be presented in the underground metro station and how these might be connected with content, *liveness*, programme, events etc., related to and coming from the DKT.

One of the focus research areas will deal with possible solutions that are attached to distraction concerns, as described above. The data derived from the camera-sensor registration regarding for example the number and density of passengers passing might be used to control the various moving image properties on the LED screen. These properties, described in Table 11.9, might also be combined in various ways.

Table 11.9 A selection of moving image properties that might be controlled with data extracted from the camera censors at installation 1

Property	Description
Speed	The speed of the moving images might be changing according to the number of people E.g. more crowded: *slower speed* Fewer people: *normal speed*
Contrast and colour intentsity	The contrast and colour intensity of the moving images might be influenced E.g. more crowded: *less contrast and lower colour intensity* Fewer people: *more contrast and higher colour intensity*
Composition	The composition of the moving images might be influenced E.g. more crowded: *fewer visual elements, and less complex composition* Fewer people: *more visual elements, and more complex composition*

This project will also focus on various aspects of *time*, which relate to the image appearance and content on the rounded LED screen from installation 1. One could for example imagine commuters passing the large curved screen daily at around the same time; let's say between 08.30 and 09.00. The DKT could then use that time space to show a still image or motion graphics related to a forthcoming premiere, perhaps revealing some extra detail each day in that week. This is just one of many possibilities of how time might be related to moving image appearance and content. This content will primarily refer to classical music performances, but ballet and opera could also be considered. Both installations (1 and 2) might be part in future events in which visuals in public spaces can be connected with live performances elsewhere.

Laboratory

The research for this project might be classified as a form of 'constructive design research', according to the description of Koskinen *et al.*, where 'design research in which construction – be it product, system, space or media – takes center place and becomes the key means in constructing knowledge' (2011: 6). As noted earlier in Table 11.3, point 6 *knowledge-building and knowledge-sharing in the Øresund region* is one of the conditions for participating in this EU Interreg project. At the present we are discussing how to share knowledge derived from constructive design research. In this case, the laboratory metaphor, or the design-lab seems useful for the partners, since it has the potential to incorporate multiple projects in multiple locations.

The illustration in Figure 11.11. highlights the metro project within other yet to be defined projects (e.g. project W, X, Y and Z) inside the preliminary laboratory construction.

Content

The development of content of interest for the DKT will be considered as the project evolves and takes shape. For now one can imagine that elements from the design projects as conceptualized by the students and described as cases, might find their way into the installations for the underground metro project in one form or another.

Conclusions

Since this chapter builds largely upon an ongoing project, it is too early to conclude, for example, on the effect these concepts and design projects might have on the otherwise declining of audience attendance at classical music events.

At the moment, students and researchers from KADK as well as from Malmö University (MEDEA) are collaborating on a new project for the DKT.

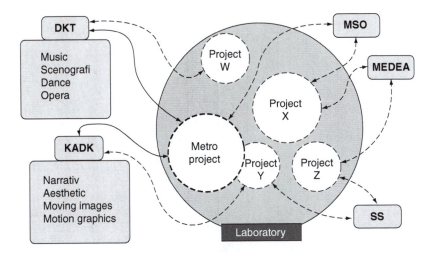

Figure 11.11 Preliminary schematic construction of a design-laboratory containing multiple projects involving all creative partners (© Arthur Maria Steijn 2013).

This project, which is part of a popular concert series for children, involves digital interactions, co-creation as well as video projected animations and motion graphics as an integrated narrative element related to the liveness of the classical music performance. In this project the *before-during-(after)* paradigm is used, in that children will cut out figures *before* the concert, which will be used as visual elements that are digitally projected *during* the concert.

The underground metro project provides an opportunity to research various aspects of onscreen visuals that might be altered in real time in response to data derived from local camera-sensor registrations of, for example, number of passing pedestrians. The resulting interactive audio-visual installations that connect to live performances produced by the Royal Theatre might become an integral part of larger future events that include classic music and experience design.

On the level of regional and interregional partnerships, a laboratory seems to be a workable metaphor for present and future collaborations between those involved in this EU Interreg project where knowledge-building and knowledge-sharing is essential.

Acknowledgements

Thanks are due to Per Galle, my supervisor; Barbara Adler, for reading, advice and corrections; and Jakob Ion Wille, my companion in this project. This Interreg IVA project was funded by the European Union under the European Regional Development Fund.

References

Auslander, P. (2008) *Liveness: Performance in a Mediatized Culture*, New York: Routledge.

Binder, T. (2007) *Why Design: Labs*, Denmark: Center for Design Research Copenhagen. Online, available at: www.nordes.org (accessed 11 December 2013).

Block, B. (2008) *The Visual Story, Creating the Visual Structure of Film, TV and Digital Media*, Oxford: Focal Press, Elsevier.

Cardiff, J. (2001) *The Forty Part Motet* [video file]. Online, available at: www.cardiff-fmiller.com/artworks/inst/motet.html (accessed 30 January 2014).

European Commission (2014) 'Creative Europe'. Online, available at: http://ec.europa.eu/culture/creative-europe/index_en.htm (accessed 10 February 2014).

Idema, J. (2012) *Present! – Rethinking Live Classical Music*, Amsterdam: Muziek Centrum Nederland.

Koskinen, I., Zimmerman, J., Binder, T., Redstrom, J. and Wensveen, S. (2011) *Design Research through Practice: From the Lab, Field and Showroom*, Amsterdam: Elsevier.

League of American Orchestras (2009) 'The League of American Orchestras'. Online, available at: www.americanorchestras.org/images/stories/knowledge_pdf/Audience_Demographic_Review.pdf (accessed 30 January 2014).

Manovich, L. (2006) 'After Effects, of Velvet Revolution: Part 2'. Online, available at: www.manovich.net/DOCS/ae_article_part2.doc (accessed 30 January 2014).

Manovich, L. (2013) *Software takes Command*, New York: Bloomsbury Academic.

Netherlands Institute for Social Research (2009) 'Digging Culture and Doing Culture'. Online, available at: www.scp.nl (accessed 30 January 2014).

Richter, H. (1952, February) 'Easel – Scroll – Film', *Magazine of Art*, 45 (February): 78–86.

Royal Danish Theatre (2011) 'Årsrapport: Det Kongelige Teater 2011'. Online, available at: http://kglteater.dk/omos/~/media/Om%20os/Organisation%20og%20Oekonomi/Det_Kongelige_Teaters_aarsrapport_2011.ashx (accessed 18 September 2013).

Steijn, A. (forthcoming) 'Imagined Spaces: Motion Graphics in Performance Spaces', in S. Shaw and A. Reilly (eds) *Embodied Performance: Design, Process, and Narrative*, Oxford: Inter-Disciplinary Press (manuscript submitted for publication).

Wille, J. and Steijn, A. (2013) *Classical Music and Experience Design Interreg Proposals, Projects and Research*, Copenhagen: Royal Danish Academy of Fine Arts, School of Design.

Wolf, T. (2006) 'The Search for Shining Eyes'. Online, available at: http://wolfbrown.com/component/content/article/42-books-and-reports/399-the-search-for-shining-eyes-audiences-leadership-and-change-in-the-symphony-orchestra-field (accessed 30 January 2014).

12 The transformation of leisure experiences in music festivals

New ways to design imaginative, creative and memorable leisure experiences through technology and social networks

June Calvo-Soraluze and
Roberto San Salvador del Valle

Introduction

Festivals and special events are becoming more and more important in society due to the positive impacts they can generate economically, socially, individually and environmentally (Lee and Crompton 2003; Pitts 2004, 2005; Sherwood 2007; Karlsen and Brandstrom 2008; Rivera *et al.* 2008; Rowley and Williams 2008). Although there is a wide range of topics in event research, a recent area of work in event studies currently focuses on imagineering (Nijs and Peters 2002; Van Pelt 2005; Hover 2008) and co-creation (Pralahad and Ramaswamy 2004a, 2004b; Jaworski and Kohli 2006; Payne *et al.* 2008; Ramaswamy and Gouillart 2010). Traditionally event research was focused on a technocratic perspective where the event industry and organizers were at the centre; in contrast, the audience just consumed what was offered. However, this situation has now changed, thanks to a number of important qualitative shifts in demand which have taken place in recent years, like the rise in education, income and status levels in the market (Richards 2007). This means that the general knowledge of the public is growing and so they have become increasingly demanding and informed. This change, along with the greater interest in experiences and creativity (Richards 2007) is forcing the event sector to change the traditional model to a new one where the main actor is the audience and what they feel and, therefore, events offer memorable *experiences* (Pine and Gilmore 1999) rather than information or just services.

On the other hand, the growing presence of social networks and the new applications of technological devices like mobile phones and tablets in daily life opens new and unsuspected horizons in the field of experiences and co-creation (Bryce 2001; Nimrod and Adoni 2012) which can be applied in the event sector. Hence, this chapter offers a reflection and a theoretical starting point into the contributions and transformations that technology can make to promote (co)creative and memorable event experiences. In order to address this issue, we will focus on a specific type of event: music festivals.

In the first section of this chapter we will examine the phenomenon of leisure experience, trying to understand the concepts and the elements that underpin these two different approaches to experiences: leisure as welfare and leisure as well-being. This allows us to better comprehend how technology has transformed, is still transforming and will transform in the future these elements of leisure experience. In the second section, we will focus on music festivals as example of leisure expression that provides first-hand experiences and emotions and examine how their design can contribute to the welfare and well-being of attendees. In this part we will highlight what festivals are about and how technology is changing their design process (pre-/during/post-event) and transforming leisure experiences. In the third section, we analyse a specific case: Heineken MyFestival. Finally, in the last section, we present a brief conclusion of the main ideas and some lines for further research.

Technology, at the origin of leisure experience transformation

Changes in the organization and experience of leisure activities and periods of leisure history have frequently been driven by technological developments. Film, TV and video (Argyle 1996; Rojek 2000) are some of the examples. Technological advances in transport and travel have also been important in providing access to leisure spaces such as beach resorts and the countryside (Argyle 1996). The invention of the phonograph, TV and film has all made it possible 'to revise ordinary orientations of leisure by dramatically increasing our sense of interdependence and our access to information and entertainment' (Rojek 2000: 24). The new information and communication technologies, personal computers, Internet and mobile phones, have deeply and drastically changed norms and practices in all life domains. Individuals' access to leisure and culture, leisure behaviours and experiences have been transformed, changing the ways in which people spend their time, determining their cultural preferences and developing their social ties and networks (Bryce 2001; Nimrod and Adoni 2012). Hence, technological change has influenced concepts of leisure and its organization, both in terms of access and experience (Bryce 2001).

Leisure experience as welfare

We can approach the issue of leisure through two different paths: the objective and the subjective approaches. Both round off the leisure experience (San Salvador del Valle 2011; Cuenca Cabeza *et al.* 2011). However, the leisure experience involves diverse experiences in different people and diverse experiences through our personal life itinerary (Kleiber 1999; Monteagudo 2008). So what are the objective and subjective conditions that make up each one? And how is technology changing those conditions?

All the objective conditions of leisure experience are oriented to achieving *welfare* (Stiglitz *et al.* 2013). The convergence between individual or group practices, activities, time budgets, uses of space and resources form objective conditions in order to produce diverse experiences.

Leisure activities offer an endless range of possibilities and they promote diverse opportunities for the person involved in them (Cushman *et al.* 2005). People participate in leisure activities for experiences that are enjoyable and personally satisfying (Kabanoff 1982), to relax and escape from the stresses of everyday life, and to improve their health (Iso-Ahola 1997). It has also been claimed that leisure is related to self-esteem, feelings of control, lifestyle and self-identity (Iso-Ahola 1980; Cuenca Cabeza 2000; Kleiber *et al.* 2011).

Technological leisure activities fulfil the same functions as traditional leisure activities; they provide relaxation, stimulation, escape, social interaction, and the development of self-identity and lifestyle. Although this suggests continuity in leisure functions, it seems that the new leisure technologies will lead to other changes in the contemporary experience of leisure (Bryce 2001).

The first consequence of the impact of the scientific-technological paradigm was the acceleration of time (Honoré 2004; Durán 2007; Rosa 2010). The impacts of the new paradigm in time are transforming the nature of different life scopes: the environment, socio-demography, the economy, education, politics and leisure (Carr 2011).

In fact, technology and the new scientific-technological paradigm (San Salvador del Valle 2000; Castells 2001) have contributed to the acceleration of time generating major changes in leisure (San Salvador del Valle 2009; Cuenca Cabeza *et al.*, 2011). In this sense, leisure is not only the consequence and origin of most changes in recent decades, but also the result of this new paradigm. Therefore, the social phenomenon of leisure is the effect of this changing lifestyle (Lipovetsky and Serroy 2010).

Hence, natural time has been recomposed, the significance of the seasons and the dichotomy between day and night have been disturbed, social time has fractured into individualized timetables and new immediate time is growing, with a direct impact on personal stress. As a consequence, leisure has undergone an important transformation, with new ways of programming, changes in timetables and time for performance with a change in the contemporary role of events. Furthermore, e-leisure[1] has reduced the distinctiveness of leisure as time considerably. The ubiquity of computers, mobile phones and the Internet both at home and in work settings, as well as in cafés, hotels, trains, buses, enables individuals to enjoy leisure activities along with their working and commuting activities (Nimrod and Adoni 2012). The traditional boundaries between work and leisure seem to disappear in a wired world (Lightman 2005).

In relation to space, the impacts of the new paradigm are also transforming the nature of different areas in life. For example, home computing and the Internet challenge traditional conceptions of the spatial and interactional organization of leisure by blurring the boundaries between domestic, virtual and commercial leisure spaces (Bryce 2001).

In cyberspace, the experience of time and interaction is altered; interaction can be both synchronous (as in MUDs)[2] and asynchronous (as in newsgroups)

(Smith and Kollock 1999). The individual may simultaneously be involved in synchronous and asynchronous interaction within virtual leisure spaces while being present in the external environment (Bryce 2001). Contemporary leisure spaces, then, may be experienced as multiple, diverse and simultaneous (Bryce 2001). This suggests the ability of technology to create 'heterotopic space [...] the juxtaposing in a single real place [of] several places' (Foucault 1986: 25). Hence, these virtual leisure spaces represent changing leisure activities and experiences, which have consequences for the societal and individual experience of leisure and well-being.

Resources are also essential when we try to complete leisure experience welfare (Tribe 1999). Economic resources guarantee enough income to pay for leisure consumption; educational skills make it easier to enjoy cultural leisure supply and social skills allow us to share leisure experiences with others. Nowadays, new technological resources allow us to experience leisure in another way. The Internet, social media (e.g. Facebook and Twitter), mobile phone applications or tablets are useful tools and valuable resources that are increasingly present in leisure, changing the variables of welfare (activities, time and space) and the way we experience things.

All the changes that technology brings in activities, time, uses of space and resources have a huge impact in different leisure fields. In the case of events these changes are even more noticeable. This is because the sporadic and unique character of events is accentuated by the influence of technology on leisure welfare. Acceleration of time, the intersection of traditional and virtual leisure spaces and new technological resources require the transformation of event design. Ticketing experience, promotion, the design and implementation of the content and all the elements surrounding the event have to be integrated with social media, mobile applications and the latest technology. Not only in order to adapt to new trends, but also to facilitate memorable and unique experiences to the audience through leisure welfare elements. Furthermore, the changes in the design of the objective leisure elements influence directly other factors, such as synchronicity of communication. Social networks and online applications allow a multiplicity of asynchronous social activities and interactions that impact in turn on the welfare of the audience.

Until now, we have only examined the objective approach to leisure experience with regard to individual and group practices, the active/passive activities carried out, the personal time budget, the leisure spaces used and the resources and skills available making up leisure experience welfare. Nevertheless, a great number of subjective aspects influence leisure experience well-being. What are the subjective conditions that comprise it? And how is technology influencing these conditions?

Leisure experience as well-being

Subjective well-being is an umbrella term which captures factors such as how satisfied people are with their lives and how happy people feel. It focuses on what people think and how they feel about their own well-being, so it includes both emotional reactions and cognitive judgements. In the current context, consumers are not looking just for physical well-being, so it is not enough to pay attention to those elements that are going to satisfy the consumer welfare, but also the aspects that satisfy consumers mentally and spiritually. In fact, emotions and feelings are what people remember most (Torralba 2010). In order to offer meaningful experiences, experiences that people will never forget, there is a need to pay attention to more subjective aspects like emotions, values, motivations, benefits and needs of the customers (San Salvador del Valle 2011). But how can technology influence these subjective aspects?

Motivations (Neulinger 1974; Iso-Ahola 1980; Nicholson and Pierce 2000, 2001; Monteagudo 2008) are push factors in the creation of leisure experiences. Investigations often reveal only a small part of the motivational factors shaping leisure behaviours and preferences (Kleiber *et al.* 2011; Nimrod and Adoni 2012). Anyway, it seems that factors influencing offline leisure affect participation in e-leisure as well (Nimrod and Adoni 2012). Therefore, the use of technology or the participation in different social networks (e.g. Facebook, Twitter) can be explained by the same factors as offline activities such as interest in the topic, the need for peer appreciation and socialization.

Needs are the known and unknown reasons that condition leisure decisions (Dower 1981; Monteagudo 2008; Cuenca Cabeza 2000). All the objective elements of leisure experiences are more or less linked to personal needs that satisfy inner dreams, desires, wants, material necessities and social recognition (Dower 1981).

Values are the pull-factors of leisure experience well-being and seem to be essential in future developments of the leisure experience decision process (Academy of Leisure Studies 1983; Monteagudo 2008; Stebbins 2007). At the same time, freedom, family, equality or work are also important. The prevalence of the values of freedom or equality creates two different leisure paradigms. First, creativity and free movement will be preserved, away from the pressure of institutional bodies, led by strong social nonprofit initiatives. Second, the solidarity and equality of opportunities will be promoted, away from the market (Stebbins and Graham 2004), guided by social movements.

Technology can be also an important element that influences values. Applied technology solutions for events promote different values taking into account the promoters' aims. There are institutional events, market oriented events and social events depending on how technology is used (Castells 2001).

Besides motivations, needs, emotions and values, the feeling of well-being is influenced by the benefits attained. They refer to the desired and expected future conditions. People expect to obtain economic, social, cultural and environmental benefits as a result of our leisure activities (Driver *et al.* 1991). All these benefits are relevant for e-leisure as well (Bryce 2001), although as in offline leisure activities, e-leisure may include risks and unpleasant experiences as well such as boredom, tension and disappointment. For this reason, it is important to know how to use technology and social networks as a way to obtain positive benefits and increase the feeling of well-being.

In the case of event design it is crucial to take into account all the elements that contribute to well-being. It is essential to know the motivations, needs, values, emotions and benefits of the audience in order to design the event according to their needs. If participation, experiences and creativity are what the current audience value most, events need to know how to use the latest tools like social networks, mobile applications and new technology to encourage these aspects of the event experience. If event managers know, for instance, that interactivity can reinforce the benefits of acceptance, satisfaction, learning and mastery, enhanced thoughtfulness, cooperation and responsibility, and heightened performance, motivation and sociability, they can design an event based on participation and co-creation through the use of new technology.

Therefore, when designing an event it is important to have in mind the factors involved in the process (Figure 12.1). Technology can be used in all aspects of the design process of event, because it helps to open new horizons in the field of experiences, intensifying audience emotions.

Music festivals, where leisure and technology meet

In this section we examine a specific type of event, music festivals, as an example of leisure expression that provides first-hand experiences and emotions. Music festivals can contribute to different levels of welfare and well-being of attendees depending on how the elements that comprise them are designed (e.g. time, space, activities). In fact, festivals are an important sub-field within event studies, and of particular interest to scholars in many disciplines because of the universality of festivity and the popularity of festival experiences and meanings (Robinson and Noel 1991; Prentice and Anderson 2003; Pitts 2004, 2005; Berridge 2006; Morgan 2006, 2008; Getz 2010). Thus, this investigation seeks to advance the field by introducing the element of technology as a way to enhance the leisure experiences of festivals.

First of all, it is important to know what we understand when we are talking about festivals. The difficulty of defining a festival lies in its etymology and in the popularity of the concept. Etymologically, the word festival comes from the Latin *festivus* and it refers to the concept of a celebration or party (Falassi

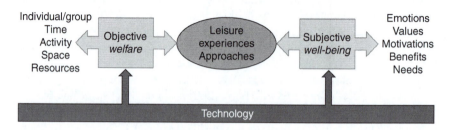

Figure 12.1 The impact of technology in leisure experiences approaches (source: author's own elaboration).

1987). It was not until the eighteenth century that it was used in English in the sense of great celebration of art, sport or exhibition (Falassi 1987; Getz 2005; Bonet 2009).

For this reason, in the analysis presented below we delimit the word festival using the following criteria:[3]

- having a distinct brand name, which encompasses all the work performed and having an outstanding character (excluding, therefore, music integrated into regular cultural programming);
- annual or biannual scheduling;
- representation of more than six different shows in single or multi-stage areas;
- duration of more than two days;
- programming of primarily professional content.

Each type of festival is the consequence of the interaction between the following key factors (Getz 1991; Getz and Frisby, 1991; Goldblatt 1990, 2005; Hall 1992; De Bres and Davis 2001; Peters and Pikkemaat 2005; Bonet 2009; Johnson *et al.* 2009):

- the place where it is located (central or geographical or cultural periphery, socio-economic level, demographic density and cultural offer, the communities that host it, educational level and cultural capital, traditions, vitality and the like);
- the institutions (ownership, governance and organizational values, management model, influential actors and participation in networks);
- the available budget (volume, development, financing and income structure, cost structure and pricing policy);
- the artistic project (specialized-interdisciplinary-eclectic, classic-contemporary, *premiere* and established hits).

These four factors interact with each other and with other external elements such as the legal framework, the market or the quality requirement, among others.

Understanding what a festival is, also requires knowledge of its mission and main objectives (Hall 1992; Long and Robinson 2004; Hall and Sharples 2008; Bonet 2009). The mission helps the managerial team to lead the organization towards its intended goal. One of the most important aspects for this to occur is that the mission of the festival transmits its values and points towards a specific meaning (Calvo-Soraluze 2011). Although with the passage of time it is appropriate to make small changes in this definition to adapt to new situations and ensure their existence in the context that surrounds them.

Not all festivals pursue the same mission and goals. The political-institutional, economic and technological environment, as well as the vitality of the local artistic sector, the existing tradition, as well as the needs and cultural habits of the population, influences the development and the mission of a festival and should be taken into account (Getz 1991, 2010; Bonet 2009). The observations of all the materials that form the event (programme, public image, media strategy, strategy funding, relationships with other institutions, etc.) allow us to distinguish between possible different festival orientations (Calvo-Soraluze 2011). Although almost all festivals have mixed interests, it is possible to differentiate between festivals according to their level of orientation towards artistic, social, financial, prestige elements, or to the attainment and the satisfaction of the audience (Bonet 2009).

Therefore, the objectives of a festival vary depending on the orientation of its mission, its social or artistic vocation, as well as the territory where it is located and its relationship with the community and their institutional and community representatives (Hall 1992). Most festivals tend to pursue a combination of purposes, and although they have potentially very diverse programmes and styles, all attempt to foster a specific kind of experience (Getz 2010). Event designers are particularly interested in knowing how their manipulation of setting, programme and various human interactions affects the audience and/or participants and whether or not the desired experiences and consequences are achieved (Berridge 2006; Brown and James 2006; Getz 2007; Morgan 2006, 2008; Pitts 2004, 2005; Calvo-Soraluze 2011). This requires knowledge of not only culture, arts and environmental psychology, but also of each of the elements that comprise leisure experience: time, space, activity, individual/group practices, resources, as a way to achieve welfare and emotions, values, needs, motivations and benefits as a way to achieve well-being (Cuenca Cabeza 2000; San Salvador del Valle 2011; Calvo-Soraluze 2011).

Moreover, despite the economic crisis, festivals are growing both in terms of spectators and revenue (SGAE Reports 2005–2011) and new ones have been created (e.g. in Spain: Bilbao BBK Live in 2008, SOS 4.8. in 2009 and Arenal Sound in 2011). Increased competition means new variables or elements are being introduced into festival experience design as a means to innovate and differentiate events, such as technology and social networks (Bryce 2001; Nimrod and Adoni 2012). These developments impact on the elements that comprise leisure experience and, as a consequence, on the experience itself. Hence, festival experience design has to take into account technology for a more complete understanding of the new situations that are currently emerging, such as the new interactions that are created among people. New leisure experiences can thus be facilitated by the festival through social networks (e.g. Facebook, Twitter), mobile phone applications (e.g. MyLife, GroupMe), new tools for online distribution and streaming, digital marketing (including ticketing systems) and new technology and systems that can change or complement live experience (e.g. Augmented Reality,[4] Holography).[5] But how is technology changing the context and the design of music festivals at the moment?

Current applications of technology in festival experience design

Technology and social media are increasingly being used in music festivals to heighten the leisure experience. Festivals around the world are beginning to use social media sites to further promote their festivals, and add another layer to the festival experience. For example, festivals are using social networks before, during and after the event in many ways.[6]

- Promotional deals for following the festival on Twitter or liking it on Facebook are used to transform the excitement of the audience about a festival into some promotional merchandise or discounts that will help them enjoy it even more. This strategy is used by many festivals like FIB (Festival Internacional de Benicàssim) and Bilbao BBK Live.
- The release of teasers through the festival social media channels. People can keep up with these on Twitter, Facebook and other sites by using the MyLife mobile app to integrate all their social network updates in one place.

  The Vans Warped Tour (USA and Canada) festival is one of the most anticipated festivals every summer and it has created a massive following in its 17 year run. The festival uses 'musical teasers' and, almost every year, they have released a Warped Tour compilation CD, and all of these have been incredibly popular and are a successful pre-festival promotion. However, online radio and music listening apps are gaining popularity and some festivals are trying to incorporate them in their design process. For instance, Warped Tour has embraced the online music listening experience by using apps like Spotify and Turntable.fm to engage the Warped Tour community in listening to the artists of past, present and future tours.

- The opportunity of sharing activities. Festivals are using social networks so that the audience can share the experiences they have at the festival. In this way, social networks become a platform where people can share what they are watching, eating, wearing and singing at the festival by tweeting, posting and using hashtags to access everything pertaining to the topic they want to follow on Twitter, Instagram, Vine and Pinterest. Moreover, integrated feed like MyLife can help ensure the audience does not miss anything in the social sphere as MyLife aggregates social feeds into one place.

  In the case of Coachella for instance (a two-weekend-long festival in Indio, California, USA) they are making their festival different by pushing GroupMe to communicate during the festival. GroupMe works on any phone that can text. Through GroupMe, you can stay in touch with a group of people through group messages, photo share and location share throughout your time at Coachella. This makes staying connected to Coachella attendees and people in your group much easier.

  On the other hand, Newport Folk Festival (in Rhode Island, USA), a festival based on tradition, is using social media as a way to keep the philosophy of the festival and creating faithful followers through the sharing of experiences. In fact, with the rise of technology and the increasing popularity of folk music, the festival has utilized social networks to preserve its traditions. Pinterest is the most recent addition to Newport's social presence, and the ability to post not only photos and videos of performances, but also certain things relevant to 'the folk'. So far, they have added boards for

'Music We Love', 'Folk Style' and 'Favorite Festival Moments' using Pinterest to promote not only the festival, but also to display the folk aesthetic to their fan base.

- Live streaming concerts. Festivals are using social media also for the people that could not make it to the festival to help them enjoy it from afar and create a loyal fan base offering live streaming through their own social media channels. Many of them also have agreements with social networks like YouTube to offer live streaming concerts or clips from the festival. For instance, Lollapalooza (Chicago, USA) partnered with YouTube and Dell to provide live streaming of the festival, engaging audiences without a ticket. According to a YouTube blog post the live streaming has done wonders for increased exposure: 'Live shows by artists like U2, Kenny Chesney and Coldplay have drawn millions of viewers to YouTube, and last year's Lollapalooza webcast saw viewers spending an average of 44 minutes watching the show' (YouTube Official Blog 3 August 2012).
- Mobile apps. Nowadays most of the festivals create their own digital application that can be downloaded to any smartphone. Most of these applications are free and contain important information about the festival. For instance, Outside Lands, created in 2008 in San Francisco, knows its audience's love of and reliance on smartphones. Steadily improving its mobile app each year, Outside Lands recently gave festival-goers a free app that included: set times, a map, the ability to scan food vendor menus, create custom schedules, rate food items or take pictures with Instagram. The app also sent push notifications during the festival notifying fans of set changes and secret pop-up shows. Hence, this is changing the interactions with and among the audience and, as a consequence, the design process of the festival.
- RFID,[7] a radio-frequency identification technology, originally used in an industrial context, has also been introduced to the entertainment industry. This technology is changing the ticketing experience. Wristbands using RFID technology created by Intellitix have been developed to address crowd control, gate crashing, counterfeiting, lost tickets, social media integration and identification of guests in case of emergency. Wristbands with these capabilities have already been implemented at major music festivals across the globe such as Coachella, Bonnaroo, Lollapalooza, SXSW, Electric Zoo and Eurosonic Noorderslag. 'Live Click Stations', featured at Coachella and Bonnaroo, allowed festival goers to automatically check into the events on Facebook (and when you register your bracelet online, Bonnaroo asks permission to update your Facebook status). A total of 30,000 guests registered for this service at Coachella and over 70,000 at Bonnaroo. Bonnaroo also featured a 'Live Click Photo Station', which made it possible for guests to take pictures that were simultaneously uploaded to Facebook. The new wristbands were also very successful at this summer's Wavefront festival in Chicago, where they easily differentiated between VIP and GA ticketholders and made the festival run smoothly. Furthermore, Serge Grimaux, the founder of Intellitix, is currently working to develop a cashless payment

system that would allow guests to make payments at festivals using their wristbands. The system would either be set up as a debit account with people transferring money before the festival or as credit with guests linking a credit card to the account. This development is expected to improve the speed of transactions and reduce fraud by introducing a way for guests to purchase goods without having to carry cash or credit cards. This would be another technological development that would change the design process and experience of the festival as we know it.

The case of Heineken MyFestival – the impacts of technology in the variables of leisure experience and event design

Heineken MyFestival is a particularly innovative initiative created and developed by Heineken in collaboration with the Why Not Challenge agency. The idea behind the festival is to establish the conditions necessary for all the people who want to create 'their own music festival, making real the festival of their dreams'. A digital application makes possible the design of 'one festival for each user'. In the words of Heineken: 'With Heineken MyFestival you are the creator and the main character' (Heineken MyFestival 2013).

The process starts when the users download the application in their smartphone. After their registration in the application they can start using it and taking decisions about the design of the festival: the name, the place, the poster the musical groups among other things. Once these issues are resolved it is time to interact with each other: listening to the playlist of other users as many times as they want, sharing their favourite festival on social networks like Facebook and Twitter and deciding which festival is the best one.

In order to promote their festival, users can paste their own posters in different places using the camera on their mobile phones and thanks to augmented reality, other users can see them. Besides, once a poster is pasted, it will appear automatically on a map from which users can access other posters, and play and save them as favourites.

The last decision is taken by all the users together. Each user can vote for their favourite festivals and the festival that has the largest number of votes is the one that wins. The votes are counted by the organization as well as the number of visits and plays of each festival. The festival that is most visited and played by all users of the application is the one that wins the prize. This consists of VIP tickets for the winner and three friends that the winner decides to enjoy the experience of going to one of the live festivals organized by Heineken. Therefore, Heineken MyFestival becomes not just a tool to enjoy good music or to live the experience of being a festival organizer but also is a way that Heineken can promote its real-life events.

In the case of Spain the first edition was in 2012 and it was a huge success. In fact, the application was the number one in general free downloads in Apple Music Store with 90,856 downloads, and with 35,527 posters created, 145,499 music playbacks and 15,423 new fans on Facebook (Heineken MyFestival 2013).

Therefore, although the ultimate goal of this initiative is not to carry out the winning project, it is a good example of involvement and participation in the organization of an event with mutual value creation results. The organization plays a crucial role in facilitating the platform that allows users to understand the process of designing a festival and let them take part in the main decisions digitally. In this sense, the model that this initiative uses and the main characteristics of the project gives clues about how technology can change some elements of the festival design process of the organization as well as the leisure experiences of the users in online communities of the festival, as they share musical tastes and experience the process of designing a festival. This can create synergies that could allow the creation of mutual value. So, how are leisure experience elements transformed with the introduction of technology into festival design?

As we have seen in Heineken MyFestival the use of technology can be a game changer, as technology and social networks introduce new and unique dimensions related to the core aspects of leisure experience. These new dimensions may have a strong impact on the individual's preferences, choices, behaviours and experiences, both offline and online, and therefore in the festival design (time management, activities, spaces etc.). But what are the dimensions that change leisure experience as welfare and well-being in the case of Heineken MyFestival?

Synchronicity of communication (changes in activity, time and space)

The use of technology and social networks in Heineken MyFestival altered the experience of time, space and the activity itself. The online application allows a multiplicity of asynchronous social activities and interactions, which has no equivalent in offline festivals. The use of the MyFestival online application allows synchronous interaction even though the participants may be miles away from each other.

Moreover, the online application extends the notion of heterotopic space (the juxtaposing in a single real place of several places) by increasing anonymity and reducing inhibition. This disembedded or cyber space is the context in which virtual communities are formed in MyFestival. From this perspective the online application can be seen as empowering, an egalitarian space and a frontier of electronic democracy (Bellamy *et al.* 1995).

Interactivity (changes in motivations and benefits)

The changes in the activity, time and space influence, in turn, the way people interact with each other. Interactivity refers to 'reciprocal communication exchanges that involve some form of media or information and communication technology' (Bucy 2004: 375).

In the case of Heineken MyFestival the use of computers and mobile technology allow the continuous two (or more) way transfer of information among a great number of users and a central point of communication, in this case,

MyFestival application. Furthermore, as the goal of the initiative is that users feel involved in the whole process with their personal participation designing a festival like Heineken does with Heineken Jazzaldia or Heineken Jammin' Festival, the process and the system are characterized by constant change, activity and progress with new users' contributions and the constant feedback. So, the use of technology is oriented towards experience and as users can interact with the organization they can develop the mutual value creation which is meaningful for both the individual and the organization.

All of these factors are intrinsically correlated with the action/activity aspect of leisure experience. They are specifically associated with the freedom of choice, the sense of control that results from such freedom, and the significance attributed to an activity (e.g. the level of involvement). Consequently, as Nimrod and Adoni (2012) argue the more interactivity users experience, the more their use of the Internet is experienced as leisure. And as the number of combinations depends on the variety of 'products'/'applications' and the whole process becomes play-like, engaging and enjoyable, the more interactive the site or the applications used the more it provides an experience of leisure and heightens the well-being of users (stronger emotions, motivations and benefits). As Rafaeli (1988) catalogued, the benefits of interactivity includes increased acceptance, satisfaction, learning and mastery, enhanced thoughtfulness, cooperation and responsibility and heightened performance, motivation and sociability. Examining these benefits through the lenses of the leisure benefits literature (e.g. Driver *et al.* 1991) leads to the conclusion that interactivity provides many psychological and social benefits (Nimrod and Adoni 2012) that heighten the festival experience even before the festival starts, as happens with Heineken MyFestival.

Participation and co-creation (changes in emotions, motivations)

Heineken MyFestival allows users to be involved in the whole process of creation. It encourages more active involvement from the audience to create a value-rich experience. Virtual reality, for instance, heightens the leisure experience by merging various user interfaces in order to create a fully integrated cyberspace experience. As Rheingold (1991) suggested, the elements of the virtual reality experience are moving, navigating or surfing in the space and creating for the users a sensation of being present or existing in a place that is different from the place in which they 'really' exist in their physical body at that time. Moreover, when virtual reality is integrated into daily life and activity, as happens with Heineken MyFestival (e.g. the use of the application and the possibility to paste their own posters in different places using the camera on their mobile phones and interacting with other users, offering them the possibility to win tickets to go to a 'real' festival) the experience is even more powerful (Nimrod and Adoni 2012).

Hence, e-leisure has introduced new, unique dimensions related to the core aspects, which were not commonly applied in traditional leisure. We can see through the case that the use of social networks and new technology influence the elements that comprise leisure experience as welfare and well-being. Changes in time, space and activity itself, impact on the synchronicity of the communication influencing as a consequence, elements of well-being such as motivations, emotions and benefits. These elements also have an effect on the level of interactivity, participation and co-creation, opening new possibilities for leisure experiences. All the processes in Heineken MyFestival attempt to enhance users' experience through the online application: sharing decisions, musical tastes, promotional posters, opinions and the like. In all these activities digital applications facilitate changes in the elements of leisure welfare (ways of programming, time of activities, changes in timetables) and well-being (increased acceptance, satisfaction, learning, cooperation). Moreover, the fact that almost everything is online influences the dimensions of synchronicity, interaction and participation and co-creation, thereby heightening leisure experience.

Changes in the festival design process

The use of technology and online applications allow the organization to stretch the process of the festival experience over time as well. In this way, even before the festival has been held, the 'users' of the application are already taking part in some of the decisions about the line-up, interacting with other 'users' through social networks and exchanging information and sharing tastes. The interaction happens not only with other users but also with the organization itself through mobile apps that can give you valuable information, teasers and ticket discounts, raising the motivation and expectation of the potential attendees. The interaction and participation is also heightened during the festival thanks to technological devices and online applications. The sharing of pictures and activities with friends and the festival community means the experience of the festival both offline and online enhances one of the main characteristics of a festival: socialization. Furthermore, once the festival is 'over' the festival community does not disappear. The post-festival phase becomes as important as the preparation and the experience of the festival itself, because technology and social networks allow people to keep sharing the experience (e.g. posting videos and pictures, writing blogs, commenting to festival groups and the whole organization regarding ticketing, camping, transport). At the same time it facilitates the communication with the organization regarding the next edition of the festival: improvements that can be made, ideas for the next edition line-up, introduction of innovative aspects in the festival and the like. Hence, although the festival is 'over' offline, the community continues online through social networks or mobile applications, becoming something that is sporadic like an event, but at the same time something continued, connected and dynamic that is all the time being changed by the 'users'.

Conclusion

Music festivals are increasing in quantity and quality. Even in the current economic crisis new festivals are being created. This is mainly because they are seen as an opportunity in many cities due to the potential economic, social and environmental benefits that they can generate. In fact, we have seen throughout the chapter that music festivals are an example of leisure expressions that aid the creation of value propositions that are meaningful for the individual consumer (Pralahad and Ramaswamy 2004a, 2004b; Jaworski and Kohli, 2006; Payne *et al.* 2008; Ramaswamy and Gouillart 2010). Thus, festivals are not just a form of civic entertainment; actually they can be unique leisure and cultural experiences, powerful travel motivators, and facilitators of community pride and development, as seen in different chapters in this volume (such as Bevolo Chapter 6 or Simons Chapter 7).

Nowadays, events succeed by providing a space and time away from everyday life in which intense extraordinary experiences can be shared (Li and Petrick 2006) and this leisure experience can be heightened by introducing technology and social networks into the festival experience design. The new dimensions that emerge with the introduction of technology (synchronicity, interactivity, participation and co-creation) transform both objective and subjective leisure experience elements, enhancing the festival experience as a whole and making it more memorable.

This chapter highlights the idea of this new context where the pace is accelerated and where technology and social networks are transforming and can keep transforming festival experience design. Welfare as well as well-being (physical, emotional and spiritual) (Stebbins 2007; San Salvador del Valle 2011) is a design output that is made concrete during the leisure experience.

However, the concepts outlined in this chapter call for further research to better understand the role that both technology and audiences can have in creating scenarios where events produce enriching, memorable and transforming experiences and therefore have a more meaningful impact on individuals.

Notes

1 E-leisure refers to the leisure that is performed in 'cyberspace'. The new information and communication technologies, personal computers, Internet and mobile phones are used as a source of information and entertainment, offering many enjoyable activities such as games, online education, shopping, dating, blogging and many more. Such activities are often described as 'online leisure', 'cyber leisure', 'virtual leisure' or 'e-leisure' (Bryce 2001; Cheng 2006; Nimrod and Adoni 2012).

2 MUD stands for Multi-User Dimension. The term refers to a multiplayer real-time virtual world, usually text based. MUDs combine elements of role-playing games, hack and slash, player versus player, interactive fiction and online chat. Players can read or view descriptions of rooms, objects, other players, non-player characters and actions performed in the virtual world. Players typically interact with each other and the world by typing commands that resemble a natural language (Hahn 1996; Bartle 2003).

3 These criteria are based on the research made for the Spanish Network of public ownership of Theatres, Auditoriums, Circuits and Festivals Escenium '08, 'Economic analysis of Art Sector in Spain'. The research was conducted by *Fundació Bosch I Gimpera* team of Barcelona University formed by L. Bonet, J. Colomer, X. Cubeles, A. De Gregorio, R. Herrera, R. and T. Tarrida.

4 Augmented reality (AR) is a live, direct or indirect, view of a physical, real-world environment whose elements are *augmented* (or supplemented) by computer-generated sensory such as sound, video, graphics or GPS data. It is related to a more general concept called mediated reality, in which a view of reality is modified (possibly even diminished rather than augmented), by a computer. As a result, the technology functions by enhancing one's current perception of reality. By contrast, virtual reality replaces the real world with a simulated one, augmentation is conventionally in real-time and in semantic context with environmental elements, such as sports scores on TV during a match. With the help of advanced AR technology (e.g. adding computer vision and object recognition) the information about the surrounding real world of the user becomes interactive and digitally manipulable. Artificial information about the environment and its objects can be overlaid on the real world (Steuer 1992; Metz 2 August 2012; Nimrod and Adoni 2012; Maxwell 2013).

5 Holography is a technique which enables three-dimensional images to be made. It involves the use of a laser, interference, diffraction, light intensity recording and suitable illumination of the recording. The image changes as the position and orientation of the viewing system changes in exactly the same way as if the object were still present, thus making the image appear three-dimensional (Hariharan 2002). This technique was used for instance by Coachella music festival in 2012 to offer a performance of the late Tupac Shakur (Ngak 9 November 2012).

6 The information is collected through the following festivals websites: FIB, BBK live, Vans Warped Tour, Coachella, Newport Folk Festival, Lollapalooza and Outside Lands and MyLife (28 June 2013), Kuchta (15 February 2012).

7 All the information about RFID was acquired through Intellitix (2013), Remling (1 June 2012) and Smith (26 July 2012).

References

Academy of Leisure Studies (1983) *Values and leisure and trends in leisure services*, State College, PA: Venture.

Argyle, M. (1996) *The social psychology of leisure*, New York: Penguin.

Bartle, R. (2003) *Designing virtual worlds*, Indianapolis, IN: New Riders.

Bellamy, C., Horrocks, I. and Webb, J. (1995) 'Exchanging information with the public: from one-stop shops to community information systems', *Local Government Studies*, 21(1): 11–30.

Berridge, G. (2006) *Event design and experiences*, Oxford: Butterworth Heinemann.

Bonet, L. (2009) 'Modelos de Dirección y Gestión de grandes Festivales', study conducted for the Instituto Nacional de las Artes Escénicas y la Música (INAEM), Ministry of Culture of Spain, University of Barcelona.

Brown, S. and James, S. (2006) 'Event design and management: ritual sacrifice?' in I. Yeoman, M. Roberon, J. Ali-Knight, S. Drummond and U. McMahon-Beattie (eds) *Festival and events management*, Oxford: Elsevier, pp. 53–64.

Bryce, J. (2001) 'The technological transformation of leisure', *Social Science Computer Review*, 19(1): 7–16.

Bucy, E.P. (2004) 'Interactivity in society: locating an elusive concept', *Information Society*, 20(5): 373–383.

Calvo-Soraluze, J. (2011) *Understanding leadership in music festivals: the analysis of management dilemmas*, Saarbrücken: Lambert Academic Publishing.

Carr, N. (2011) *Superficiales: ¿Qué está haciendo internet con nuestras mentes?* Madrid: Taurus.

Castells, M. (2001) *La galaxia internet*, Madrid: Areté.

Cheng, S.-L. (2006) 'Relationship between demographics, internet experience and social capital', Thesis, Chapel Hill, NC. Online, available at: http://dc.lib.unc.edu/cdm/ref/collection/etd/id/468 (accessed 25 June 2014).

Cuenca Cabeza, M. (2000) *Ocio humanista: Dimensiones y manifestaciones actuales del ocio*, Bilbao: Universidad de Deusto.

Cuenca Cabeza, M., Aguilar Gutierrez, E. and Ortega Nuere, C. (2011) *Ocio para innovar*, Bilbao: Universidad de Deusto.

Cushman, G., Veal, A. and Zuzanek, J. (2005) *Free time and leisure participation: international perspectives*, Wallingford: CAB International.

De Bres, K. and Davis, J. (2001) 'Celebrating group and place identity: a case of a new regional festival', *Tourism Geographies*, 3(3): 326–337.

Dower, M. (1981) *Leisure provision and people's needs*, London: HMSO.

Driver, B.L., Brown, J.P. and Peterson, G.L. (1991) *Benefits of leisure*, State College, PA: Venture.

Durán, M.A. (2007) *El valor del tiempo*, Barcelona: Espasa.

Falassi, A. (ed.) (1987) *Time out of time: essays on the festival*, Albuquerque, NM: University of New Mexico Press.

Foucault, M. (1986) 'Spaces, knowledge and power', in P. Rabinow (ed.) *Michel Foucault: beyond structuralism and hermeneutics*, Harmondsworth: Penguin, pp. 239–256.

Getz, D. (1991) *Festivals, special events and tourism*, New York: Van Nostrand Reinhold.

Getz, D. (2005) *Event management and event tourism*, New York: Cognizant.

Getz, D. (2007) *Event studies: theory, research and policy for planned events*, Oxford: Butterworth Heinemann.

Getz, D. (2010) 'The nature and scope of festival studies', *International Journal of Event Management Research*, 5(1): 1–47.

Getz, D. and Frisby, W. (1991) 'Developing a municipal policy for festivals and special events', *Recreation Canada*, 19(4): 38–44.

Goldblatt, J.J. (1990) *Special events: the art and science of celebration*, New York: Van Nostrand Reinhold.

Goldblatt, J.J. (2005) *Special events: event leadership for a new world*, New York: John Wiley & Sons.

Hahn, H. (1996) *The internet complete reference*, New York: Osborne, McGraw-Hill.

Hall, C.M. (1992) *Hallmark tourist events: impacts, management and planning*, London: Belhaven.

Hall, C.M. and Sharples, L. (eds) (2008) *Food and wine festivals and events around the world: development, management and markets*, Oxford: Butterworth Heinemann.

Hariharan, P. (2002) *Basics of holography*, Cambridge: Cambridge University Press.

Heineken MyFestival (2013) *Heineken MyFestival*. Online, available at: www.mtvheinekenmyfestival.com (accessed 20 June 2013).

Honoré, C. (2004) *Elogio de la lentitud*, Madrid: RBA.

Hover, M. (2008) 'Imagine your event: imagineering for the event industry', in U. Wünsch (ed.) *Facets of contemporary event management: theory and practice for event success*, Bad Honnef: K.H. Bock, pp. 37–62.

Intellitix (2013) 'Intellitix, smart solutions for smart events'. Online, available at: www.intellitix.com/ (accessed 10 October 2013).

Iso-Ahola, S. (1980) *Social psychology of leisure and recreation*, Dubuque, IA: Brown Company.

Iso-Ahola, S. (1997) 'A psychological analysis of leisure and health', in J.T. Haworth (ed.) *Work, leisure and well-being*, London: Routledge, pp. 131–144.

Jaworski, B. and Kohli, A.K. (2006) 'Co-creating the voice of the customer', in R.F. Lusch and S.L. Vargo (eds) *The service-dominant logic of marketing: dialog, debate and directions*, Armonk, NY: M.E. Sharpe, pp. 109–117.

Johnson, A., Glover, T. and Yuen, F. (2009) 'Supporting effective community representation: lessons from the festival of neighborhoods', *Managing Leisure*, 14(1): 1–16.

Kabanoff, B. (1982) 'Occupational and sex differences in leisure needs and leisure satisfaction', *Journal of Occupational Behaviour*, 3(3): 233–245.

Karlsen, S. and Brandstrom, S. (2008) 'Exploring the music festival as a music educational project', *International Journal of Music Education*, 26(4): 363–372.

Kleiber, D.A. (1999) *Leisure experience and human development*, New York: Basic Books.

Kleiber, D.A., Walker, G.J. and Mannell, R.C. (2011) *A social psychology of leisure*, 2nd edn, State College, PA: Venture.

Kutcha, K. (15 February 2012) 'WERW Wednesday: how are music festivals using social media?' Online, available at: http://infospace.ischool.syr.edu/2012/02/15/werw-wednesday-how-are-music-festivals-using-social-media/ (accessed 10 October 2013).

Lee, S. and Crompton, J. (2003) 'The attraction power and spending impact of three festivals in Ocean City, Maryland', *Event Management*, 24(1): 1–11.

Li, R. and Petrick, J. (2006) 'A review of festival and event motivation studies', *Event Management*, 9(4): 239–245.

Lightman, A. (2005) *A sense of the mysterious: science and the human spirit*, New York: Random House.

Lipovetsky, G. and Serroy, J. (2010) *La cultura-mundo*, Barcelona: Anagrama.

Long, P. and Robinson, M. (2004) *Festivals and tourism: marketing, management and evaluation*, Sunderland: Business Education Publishers.

Maxwell, K. (2013) 'Augmented reality', *Macmillan Dictionary Buzzword*. Online, available at: www.macmillandictionary.com/buzzword/entries/augmented-reality.html (accessed 10 October 2013).

Metz, R. (2 August 2012) 'Augmented reality is finally getting real', *Technology Review*. Online, available at: www.technologyreview.com/news/428654/augmented-reality-is-finally-getting-real/ (accessed 10 October 2013).

Monteagudo, M.J. (2008) *La experiencia de ocio*, Bilbao: Universidad de Deusto.

Morgan, M. (2006) 'Making space for experiences', *Journal of Retail and Leisure Property*, 5(4): 305–313.

Morgan, M. (2008) 'What makes a good festival? Understanding the event experience', *Event Management*, 12(2): 81–93.

MyLife (28 June 2013). 'Rocking social media at summer music festivals', *MyLife*. Online, available at: www.mylife.com/blog/rockin-social-media-at-summer-music-festivals/ (accessed 10 October 2013).

Ngak, C. (9 November 2012) 'Tupak Coachella hologram: behind the technology', *CBSnews*. Online, available at: www.cbsnews.com/8301-501465_162-57415126-501465/tupac-coachella-hologram-behind-the-technology/ (accessed 10 October 2013).

Neulinger, J. (1974) *The psychology of leisure*, Springfield, IL: Charles Thomas.

Nicholson, R. and Pearce, D. (2000) 'Who goes to events? A comparative analysis of the profile characteristics of visitors to four South Island events in New Zealand', *Journal of Vacation Marketing*, 6(3): 236–253.

Nicholson, R. and Pearce, D. (2001) 'Why do people attend events: a comparative analysis of visitor motivations at four South Island events', *Journal of Travel Research*, 39(4): 449–460.

Nijs, D. and Peters, F. (2002) *Imagineering: the creation of experience worlds*, Amsterdam: Boom.

Nimrod, G. and Adoni, H. (2012) 'Conceptualizing e-leisure', *Loisir et Société/Society and Leisure*, 35(1): 31–56.

Payne, A.F., Storbacka, K. and Frow, P. (2008) 'Managing the co-creation of value', *Journal of the Academy of Marketing Science*, 36: 83–96.

Peters, M. and Pikkemaat, B. (2005) 'The management of city events: the case of Bergsilvester in Innsbruck, Austria', *Event Management*, 9(3): 147–153.

Pine, B.J. and Gilmore, J.H. (1999) *The experience economy: work is theatre and business a stage*, Boston, MA: Harvard Business School Press.

Pitts, S. (2004) ' "Everybody wants to be Pavarotti": the experience of music for performers and audience at a Gilbert and Sullivan festival', *Journal of the Royal Musical Association*, 129(1): 143–160.

Pitts, S. (2005) 'What makes an audience? Investigating the roles and experiences of listeners at a chamber music festival', *Music and Letters*, 86(2): 257–269.

Prahalad, C.K. and Ramaswamy, V. (2004a) 'Co-creation experiences: the next practice in value creation', *Journal of Interactive Marketing*, 18(3): 5–14.

Pralahad, C.K. and Ramaswamy, V. (2004b) *The future of competition: co-creating unique value with customers*, Boston, MA: Harvard Business School Press.

Prentice, R. and Anderson, V. (2003) 'Festival as creative destination', *Annals of Tourism Research*, 30(1): 7–30.

Rafaeli, S. (1988) 'Interactivity: from new media to communication', in R. Hawkins, J. Wiemann and S. Pingree (eds) *Advancing communication science: merging mass and interpersonal processes*, Newbury Park, CA: Sage, pp. 110–134.

Ramaswamy, V. and Gouillart, F. (2010) *The power of co-creation: build it with them to boost growth, productivity, and profits*, New York: Free Press.

Remling, A. (1 June 2012) 'RFID wristband: about the latest in music festival technology at Bonnaroo, Bamboozle, Coachella and more', *International Business Times*. Online, available at: www.ibtimes.com/rfid-wristband-about-latest-music-festival-technology-bonnaroo-bamboozle-coachella-more-705702 (accessed 10 October 2013).

Rheingold, H. (1991) *Virtual reality: identity and community in cyberspace*, New York: Summit Books.

Richards, G. (ed.) (2007) *Cultural tourism: global and local perspectives*, New York: Haworth Press.

Rivera, M., Hara, T. and Kock, G. (2008) 'Economic impacts of cultural events: the case of the Zora festival', *Journal of Heritage Tourism*, 3(2): 121–137.

Robinson, A. and Noel, J. (1991) 'Research need for festivals: a management perspective', *Journal of Applied Recreation Research*, 16(1): 78–88.

Rojek, C. (2000) *Leisure and culture*, London: Macmillan.

Rosa, H. (2010) *Accéleration: une critique sociale du temps*, Paris: La Découverte.

Rowley, J. and Williams, C. (2008) 'The impact of brand sponsorship of music festivals', *Marketing Intelligence and Planning*, 26(7): 781–792.

San Salvador del Valle, R. (2000) *Políticas de ocio*, Bilbao: Universidad de Deusto.

San Salvador del Valle, R. (2009) 'La aceleración del tiempo y el fenómeno del ocio', in M. Cuenca Cabeza (ed.) *El tiempo del Ocio: transformaciones y riesgos en la sociedad apresurada*, Bilbao: Universidad de Deusto, pp. 23–44.

San Salvador del Valle, R. (2011) 'La experiencia de ocio y los museos del siglo XXI', in J.C. Rico (ed.) *Museos: del templo al laboratorio*, Madrid: Silex, pp. 329–343.

SGAE reports (2005–2011) *Anuario de las artes escénicas, musicales y audiovisuales*, Fundación Autor. Online, available at: www.anuariossgae.com/home.html (accessed 15 June 2013).

Sherwood, P. (2007) 'A triple bottom line evaluation of the impact of special events: the development of indicators', unpublished doctoral dissertation, Victoria University, Melbourne.

Smith, C. (26 July 2012) 'Social media check-ins at major music festivals signal next phase for RFID wristbands'. Online, available at: www.hypebot.com/hypebot/2012/07/social-media-check-ins-at-major-music-festivals-signal-next-phase-for-rfid-wristbands.html (accessed 10 October 2013).

Smith, M.A. and Kollock, P. (eds) (1999) *Communities in cyberspace*, London: Routledge.

Stebbins, R. (2007) *Serious leisure: a perspective for our time*, New Brunswick, NJ: Transaction Publishers.

Stebbins, R. and Graham, M. (2004) *Volunteering as leisure/leisure as volunteering*, Wallingford: CAB International.

Steuer, J. (1992) 'Defining virtual reality: dimensions determining telepresence', *Journal of Communication*, 42(4): 73–93.

Stiglitz, J.E., Sen, A. and Fitoussi, J.-P. (2013) *Medir nuestras vidas: Las limitaciones del PIB como indicador de progreso*, Madrid: RBA.

Torralba, F. (2010) *Inteligencia espiritual*, Barcelona: Plataforma.

Tribe, J. (1999) *The economics of leisure and tourism*, Oxford: Butterworth Heinemann.

Van Pelt, P. (2005) *The imagineering workout*, New York: Disney Editions.

YouTube Official Blog (3 August 2012) 'Watch Lollapalooza live all weekend on YouTube'. Online, available at: http://youtube-global.blogspot.com.es/2012/08/watch-lollapalooza-live-all-weekend-on.html?utm_source=feedburnerandutm_medium=feedandutm_campaign=Feed:+youtube/PKJx+%28YouTube+Blog%29 (accessed 14 December 2013).

13 Traditional gastronomy events as tourist experiences

The case of Santarém Gastronomy Festival (Portugal)

Marta Cardoso, Goretti Silva and Carlos Fernandes

Introduction

The interrelationship between food and tourism is nowadays unquestionable, not only because it is an obligatory part of the tourism experience but also because it is being increasingly recognized as a contextual and evolving social practice (Mak *et al.* 2012). In some cultures, cooking is considered an art, and good cooks are ranked with artists. In fact, if we look back in history one will notice that cooking books were second to bibles as the most commonly printed type of information. As ideas about food spread, food patterns and customs developed deep cultural meanings. Those patterns that do not have deep meaning are open to change rather easily, such changes often being the result of the need to appeal to certain consumer groups, for example. This is visible from the influx of tourists searching for unique, engaging and memorable experiences that are authentic to the place they are visiting, including local gastronomy.

In view of the contemporary expansion of the concept of cultural tourism which encompasses progressively more elements of 'popular' culture, and given the rigidity of iconic structures, which are losing their status as differentiation elements, event-led strategies are becoming increasingly attractive (Richards and Wilson 2004). As noted by Whelan and Wholfeil (2006), one of the constructive features regarding event marketing is their experience orientation and interactivity since, when talking about events, the consumer is more prone to take on active roles in experiences aimed at influencing their emotions, rather than being simply a passive subject.

Gastronomy festivals, as multisensory events which call for a greater involvement from the visitors and even the co-production of experiences themselves, can thus act as a link between the traditional aspects of each culture and the contemporary demands of the tourism market.

One of southern Europe's biggest gastronomy festivals is hosted every year in Santarém, situated an hour north of Lisbon, Portugal. During ten days, this event provides the visitor with the opportunity to experience the gastronomic heritage of Portugal's diverse regions. Every region of Portugal is represented and seeks to present its typical dishes along with traditional folklore and other forms of entertainment. The objective of this chapter is to determine if the design of the festival provides visitors with the adequate infrastructure and environment in which memorable experiences can flourish. Results draw upon a visitor survey carried out during the festival in November 2012 designed to cover some of the main concerns for event managers and destinations, including the experience of the event and consumption patterns. The results of this research suggest that the festival has the potential to become a landmark for the city and even the country, if it makes the necessary adjustments needed to exceed customers' expectations by developing unique experiences that engage visitors.

Experiences in gastronomy and the distinctiveness of tourism destinations

Historically, elements such as food and beverage have served a supporting role in the tourism economy since they were not normally considered strong enough attractions to bring tourists to a destination. However, taking into account gastronomy's growing appeal to the tourism industry, studies suggest that an increasing number of tourism destinations have become more sought after due to their unique gastronomy. For these destinations, gastronomy is a central feature and main element of attraction (Kivela and Crotts 2005). Scarpato (2002) goes even further by saying that in tourism industries facing the consequences of the global crisis, destinations often resort to gastronomy as a driving force in order to revitalize their cultural capital, preventing as a result the decline of their existing products.

Wolf (2002, cited in Kivela and Crotts 2005: 42) defines gastronomy tourism as 'travelling for the purpose of exploring and enjoying the destination's food and beverage and to savour unique and memorable gastronomy experiences'. Thus, gastronomy is considered nowadays an integral part of the overall tourist experience. Not only does the food structure the tourist's day but many tourism experiences occur while consuming food and drink, gastronomy thereby being regarded as an inseparable part of the holiday experience (Richards 2002). Experiences need to be carefully developed and managed in order to distinguish the destination from its competitors and ultimately to succeed in attracting special interest tourists. It is argued that as global competition between tourism destinations increases in the marketplace, so does the demand for distinctive products. This means that tourism should be developed according to the market characteristics and the destinations' resources – theoretically creating a balance between the destination and visitors' needs. By doing so, the destination provides a venue for new experiences, whereby visitors increase their engagement and possibly co-create the experiences in which they are taking part and generally leading to a 'WOW' effect and response. This will ensure the satisfaction of the visitors, which in turn should improve destination performance (Ryan 2002).

As explained by Pine and Gilmore (1998: 98), according to the progression of economic value, we moved from extracting commodities and making goods to delivering services and more recently to staging experiences, which will be the 'next competitive battleground'. Clifford and Robinson (2012) also highlight that contemporary economies are progressing along a continuum from commodity to service to experience-centred interactions, meaning that the development of these experiences is becoming a mandatory element of differentiation. In this sense, Xu (2010) argues that tourism products are evaluated in a holistic manner, where the lived experience should fulfil the tourist's various needs and provide conforming benefits. This notion was formalized by Smith (1994) by saying that tourism is not just something that is experienced but an experience in itself. Richards (2011) also supports these positions by saying that we have entered a new, networked economy where the concept of tourism has definitely moved away from its dependence on infrastructures. This is because unlike commodities – fungible by nature – goods or to a lesser extent services, experiences are memorable and can therefore leave a lasting impression on the visitor, at the same time increasing their satisfaction and adding value to the products (Pine and Gilmore 1998). In fact, it is widely recognized that in today's environment of ever more sophisticated consumers, those who deliver memorable customer experiences consistently create superior value and competitive advantage (Ritchie and Crouch 2003). Moreover, the development of authentic and adequate experiences has become essential to the success of products and destinations, since they will influence the satisfaction and perceptions of value, for example by raising involvement levels of tourists.

Experiences in tourism are defined as highly subjective and individually significant phenomena, which result from each individual's response to a range of physical, social, product and service stimuli, including food, which are influenced by each one's 'personal realm', in other words, the elements inherent to individuals, such as motivation, expectation, knowledge, memory, perception, self-identity and emotion (Cutler and Carmichael 2010). This interaction creates therefore a succession of ambiences, feeling and emotions which experiences are made of (Bialski 2007). Evaluation of events related to the experience begins before and happens during and after the experience. In this sense, and since experiences flourish from the interaction between the staged event and state of mind of each individual (due to its subjective and personal nature), each experience is unique to each individual and cannot be equally experienced by others.

As reported by Clifford and Robinson (2012) while the core of touristic experiences has been up until now the gaze, based on 'heritage mining' experiences (Richards and Wilson 2006), the literature illustrates the importance and appeal of experiences from other perspectives. For example, gastronomy comes across as a privileged element around which many experiences can be created, encouraging destinations to incorporate local food and beverages into the tourism product, following market trends of seeking authentic and unique experiences. As Plummer *et al.* (2005) argue, the consumption of local food and beverages brings the tourist closer to the host culture. MacDonald and Deneault (2001, cited in Plummer *et al.* 2005) emphasize this relationship between gastronomy and experiences by arguing that tourists hope to involve and get to know the host culture through participation in authentic and engaging experiences with people, cuisine, wine and other cultural elements, and only then can they fulfil their expectations. Gastronomy is then not only identified with food products, but it often involves a composed experience of food, wine, heritage, traditions and landscape (Mason and Paggiaro 2012; Mak *et al.* 2012). This is particularly relevant in today's context where globalization is a well-established concept and destinations compete in order to diversify its offer and endow their products with competitive advantages which can meet contemporary visitors' needs, giving emphasis to identities and the unique aspects of the local food and their cultural significance (Mak *et al.* 2012) and intangible characteristics such as the authenticity of gastronomy (Chang *et al.* 2011).

However, many gastronomy experiences are frequently taken for granted, because eating is regarded as a necessity rather than a leisure activity. Quan and Wang (2004) note this trend and state that the tourist experience has been up until now regarded in the literature as the 'pure' or 'peak' experience, rather than 'supporting' experiences such as eating or sleeping, although this trend is currently starting to shift as tourists demand a higher standard in quality. Accordingly, the task in developing gastronomic tourism is to increase the value perceived by the tourist with regard to their eating experience (Richards 2002). Some businesses have indeed started addressing the role of the experiences and gastronomy. Extreme examples of this are theme restaurants such as the Hard Rock Café or Planet Hollywood. For these restaurants, food is just the backdrop of what Pine and Gilmore (1998) define as 'eatertainment'. The increasing literature on the experience economy and the relevance for tourism places additional pressure on tourism destinations for a new management paradigm that fosters the transition from service delivery to experience creation.

Selling experiences through event creation

Events, and cultural events in particular, can be considered good examples of tourism experiences, with the potential to have great impact on destinations' competitiveness. They have the ability to attract visitors and investment – since they are an important motivator of tourism, stimulate cultural consumption among residents and stimulate destination development and regeneration. Moreover, events are frequently used in destination marketing.

Since many products and services have matured to a point where they cannot be differentiated purely on quality and functional benefits alone (Whelan and Wholfeil 2006), and considering the growth of the experience economy, the experiential nature of events becomes particularly pertinent. Getz (2007) also acknowledged that events are intrinsically experiential phenomena and the experience of stakeholders and attendees is the core element for event management and these should be designed or planned aiming at facilitating visitors' needs, and maximizing their satisfaction.

The design of the festival is an extremely important aspect. First of all, the elements of graphic design add value to the event, as highlighted by Raymond Loewy (1893–1986, cited in European Commission 2009: 49), who alerts us to the impact of form and aesthetics for sales, by declaring that 'ugliness does not sell'. In his statement, the value of design as a way of amplifying product's perceived value was first addressed. If this element is unpacked, other issues related to a broader sense of *design* are raised.

In a first approach, graphic design can evidently be considered as one of the relevant aspects of the National Festival of Gastronomy. It is believed to be an element of differentiation, which distinguishes products from their competition. In fact, here, design and aesthetics are considered some of the features incorporated in goods and services as a form of increasing its value (Sacco and Segre 2006).

It is the *touchpoint* between the organizations' or destinations' values and perceived consumer demand, and should create a 'harmonious balance' between them in the production of the service, or experience. It is also a means of creating meaning that should be based on the observation of lifestyles and behaviours, the individuals' characteristics and collective needs and desires (European Commission 2009).

Additionally, as the Gottlieb Duttweiler Institute (2006) report notes, travel markets are by their nature relationship markets. It is important then to highlight the fact that design can facilitate the feeling of belonging that festivals should facilitate within a community. This was noted by Richards (2011), referring to the rapid pace of everyday life that causes a growing isolation amongst individuals, creating the need for moments of co-presence and social cohesion (see also Richards, Chapter 2 and Simons, Chapter 7). Events have the capacity to promote relationships with and among customers and trigger emotional outcomes (Grönroos 1994). These opportunities can be exacerbated by adequate event design and organization.

The range of potential event experiences is truly broad, from leisure and entertainment to the spirituality of religious rituals (Getz 2008; Trono and Rizzello, Chapter 8). Cultural celebrations such as gastronomy festivals have the potential to be a perfect backdrop for enriching, culture-led experiences. These events are above all polysensorial experiential units which share a hedonistic nature, mainly targeted at emotions. It is thus suggested in the literature that gastronomy events and food experiences are privileged frameworks in terms of engaging consumers into different cultural, spiritual, spatial and temporal 'places' (Clifford and Robinson 2012). Similarly, Mason and Paggiaro (2012) state that the final output of gastronomy events is related to the tourist's personal evaluation and enjoyment in regard to the event, the level of involvement experienced and the degree of interaction with the visited location. Designing such experiences should therefore take these elements into account.

National Gastronomy Festival at Santarém (Portugal)

Each year, Santarém, a relatively small town north of Lisbon, Portugal, hosts the National Gastronomy Festival. This festival is the oldest and biggest gastronomy fair in Portugal and aims to raise awareness of the best national cuisine as well as to promote the cultural values of Portuguese recipes. In its thirty-second edition in 2013, the festival presented various regional cuisines, which compose part of the cultural heritage of the country. In spite of this edition being slightly smaller due to the difficult economic situation, the organizers of the festival ensured that it retained its essential characteristics, with the usual stalls ('tasquinhas'), spaces for selling regional sweets and other national products of reference, such as cheeses, smoked meats and sausages along with crafts, culinary exhibitions and eateries. Furthermore, there is an area with restaurants that represent the Portuguese regions in the festival, and that participate in organized contests such as the 'Snack and Soup' contest, where the region with the best snacks and soups is selected and rewarded. Musical entertainment is also featured in the programme.

Research design

Recent tourism studies witnessed a great diversity of methods employed to understand the meaning associated with travel experiences (Coghlan and Filo 2012). In this research, it was decided to adopt a survey based on a quantitative approach, through the completion of a questionnaire, which, according to relevant literature (e.g. Kivela and Crotts 2005; Plummer *et al.* 2005), is a technique often used to research themes like gastronomy and tourism experiences.

The design of the data collection instrument derived from the Association for Tourism and Leisure Education and Research (ATLAS) event visitor survey, aimed at unveiling main social, cultural and economic impacts of events/festivals that would enable comparisons between studies. Some questions were adapted in order to better meet the specific objectives of the research, namely the visitors' perceptions regarding their overall experience and the different dimensions of the experience. In order to analyse these elements, a five point Likert-type scale was used to rate a set of statements drawn from the literature review, for obtaining data on activities undertaken, outcomes from participation, and general feedback and perceptions about the festival.

For example, Schmitt (2003, cited in Mason and Paggiaro 2012) states that it is important to offer the visitors an holistic experience which results from the interaction of sensorial (sense), affective (feel), cognitive (think), behavioural (act) and social (relate) experiences, thus a set of six statements was introduced reflecting each of these dimensions. Following these statements, the questionnaire focused on the evaluation of the performance and quality of the festival, namely its infrastructures, services provided and quality of the food and drink. The aim was to cover most aspects of the festival's design in order to understand if its concept is adequate to current market trends. It also covered the authenticity of the experience since the provision of a perceived authentic experience can be considered as a part of the event product and can increase tourist satisfaction (Getz 1994, cited in Clifford and Robinson 2012). Considering that it is only when the customer is engaged in a unique and memorable moment in a participative manner, that the experience takes place (Morgan 2006), elements such as the diversity of the programme, availability of activities in which the visitor could engage, uniqueness and distinctiveness of the festival were included in the questionnaire. Other sections of the instrument focused on the behaviour of the visitors, their main motivations for the visit as well as questions about the overall level of satisfaction, the probability of repeating the visit and of recommending the event. The last section of the instrument was designed to obtain demographic data in order to better determine the visitor profile. A pilot test was conducted and necessary adjustments were made to the instrument.

Sampling procedures and data collection

The population of the study was the visitors to the National Gastronomy Festival in Santarém 2013. A non-probability sampling method was selected for this research. Although it is unlikely that valid inferences can be made regarding the entire population using non-probability sampling, as the sample selected is not representative, Altinay and Paraskevas (2008) argue that this type of sampling is the most appropriate if the purpose of the study is to explore the idea behind the range of responses collected, as is the case with this research.

A total of 278 valid questionnaires were collected. The survey time-frame was designated from 26 October and 4 November – the dates of the festival – and it was administered twice per day, three times. The survey was conducted with the authorization of the organizational committee of the festival and with the support of the Tourism Board of Porto and the North of Portugal. In order to reduce bias, the survey was applied at different times of the day and different times during the week (weekdays and weekend) and at different points in the venue.

A team of four interviewers, undertook the task of surveying, and the entire process was conducted on a face-to-face basis. The participants were clearly and fully informed of the purpose of the research study.

Data analysis

The results of primary data presented in this study are based on the analysis of questionnaire data, using SPSS. To accomplish the proposed objectives, diversified data analysis procedures were used, namely descriptive statistics and inferential statistics. Inferential analysis is conducted in order to explore the existence of differences between groups of visitors based on their previous experience (never visited before, visited once, visited more than once). Non-parametric tests were applied, since they do not make assumptions about the underlying population distribution and have less requirements, when compared to the parametric alternatives (Altinay and Paraskevas 2008; Field 2009; Pallant 2010). The specific tests used were the Kruskal–Wallis Test and Spearman Rank Order Correlation. The Kruskal–Wallis Test allows comparisons between the scores on some continuous variable for three or more groups. In this case, respondents were grouped in three categories in order to understand if there were significant differences regarding the perceptions of the experience amongst the group of visitors. In order to understand the strength of the relationship between continuous variables such as levels of satisfaction and probability to return and to recommend the festival, the Spearman Rank Order Correlation was used.

Discussion of the results

Visitor profile

As shown in Table 13.1, the distribution of respondents by gender is fairly homogeneous, although more males (52.3 per cent) than females (47.7 per cent)

Table 13.1 Profile of the sample

	Total	
	N (frequency)	% (valid per cent)
Gender		
Male	145	52.3
Female	132	47.7
Total count	277	
Age group		
≤29	71	25.6
30–39	106	38.3
40–49	73	26.4
49–59	16	5.8
59–69	11	4.0
Total count	277	
Origin		
Portugal	269	96.8
Abroad	9	3.2
Total count	278	
Educational level		
Primary school	10	3.7
Secondary school	77	28.4
Further education	16	5.9
Higher education (first degree)	108	39.9
Postgraduate	60	22.1
Total count	271	
Occupational group		
Director or manager	57	21.9
Academic professions	28	10.8
Technical professions	81	31.2
Clerical/administration	38	14.6
Service and sales personnel	29	11.2
Manual or crafts worker	4	1.5
Student	23	8.8
Total count	260	

completed the survey, with ages mainly between 30 and 49 years old. Visitors are in general quite educated (with an important percentage of university graduates) and mostly with technical professions (31.2 per cent) or holding management positions. The main monthly household gross income ranges between 1,001 and 2,000 euros (31.4 per cent).

It seems that the festival attracts mainly Portuguese visitors (96.8 per cent) mostly from the district of Santarém (34 per cent) or districts within a radius of 100 km, namely Lisbon and Leiria (50.8 per cent). This figure leads us to question whether the festival is a national event, or rather a regional event as the origin of the visitors suggests.

Characteristics and purpose of visit

The majority of visitors usually attend the festival in pairs and most of the groups did not include children (74.3 per cent). It is significant that for more than half of the respondents (61.7 per cent) this is not the first time they visited the festival although the majority (69.6 per cent) stay for only one day with 86.9 per cent of respondents returning home. There is then no need for local accommodation facilities. For those who stayed at the destination, the preferential types of accommodation are hotels and staying with friends and family.

Results suggest that visitors first heard about the festival through friends or family, highlighting the importance of word-of-mouth communication of the festival. In contrast, tourist information offices and websites (both event website and others) were the least frequently mentioned source of information about the event.

As illustrated in Table 13.2, the main motivations to attend the event were the opportunity to 'spend time with family/friends' (34.9 per cent), classifying therefore the festival as a place to visit with family, or just because people 'like the festival' (30.2 per cent), which is in line with the high percentage of repeating visitors. Very few respondents expected to 'try something new' or 'to learn something'.

Table 13.2 Main reasons for attending the event

	Total	
	N (frequency)	% (valid per cent)
I like the festival	110	30.2
Entertainment	29	8.0
Spend time with family/friends	127	34.9
Special occasion	12	3.3
The music programme	2	0.5
Visiting the area	22	6.0
To learn something	5	1.4
To try something new	36	9.9
Other	21	5.8
Total count	364	

The National Gastronomy Festival experience

One of the main focuses of the research was on the respondents' perception about the holistic experience in the festival, both with regard to the quality of the event, in its different dimensions and with regard to the outcomes and satisfaction at the personal level. As described in the methodology section, a set of items representing the different aspects that should be measured when analysing perceptions and experiences at festivals was identified, and answers were given on a five point Likert-type scale (1 = totally agree, to 5 = totally disagree).

Results summarized in Table 13.3 indicate that most respondents especially value the more functional aspects of the event, for example the quality of the

Table 13.3 Items and indicators

	Total	
	N (frequency)	Mean
Food		
The quality of the food was excellent.	254	4.14
The quality of the beverages was excellent.	256	4.12
The food and drink is good value for money.	259	3.18
The food and wine was representative of the traditional Portuguese gastronomy.	264	4.02
The festival		
I think the event is well produced/staged.	264	3.91
The staff have been friendly and helpful.	260	3.86
The event ticket is good value for money.	262	3.57
The facilities and layout were adequate to host the event.	266	3.67
I think the event is doing a good job of limiting its environmental impact.	211	3.63
Programme of the festival		
The cultural programme of the event was diverse.	206	3.50
The programme comprised various activities in which I could participate.	221	3.24
The entertainment activities (music programme) were of good quality.	192	3.57
Dimensions of the experience		
This event made me think a lot.	252	2.71
I was physically active during the event.	264	3.50
This event engaged all my senses.	260	3.78
I felt emotionally involved during the event.	261	3.63
This event offered me an opportunity to connect with other people.	268	3.68
Outcomes of the experience		
Overall this event left a lasting impression on me.	267	3.90
My overall experience transcended my original expectations.	262	3.24
This event improved my image of Portuguese gastronomy.	265	3.88
This event provided me an authentic gastronomic experience.	264	3.97
The event provided unique and distinctive experiences.	253	3.34

food and beverages (means of 4.13 and 4.12 respectively) and the staging of the event (3.91). The authenticity aspect of the experience ranked 3.96 points, suggesting that the festival was moderately able to provide an authentic gastronomic experience. In contrast, however, the festival scores low in providing distinctive and unique experiences (3.35).

According to the results, the more subjective dimensions of the experience show a relatively weaker rating when compared to the functional characteristics of the event. As referred to above, Schmitt (2003, cited in Mason and Paggiaro 2012) mentions the importance of offering visitors an experience derived from the interaction between sensorial, affective, cognitive, behavioural and social stimuli. As can be seen from table 13.4, these dimensions range from 2.71 to 3.78 points, suggesting that these aspects do not really stand out from the visitors' perspective. To note, the highest value in this scale is given to the statement 'this event engaged all my senses', which is not surprising due to the sensorial nature of gastronomy experiences in general. On the other hand, the festival failed to provide an opportunity for the visitors to think and consequently to engage in explorative behaviour. The programme of the festival was considered its weakest point in terms of number and diversity of activities available. Morgan (2007) adds that people want to have the freedom to choose between a wide range of offers available, regardless of whether or not they could enjoy all these possibilities in the amount of time spent at the event.

As stated above, the existence of differences in the perception of the festival between different groups of visitors, based on their previous visit to the festival (independent variable) were also investigated. Three groups of respondents were identified (never visited before, visited only once, visited more than once), and perceptions (agree/disagree, five point Likert-type scales) compared through a Kruskal–Wallis test (see Appendix). Overall, respondents who have never visited the festival (first time visitors) tend to evaluate the festival in a more negative way both with regard to the more tangible characteristics (e.g. adequateness of the festival's facilities and layout) as well as the intangible features (e.g. the festival's ability to leave a lasting impression on the visitors). On the other hand, visitors who have visited the festival before, even if only once, tend to evaluate the festival in a more positive way, in all its dimensions (detailed results in Appendix). In general, respondents consider their participation in the festival as positive, the event was able to leave a lasting impression on them and it improved their perception of Portuguese gastronomy. However, the overall experience did not transcend their original expectations. The relationship between the uniqueness and distinctiveness of the festival and the ability of the festival to transcend visitors' expectations was highlighted with a positive Spearman's Rank Order Correlation value of 0.594 (Table 13.4), which is regarded as a strong correlation (Pallant 2010). This positive correlation indicates that the more visitors perceive the festival as being a unique and distinctive experience, the more they consider it as able to transcend their original expectations.

All of these factors also have an effect on how the visitors perceive the relationship between quality and price, which is yet another aspect that should be

Table 13.4 Correlation between experience outcomes and transcending expectations

	Spearman's Rank Order Correlation (rho)
My overall experience transcended my original expectations.	
The event provided unique and distinctive experiences.	0.594**
Overall, how satisfied are you with your experience at the festival?	
How likely are you to visit this event again in the future?	0.504**
How likely are you to recommend this event to family/friends?	0.587**

Notes
** Correlation is significant at the 0.01 level (2-tailed).

improved in the festival. In fact, although the quality of the food and drink is considered good, the perceived value for money is one of the aspects that need improvement, with a mean of only 3.18 (cf. Table 13.3). Nevertheless, visitors in general expressed a good level of satisfaction with their visit to the festival (mean of 3.72 out of 5). Although a considerable percentage of the sample were repeat visitors, no significant differences were identified between the number of previous visits in terms of the level of overall satisfaction. Consequently, respondents consider that there is also a strong possibility for them to return to the festival (4.14) and recommend the festival to their friends and family (4.17). There is therefore a strong positive correlation between levels of satisfaction and probability to return (*rho*=0.504) and to recommend the festival (*rho*=0.587), as illustrated in Table 13.4.

Conclusion and implications

The overall aim of the research was to examine the extent to which experience design contributes to the overall visitor experience at the National Gastronomy Festival in Santarém. The results indicate that the festival is considered by respondents as a good practice and has succeeded in providing them with a pleasant experience leaving the visitor with a lasting impression. It is therefore not surprising that levels of satisfaction and probability of revisiting the festival are also high, taking into account the recognized importance of memorable experiences in increasing product value and customer satisfaction and loyalty. In fact, analysis emphasized the correlation between visitors' intention to revisit and their level of satisfaction. Results with regard to previous visits and intention to return are also in accordance with the belief that the gastronomy motivated tourist is a loyal market, an argument evidenced in the literature review (e.g. Kivela and Crotts 2005).

Regardless of the overall positive feedback obtained from visitors who assert that the concept of the festival is still attractive, its outcomes seem, however, to be declining, suggesting that some adjustments are required, namely with regard to the design, and to the development and implementation of a range of experiences.

We believe that the festival can still make the most out of its potential as a national event and provide expected economic and socio-cultural benefits both to the region and to the visitor. But the festival needs to direct its efforts to improve more intangible characteristics, namely those which will enable a greater contact between visitors and the community and engage them in a participatory manner.

Furthermore, the festival needs to design a more holistic experience that can distinguish it and consequently attract more visitors each year. At the moment, the results imply that the ability to attract visitors is not significant, since the majority of visitors are from a regional or local radius. This is possibly due, amongst other aspects, to the fact that the festival needs to reposition itself in the marketplace. This is given that functional/tangible characteristics appear to be losing their importance in favour of more intangible elements when it comes to the evaluation of the gastronomy experience, as above mentioned.

Given the sensorial appeal of gastronomy and the experiential nature of such events, this gastronomy festival should act as an engagement platform for visitors seeking experiences (see Crowther and Orefice, Chapter 10), going beyond the staged event itself. In the case of this particular event, organizers need to link the culinary offerings with different activities that increase the experiential elements of the festival (seeing, doing, learning and entertaining). According to the literature review, taking into account the importance of the 'symbolic' aspects of food consumption, traditions and local food customs should be promoted in order to enhance the interest of the visitors, particularly since it is argued that those elements which are unique and culturally relevant to each destination can help minimize the impacts of globalization (Mak *et al.* 2012; Mason and Paggiaro 2012). The festival needs a design solution that makes opportunities available for visitors to engage in gastronomic experiences, which involve not only seeing, listening, smelling and tasting, but also learning, and other aspects of the four experience realms defined by Pine and Gilmore (1998). In addition, gastronomic experiences should provide moments of entertainment, where visitors can feel that they are living and experiencing something new and/or unique. For example, when comparing the ratings given by the respondents who visited the festival once before, more than once before or those who never visited the festival, first time visitors consistently gave lower ratings, reflecting higher expectations with regard to the festival as a gastronomic experience. This implies then that first time visitors should be given special attention in terms of the experience design in its tangible and intangible elements (like food and beverages, or physical participation and sensory immersion).

What visitors seek nowadays is the social context associated with the sharing of experiences with friends and the host community, in turn generating emotional energy, also referred to by Richards (Chapter 2) and Simons (Chapter 7). The festival should therefore act as a facilitator for this purpose. In preparing future editions, the organizers should redesign their approach, taking into consideration the current and emerging trends in the tourism market, particularly the shift towards the consumption of gastronomic experiences as an integral part of the tourism product (Richards 2012).

Appendix

Table 13.a.1 Significant differences between groups

	N	M	Md	MR
The food and drink is good value for money.				
Visited the festival more than once	163	3.28	4.00	136.20
Visited the festival once	26	3.46	4.00	146.67
Never visited the festival before	70	2.84	3.00	109.37
Total	259	3.18	4.00	
Kruskal-Wallis test results	$x^2=8.403$, df$=2$, $p=0.015$			
The quality of the food was excellent.				
Visited the festival more than once	159	4.08	4.00	119.85
Visited the festival once	26	4.62	5.00	169.02
Never visited the festival before	69	4.09	4.00	129.49
Total	254	4.14	4.00	
Kruskal-Wallis test results	$x^2=12.015$, df$=2$, $p=0.002$			
The staff have been friendly and helpful.				
Visited the festival more than once	159	3.89	4.00	131.81
Visited the festival once	27	4.26	4.00	159.72
Never visited the festival before	74	3.64	4.00	117.02
Total	260	3.86	4.00	
Kruskal-Wallis test results	$x^2=7.518$, df$=2$, $p=0.023$			
The facilities and layout were adequate to host the event.				
Visited the festival more than once	164	3.76	4.00	139.43
Visited the festival once	28	3.82	4.00	146.27
Never visited the festival before	74	3.39	4.00	115.52
Total	266	3.67	4.00	
Kruskal-Wallis test results	$x^2=6.926$, df$=2$, $p=0.031$			
I think the event is doing a good job of limiting its environmental impacts.				
Visited the festival more than once	135	3.59	4.00	103.76
Visited the festival once	18	4.17	4.00	140.81
Never visited the festival before	58	3.53	4.00	100.41
Total	211	3.63	4.00	
Kruskal-Wallis test results	$x^2=7.314$, df$=2$, $p=0.026$			
The entertainment activities (music programme) were of good quality.				
Visited the festival more than once	126	3.49	4.00	91.51
Visited the festival once	18	4.17	4.00	128.92
Never visited the festival before	48	3.56	4.00	97.44
Total	192	3.57	4.00	
Kruskal-Wallis test results	$x^2=8.195$, df$=2$, $p=0.017$			
The cultural programme of the event was diverse.				
Visited the festival more than once	130	3.45	4.00	99.66
Visited the festival once	22	4.23	4.00	147.09
Never visited the festival before	54	3.30	4.00	94.98
Total	206	3.50	4.00	
Kruskal-Wallis test results	$x^2=15.046$, df$=2$, $p=0.001$			

continued

	N	M	Md	MR
The programme comprised various activities in which I could participate.				
Visited the festival more than once	141	3.19	3.00	107.08
Visited the festival once	21	3.95	4.00	155.48
Never visited the festival before	59	3.12	3.00	104.53
Total	221	3.24	3.00	
Kruskal-Wallis test results	$x^2=12.509$, df$=2$, $p=0.002$			
This event offered me an opportunity to connect with other people.				
Visited the festival more than once	165	3.78	4.00	142.07
Visited the festival once	28	3.89	4.00	144.52
Never visited the festival before	75	3.39	4.00	114.11
Total	268	3.68	4.00	
Kruskal-Wallis test results	$x^2=8.154$, df$=2$, $p=0.017$			
My overall experience transcended my original expectations.				
Visited the festival more than once	162	3.19	3.00	127.09
Visited the festival once	27	3.78	4.00	169.28
Never visited the festival before	73	3.18	3.00	127.32
Total	262	3.24	3.00	
Kruskal-Wallis test results	$x^2=8.326$, df$=2$, $p=0.016$			
Overall, this event left a lasting impression on me.				
Visited the festival more than once	164	3.99	4.00	141.74
Visited the festival once	28	4.04	4.00	140.36
Never visited the festival before	75	3.65	4.00	114.69
Total	267	3.90	4.00	
Kruskal-Wallis test results	$x^2=7.595$, df$=2$, $p=0.022$			
The event provided unique and distinctive experiences.				
Visited the festival more than once	158	3.27	3.00	122.18
Visited the festival once	27	3.78	4.00	157.85
Never visited the festival before	68	3.34	3.00	125.95
Total	253	3.34	3.00	
Kruskal-Wallis test results	$x^2=6.099$, df$=2$, $p=0.047$			
How likely are you to visit this event again in the future?				
Visited the festival more than once	170	4.2912	4.50	150.13
Visited the festival once	27	4.2778	4.50	138.80
Never visited the festival before	76	3.7500	4.50	106.99
Total	273	4.1392	4.50	
Kruskal-Wallis test results	$x^2=16.858$, df$=2$, p$=0.000$			

Notes
N=cases; M=mean; Md=median; MR=mean rank; x^2=Chi-square; df=degrees of freedom; p=significance level.

References

Altinay, L. and Paraskevas, A. (2008) *Planning Research in Hospitality and Tourism*, Oxford: Butterworth Heinemann.

Bialski, P. (2007) 'Friendships in a State of Mobility: The Case of the Online Hospitality Network'. Online, available at: http://intimatetourism.files.wordpress.com/2007/07/paulabialski-thesisma-intimatetourism.pdf (accessed 15 June 2013).

Chang, M., Kivela, J. and Mak, A. (2011) 'Attributes that Influence the Evaluation of Travel Dining', *Tourism Management*, 32(2): 307–316.

Clifford, C. and Robinson, R. (2012) 'Authenticity and Festival Foodservice Experiences', *Annals of Tourism Research*, 39(2): 571–600.

Coghlan, A. and Filo, K. (2012) 'Using Constant Comparison Method and Qualitative Data to Understand Participants' Experiences at the Nexus of Tourism, Sport and Charity Events', *Tourism Management*, 35: 122–131.

Cutler, S.Q. and Carmichael, B. (2010) 'The Dimensions of the Tourist Experience', in M. Morgan, P. Lugosi and B.J.R. Ritchie (eds) *The Tourism and Leisure Experience: Consumer and Managerial Perspectives*, Clevedon: Channel View Publications, pp. 3–26.

European Commission (2009) *The Impact of Culture on Creativity*, Brussels: European Affairs. Online, available at: http://ec.europa.eu/culture/key-documents/doc/study_impact_cult_creativity_06_09.pdf (accessed 6 June 2013).

Field, A. (2009) *Discovering Statistics Using SPSS*, 3rd edn, London: Sage.

Getz, D. (2007) *Event Studies: Theory, Research and Policy for Planned Events*, Oxford: Elsevier.

Getz, D. (2008) 'Event Tourism: Definition, Evolution, and Research', *Tourism Management*, 29(3): 403–428.

Gottlieb Duttweiler Institute (2006) *The Future of Leisure Travel: Trend Study*, Zurich: Gottlieb Duttweiler Institute.

Grönroos, C. (1994) 'From Marketing Mix to Relationship Marketing: Towards a Paradigm Shift in Marketing', *Management Decision*, 32(2): 4–20.

Kivela, J. and Crotts, J. (2005) 'Gastronomy Tourism', *Journal of Culinary Science and Technology*, 4(2/3): 39–55.

Mak, A.H.N., Lumbers, M. and Eves, A. (2012) 'Globalisation and Food Consumption in Tourism', *Annals of Tourism Research*, 39(1): 171–196.

Mason, M. and Paggiaro, A. (2012) 'Investigating the Role of Festivalscape in Culinary Tourism: The Case of Food and Wine Events', *Tourism Management*, 33(6): 1329–1336.

Morgan, M. (2006) 'Making Space for Experiences', *Journal of Retail and Leisure Property*, 5: 305–313.

Morgan, M. (2007) 'Festival Spaces and the Visitor Experience', in M. Casado-Diaz, S. Everett and J. Wilson (eds) *Social and Cultural Change: Making Space(s) for Leisure and Tourism*, Eastbourne: Leisure Studies Association, pp. 113–130.

Pallant, J. (2010) *SPSS Survival Manual*, 4th edn, London: McGraw-Hill Education.

Pine, J. and Gilmore, J. (1998) 'The Experience Economy', *Harvard Business Review*, July/August: 97–105.

Plummer, R., Telfer, D., Hashimoto, A. and Summers, R. (2005) 'Beer Tourism in Canada along the Waterloo: Wellington Ale Trail', *Tourism Management*, 26(3): 447–458.

Quan, S. and Wang, N. (2004) 'Towards a Structural Model of the Tourist Experience: An Illustration from Food Experiences in Tourism', *Tourism Management*, 25(3): 297–305.

Richards, G. (2002) 'Gastronomy: An Essential Ingredient in Tourism Production and Consumption?' in A.M. Hjalager and G. Richards (eds) *Tourism Gastronomy*, London: Routledge, pp. 3–20.

Richards, G. (2011) 'Cultural Tourism Trends in Europe: A Context for the Development of Cultural Routes', in K. Khovanova-Rubicondo (ed.) *Impact of European Cultural Routes on SMEs' Innovation and Competitiveness*, Strasbourg: Council of Europe Publishing, pp. 21–39.

Richards, G. (2012) 'Food and the Tourism Experience: Major Findings and Policy Ori-entations', in D. Dodd (ed.) *Food and the Tourism Experience*, Paris: OECD, pp. 13–46.

Richards, G. and Wilson, J. (2004) 'The Impact of Cultural Events on City Image: Rotter-dam, Cultural Capital of Europe 2001', *Urban Studies*, 41(10): 1931–1951.

Richards, G. and Wilson, J. (2006) 'Developing Creativity in Tourist Experiences: A Solu-tion to the Serial Reproduction of Culture?' *Tourism Management*, 27(6): 1209–1223.

Ritchie, J. and Crouch, G. (2003) *The Competitive Destination: A Sustainable Tourism Perspective*, Cambridge, MA: CABI Publishing.

Ritchie, J. and Tung, V. (2011) 'Exploring the Essence of Memorable Tourism Experi-ences', *Annals of Tourism Research*, 38(4): 1367–1386.

Ryan, C. (2002) *The Tourist Experience*, London: Continuum.

Sacco, P.L. and Segre, G. (2006) 'Creativity, Cultural Investment and Local Develop-ment: A New Theoretical Framework for Endogenous Growth', DADI Working Paper 8/06, Università IUAV di Venezia.

Scarpato, R. (2002) 'Gastronomy as a Tourist Product: The Perspective of Gastronomy Studies', in A.M. Hjalager and G. Richards (eds) *Tourism and Gastronomy*, London: Routledge, pp. 93–106.

Smith, S. (1994) 'The Tourism Product', *Annals of Tourism Research*, 21(3): 582–595.

Whelan, S. and Wholfeil, M. (2006) 'Communicating Brands through Engagement with "Lived" Experiences', *Brand Management*, 13(4/5): 313–329.

Xu, J. (2010) 'Perceptions of Tourism Products', *Tourism Management*, 31: 607–610.

14 Event design

Conclusions and future research directions

Greg Richards, Lénia Marques and Karen Mein

The contributions to this volume underline the wealth of different approaches that can be taken to event design and the study of how events are designed. Event design can be approached as far more than a simple physical act of arranging event elements or the look and feel of an event. In particular this volume points to the important role played by the social context of events in the design process. Event design needs to involve a wide range of stakeholders and to encompass a wide range of elements before, during and after the event, at the event location but also in other places and (virtual) spaces.

The main issues arising from the volume and some potential directions for future research are outlined in the following sections.

The purpose of design

As Richards and Palmer (2010) have argued in *Eventful Cities*, events are designed to serve a range of different purposes, and the effectiveness of events, and therefore event design strategies, should be judged in terms of how well the aims of the event and its different stakeholders are met.

It is clear that different stakeholders will have different priorities, but all are engaged in creating value through events, whether this is economic, social, cultural, environmental or creative value. Event design can therefore be seen as a strategy for generating (stakeholder) value from events. Events may also be 'designed for success', where success can also vary according to the perspectives of different stakeholders, and the value that design delivers to them.

For example, Gerritsen and van Olderen (Chapter 5) contrast the views of event organizers, participants and 'mystery guests', and find that what is important in terms of event design for the organizers is often less important for the participant. Similarly, the challenge for the National Gastronomy Festival in Santarém in Portugal is seen by Cardoso, Silva and Fernandes (Chapter 13) as a need to design more engaging experiences, without which the event is in danger of losing its appeal in increasingly competitive national and international markets.

Participation–involvement–engagement

Events can be seen as value creation platforms where levels of involvement by the different stakeholders can vary significantly. This can be seen as a continuum ranging from participation (which can be relatively passive, as in the spectator role) to involvement (which implies a more active role by those attending) to engagement (where there is ongoing commitment and co-creation on the part of stakeholders).

This continuum is illustrated by Trono and Rizzello (Chapter 8) in their analysis of the Holy Week celebrations in Puglia. Although the event is attended by thousands of spectators, the level of commitment and engagement increases significantly as people reach the heart of the ritual and begin to play an active role in its creation and reproduction. Such is the desire for direct engagement with the central rituals of the festival that people are willing to pay large sums of money for the honour of carrying the effigies. Although this system is driven by religious motivations, it mirrors many other situations in which 'interaction rituals' can be seen (Collins 2004).

Co-creation

Along a continuum that runs from participation to engagement, co-creation seems to be one strategy for getting visitors more engaged in events. The network economy is a growing arena of co-creation, where distinctions between producers and consumers are becoming increasingly vague. Events are also co-created to a greater or lesser extent. At a basic level one could argue that all events involve co-creation, because they bring people together in physical co-presence, which means that every participant is also helping to create the 'atmosphere' or generate the 'emotional energy' of the event, even if they are not actively involved in creation or programming. Crowther and Orefice (Chapter 10) argue that this can be seen as a form of 'co-creation by default', which contrasts with the active 'co-creation by design' being stimulated by other events in order to achieve specific outcomes. In principle, as events move from passive to active co-creation, they should be able to generate more value for all stakeholders.

It is interesting to speculate, however, just how much co-creation is really happening in the events covered in the present volume, and at events in general. Very often the way in which events are staged and physically organized militate against co-creation, because there is a strict division between producers and consumers, spectators and performers. The challenge for event designers will be to find strategies that facilitate interaction between these groups while still maintaining the overall shape or 'feel' of the event. Recent research indicates that co-creation and self-organization of activities can provide a fruitful avenue for event design. For example, Rihova *et al.* (2013) examine the potential for festival visitors to co-create value with each other, even in the absence of intervention by the organizers. Such interactions are often facilitated by new technology, enabling visitors to interact with each other before and after the event. In the terms of Boswijk *et al.* (2007), this is also evidence of a higher level of experience creation, moving on from the simple production of experiences for consumers (first generation experiences) to co-creation between producers and consumers (second generation) and eventually towards third generation experiences, where communities of consumers and producers begin to form around shared interests. Rihova *et al.* (2013) also identify 'ongoing neo-tribes' as part of the emerging 'consumer-to-consumer' co-creation process, reflecting the social practices of members of consumer subcultures and neo-tribes. At events, membership of such tribes may be expressed through clothing and other symbols, but it may also be reflected in behaviour, such as Volkswagen campervan owners or Harley-Davidson bikers, who tend to gather together physically at festival camp sites.

Calvo-Soraluze and San Salvador del Valle (Chapter 12) point out that event visitors are also co-creating experiences with each other via social media. They are coordinating their experiences during music festivals via applications such as GroupMe. Event organizers are now beginning to facilitate such interaction by providing free apps for participants, and by utilizing an increasingly wide range of different technologies, including augmented reality, holography and smart clothing. For example, the 2013 Way Out West Festival in Gothenburg, Sweden used RFID wristbands to enable visitors to access to festival content:

> By checking-in at the RFID stations before/after each performance, festival-goers will be able to build a free Spotify festival diary containing exclusive playlists for each artist they watched, along with images and bios. The Spotify diary is automatically sent each day via email, although those registering via Facebook can gain instant access.
>
> (Intellitix 2013)

Hede and Kellett (Chapter 9) also emphasize the changes that are needed in event design as a consequence of new technology. They underline the fact that imagineering with Web 2.0 applications is also a means of connecting with internal as well as external target groups. High performance work systems can be designed to deliver a range of different human resource management solutions that can improve efficiency and effectiveness in event organizations.

Arguably such technological applications will allow even more co-creation between producers and consumers in future. This in turn should allow more value to be generated by events, as more co-creation should equal more value, and help events to achieve distinction in an increasingly crowded marketplace.

Collaborative design

Interesting possibilities exist for events to be collaboratively designed. This already happens to a small extent with flash mobs. However, there are problems with collaborative design:

We have most difficulties with collaboration, because it is new. Collaboration allows access to the work-flow by self-selected outsiders. The idea is to make the work flow modular, granular, and redundant, so that very different contributions can be integrated without endangering the quality of the output. A collaboration platform must be governed by a combination of self-enforcing code, simple but strong core principles, and an inclusive culture.

(Mueller 2009)

Event design can also be a collaborative process. Increasingly we are not talking simply about the design of experiences or events for a clearly defined target group of people, but for a range of individuals. The individualization of postmodern society poses a growing challenge for the event designer and manager. However, it is not simply that everything is becoming more individual, because the individualization process of itself is producing new social forms to design for. As Bawens (2010) points out, along with growing individualization there are also efforts at reconstructing collective identities – for example through peer-to-peer relationality. The new relationality (Richards 2013) is constructed not in terms of similarities in age, class or lifestyle, but around shared goals. As Bawens (2010) puts it, new forms of relationality, such as open source software, rely on 'the ability to connect their own ends, with some transcendental collective goal'. The challenge for event designers in future, therefore, may well revolve around their ability to identify such goals – which can lie, for example, in sustainability, education or well-being – and design these elements into the event itself. In other words, the success of some events will revolve around their ability to incorporate social design as a key aspect of their business model.

Curating events

Value can also be created through other strategies, such as the curation of events. The art of curation has moved out of the museum, and has increasingly become a process of design and programming that is applied to a wide range of phenomena. For example, there is a growing range of approaches to 'curating the city', which include different architectural visions (Wiszniewski 2010) or organizing events (Richards and Palmer 2010). The idea of having a curator as an artistic leader to curate events is beginning to catch on in many cultural events (for example, David Bowie was a guest curator at the High Line Festival in New York in 2007). The concept of curation is also being applied to music, both in terms of live programming and music streaming services such as Spotify (Owinski 2013).

It is interesting to speculate on the relationship that emerging models of event curation might have on co-creation within events. Effectively curation is a means of injecting vision and leadership into the relationship between an event and its audiences. By curating content, an event can innovate content that can subsequently be co-created with participants, creating new levels of (emotional and intellectual) engagement. For example, by developing a curated programme of music or art, an event can then share its curated choices with other stakeholders and elicit their reactions and feedback, helping to develop more collaborative models of content creation.

Organic change vs radical change in events

The speed with which an event changes can have an important recursive relationship with design. Many mega-events, for example, are designed to be catalysts for change, and as such are also designed to break with the past in a radical way. Such 'pulsar events' (Kammeier 2002) have an important influence in changing mindsets and perceptions of locals and visitors alike, as the experience of the European Capital of Culture in Glasgow 1990, or the 1992 Barcelona Olympics have shown (Richards and Palmer 2010). Many other events, and particularly smaller scale events, are subject to more incremental change, which may be imperceptible at the level of individual editions of the event.

Taking Sewell's (1996) definition of a historical event as a 'gap between expectation and reality', there is often a need to design change and innovation into events, so that the element of surprise or novelty enhances the event experience. This is an interesting discussion in the context of traditional events, where there is usually an emphasis on continuity, but where there is also a need to stimulate change to respond to changing generations of event users.

Simons (Chapter 7) shows how the holding of an event at relatively infrequent intervals can have interesting effects on its relationship to participants, spectators and the local community. In a world where novelty value seems increasingly important, the idea of staging an event once every seven years may seem outdated. But the effect is to let the event grow with the community, so that changes in the event are acceptable and accepted. Each generation can put its own stamp on the event, rather than being totally fixed into a schedule that is repeated from year to year.

Time and space in event design

Events are a temporal phenomenon and therefore the time dimension is crucial in design. This covers many different design attributes, including duration, speed, frequency/recurrence or regularity. Simons (Chapter 7) illustrated how some events can become 'slow' by design, which contrasts with the kind of 'fast events' that have to generate a large number or a wide range of outputs (economic impacts, image change, social cohesion, among others).

As Hede and Kellett (Chapter 9) have emphasized, new technology is enabling the experience of an event to stretch far beyond the temporal and spatial confines of the event itself. Gerritsen and van Olderen (Chapter 5) identify a range of touchpoints that extend from the point of first engaging with an event to the post-event phase. They also underline significant differences in the importance and perception of touchpoints between organizers and visitors, which occur mainly in the pre-exposure phase. The organizers tend to emphasize touchpoints related to general event promotion and marketing, whereas visitors have a much broader interest related to the context of the event and the people involved.

Design processes therefore also have to consider how the spatial and temporal elements of the event can be extended. Although the actual event itself (or the 'direct-exposure phase') is evidently the most important design focus, increasingly efforts will need to be directed at other aspects of the event as well. An interesting example comes from the 1992 Barcelona Olympics, where the diving pool was purposefully designed to provide photographers and film crews with the opportunity to capture divers against the backdrop of the city. The spectacular setting of the diving pool not only meant that it attracted attention at the time, but it also extended the impact of the event for years afterwards, as it was used, for example, for shooting Kylie Minogue's video for the song 'Slow' in 2003. In 2012 a stunt-man dived through a car into the pool for the TV advert showcasing the new Ford B-MAX, to demonstrate the lack of a pillar between the front and rear doors.

As Steijn (Chapter 11) shows, elements of performance such as live music can be moved into new temporal and spatial settings, which changes the context of the content and expands the potential audience. Just as 'live performance' was a concept created by the rise of radio and television, so there will doubtless be new concepts of performance created by the rise of the Internet and new virtual technologies. However, an interesting point that Steijn raises is that even with shifts in technology, the basic narrative form of a story or performance remains unchanged and may even have been reinforced. This is because the basic intention remains to engage and involve the audience.

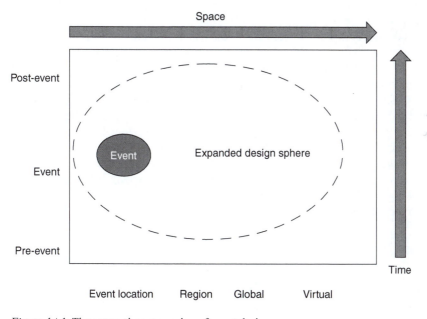

Figure 14.1 The space–time expansion of event design.

Given the importance of engagement, as the spatial and temporal 'reach' of event extends, then attention will also need to be paid to making the event period itself special. If people can access the content you are providing before they even get to the event, then why should they come? One obvious key factor is the atmosphere and 'emotional energy' generated by the physical co-presence of large numbers of people (Collins 2004), which is for example very clear in music festivals (Prentice and Andersen 2003). Therefore the ritual context for emotional energy to take place also needs to be a design concern. How can the emotional energy of the event be increased? Looking at the conditions outlined in Collins' model, the solution might lie in the physical co-presence, establishing boundaries to outsiders, creating a mutual focus of attention and shared mood. These features can already be observed in many events, including traditional and more contemporary events (e.g. Richards 2007).

Events can also be designed to be spatially distinctive, for example through designing the 'look' and 'feel' of the event. This comes close to what Getz (2012) describes as 'events as theatre' and the experience design approach described by Bladen *et al.* (2012). The experience of being 'out of the ordinary' can be achieved by changing the nature of space, as Richards (Chapter 2) describes in the context of the Festes de Gràcia in Barcelona. Staging the event is creating this special moment in space but also in time. Temporal distinction can also be created by changing the overall 'speed' of the event, and changes in rhythm and tempo during the event itself can also add to the design of the event. For the Oerol Festival on the island of Terschelling in the Netherlands, the clocks were turned back to Greenwich Mean Time (two hours behind normal summer time) to create a feeling of being in a special place for the festivalgoers (Richards and Palmer 2010).

Hede and Kellett (Chapter 9) also point out the particular nature of events as iterative and pulsating, which creates specific challenges for event organizers. Event design therefore poses different challenges from traditional design approaches, as it requires constant redesign of the experience as different editions of the event are staged. This means that particular attention needs to be paid to maintaining organizational memory. This is less of a challenge for events that are consistently staged in the same place, but becomes a major problem for events that circulate between different locations. Richards and Palmer (2010) have shown that the European Capital of Culture suffers from major 'memory loss' each time it is staged, as the knowledge built up by those working on the event is usually lost afterwards as staff leave after the programme finishes.

Design level

The contributions to the current volume make it clear that design can be employed at different levels in an event or event programme. The use of design at operational, tactical, strategic or systemic levels will involve very different challenges and outcomes, as also mentioned by Ouwens in Chapter 4.

For example, as Bevolo (Chapter 6) shows in the case of Eindhoven, the design of events can be part of the urban system as a whole. Not only is the event influenced by its setting in a particular context, but the city or place is also influenced by the way in which the event develops and reacts to that context. In terms of designing a portfolio of events for a city or region, therefore, it is important to consider not just what events currently 'fit' with the aims and objectives of the city, but also what trajectory the city wants to create towards the future. Very often cities feel that their portfolio needs to contain a film festival or a fashion show because their competitors have them. However the design of an events portfolio is not just about competitive edge, but also about feeding the DNA of the city. If film or fashion are not already an integral part of the cultural life of a city, it is unlikely that such transplanted events will succeed. In the case of Eindhoven, design is deeply rooted into the everyday life and the cultural and creative sector of the city, ensuring that events such as the Dutch Design Week can successfully mesh with the cultural, social and economic context.

At more tactical levels, more attention needs to be paid to the changes in the visitor experience as the event develops. As Gerritsen and van Olderen (Chapter 5) show, particular attention needs to be paid to those elements of the experience (or 'touchpoints') that matter to visitors and which play an important role in shaping their event experience. It is often also important to link these touchpoints by means of a 'story' that increases the value of the individual elements of event experience, as Miettinen, Valtonen and Markuksela explain in Chapter 3.

At operational level, the flow of visitors around touchpoints also becomes an important consideration. The Festes de Gràcia, in Barcelona, because of their integration into public space, require design at a neighbourhood level as well as a street level, because of the immense flow of visitors (two million visits in ten days). The City of Barcelona supports the festival by planning traffic and pedestrian flows around the Gràcia area, with suggested routes for seeing the decorations.

Different scales of event

The scale of event also has a close relationship with design processes. Large scale events, which usually need to be designed via top-down processes, will tend to involve more structured and formal design strategies than smaller scale events organized in a more ad hoc or bottom-up way. Much of the academic critique that is currently levelled at events focuses on 'mega-events' (e.g. Rojek 2014), but many of the complaints about alienation, manipulation and inauthenticity are much less applicable to smaller scale events.

For example, the Dragon Slaying event described by Simons is very much organized in a bottom-up fashion, with residents of Beesel using collective decision-making processes to design each festival (Chapter 7). A similar situation exists in the case of the Festes de Gràcia in Barcelona, where, as Richards describes, local residents decide their own design themes, even if they may then call on professional designers to help in the execution (Chapter 2).

In Portugal, in contrast, the National Gastronomy Festival in Santarém has been designed in a very top-down fashion. As Cardoso, Silva and Fernandes (Chapter 13) show, this is a much less flexible way of designing events, and it has produced problems in the fit between the design of the event and the needs of visitors over time. On the other hand, for many events a top-down approach is often the only feasible option. In the case of Den Bosch, for example, the celebrations around the 500th anniversary of Hieronymus Bosch have been planned and controlled by a small group of people linked to the Municipality (Chapter 2). However, it can be argued that the knowledge and skills required to design and organize an event of this kind, which has significant international, scientific and political dimensions, are only available to specialists.

Changes in event design

The foregoing analysis implies many potential changes in the practice of event design. In particular, it is clear that the advent of new technology is already having a significant effect (Adema and Roehl 2010). As Hede and Kellett (Chapter 9) state: 'Web 2.0 is allowing events to be *imagineered* – or themed using creative imagination and technological engineering to enhance the experience of those who participate in them'. This applies not just to the core experience of the event itself, but also to the pre- and post-event experience, and to the extension of event experiences into extra-event space and into the virtual world. It is clear that event designers will therefore have to become conversant with a wider range of technologies and techniques in future. There is a clear need to develop learning strategies to deal with this, which may include the kind of informal 'on-the-job' learning implied in Chapter 9, but which will almost inevitably involve the development of formal curricula in event education as well.

One of the areas that will almost certainly require more attention is change management. The current economic challenges in many countries are stimulating events to rethink their basic economic design, or business model. Following a period of unprecedented growth in the number of events, the onset of the crisis in 2007 produced a situation in which there was suddenly far more competition to attract audience and funding. In particular, cuts in public sector funding had serious consequences for many events, particularly in the cultural sector. Many events have therefore had to redesign their business models to attract new audiences, new sources of funding or to reduce their need for resources. For example, crowdfunding has now become an interesting option for many events. For example, the One Spark Festival in Jacksonville, Florida raised a third of its $300,000 budget through crowdfunding (Kritzer 2012). The festival itself provided a platform for funding pitches by entrepreneurs in a variety of different fields. As Kiger (2013) remarked, the 'Jacksonville event may be one harbinger of a promising new international phenomenon – civic festivals that aim to promote local communities by incorporating crowdfunding both as a source of capital and as a tool for engaging visitors and residents'.

Some would argue that festivals and events are particularly suited to crowd-funding, because their time-limited nature creates a natural sense of urgency among potential funders, who can also be offered a range of festival-related experiences in return for their backing as the essential incentive. The need to engage with potential backers is therefore something that may need to be taken into account in event design in the future.

The growth of crowdfunding and its extension of the direct stakeholders of events into broader social and economic networks is a good example of what Richards *et al.* (2013) call the 'network approach' to events. Networks require coordination mechanisms to ensure a common focus of attention in an environment in which attention is becoming an increasingly scarce commodity, particularly for the consumer (Richards 2013). In the network society we need new means of bringing people together and creating new social bonds (van Ingen and Dekker 2011). The kind of interaction rituals described by Collins (2004) and applied in this volume to events such as the Hieronymous Bosch anniversary or the Festes de Gràcia in Barcelona (Chapter 2) provide one means of developing such a focus and creating bonding and engagement.

Challenges of event design research

Events are an important catalyst for different economic, social and cultural processes. Designing events is also about configuring the relationships between different and sometimes conflicting event dimensions that increasingly need to be interconnected. Events can act as platforms which mediate exchanges between local and global, old and new, tradition and innovation. The dialogue and exchange created can be embedded in the design of the event and the event becomes a means of announcing and simultaneously of overcoming disjuncture. An event can therefore represent a particular node in space and time, which as Sewell (1996) argues from a historical perspective, can mark the gap between reality and aspiration. Successful event design therefore involves first revealing this gap, and therefore the potential for change, and subsequently closing the gap by turning aspirations into reality. As Bevolo points out in Chapter 6, 'design' and design events are tools through which cities seek to improve their physical reality by aspiring to a specific dream of urban progress. However, the downside is that designing events as a strategy may also harbour potential dangers. The fact that design concepts are easily transferable between events and locations means that formats and programming can be relatively easily copied and events commoditized (Richards and Wilson 2006). There is therefore a need to ensure that design is anchored into the cultural DNA of the city and/or location so that this essential element of event design is difficult to reproduce.

The importance of design is also underlined by Berridge (2012: 284) when describing the structure and chain of steps that are linked to event design:

> Design should be regarded as the basis of the framework for successful event experience production. Event design is the concept of a structure for

an event, the manifest expression of that concept expressed verbally and visually which leads, finally, to the execution of the concept.

The concept of event as framework also implies that effects of event design stretch far beyond the tangible event itself. The stance taken towards events and event design taken in this volume also attempts to go beyond the tangible realm, and to tell a distinct story about events and their role in social contexts. In this vein Hall and Page (2012: 149) note:

> the seeming inability of event studies to achieve a substantial shift in the thinking associated with the area to move it from an empiricist-rational tradition to one that also adopts a more critical and social constructionist stance in the analysis of event-related phenomenon.

This is also a need outlined by Rojek (2013), who criticizes the 'myopia' of the event management literature. In our view, at the very least the analysis of events needs to be set in a broader social and political context which makes their role as contemporary social phenomena clearer. Most of the contributions in this volume therefore attempt to go beyond the narrow management perspective and also further than traditional (physical) approaches to event design. Effective design is not just a means of enhancing the visitor experience or generating more income, but it can become a means of achieving much broader social, cultural and creative objectives. Given the scope and power of effective design, this also implies that it can ultimately have intended or unintended negative consequences as well. It can indeed be a means for quashing some voices or excluding specific groups of participants. These issues also need to be taken on board by event designers and event researchers in their practices.

From the point of view of research, the event studies field still has to fully examine the implications of the cultural turn, the creative turn and the relational turn in the social sciences. These perspectives have important implications for design, because they mark the increasing symbolic and relational content of events as social phenomena, which in turn are reflected in the design of events as catalysts for cultural change, image change and social cohesion.

Besides these different perspectives, other temporal and spatial levels should also be taken into account when designing events. As Hall and Page (2012) point out, there is a temporal level to be considered which makes evident the long-term and short-term outputs of the event (programme). This also questions the level where analysis (and design) should be undertaken, whether it should be more focused on the scale on the event itself or the event programme. Standard event management practice tends to deal with the level of individual events, whereas many of the outputs of events are generated at a programme level (e.g. Richards and Palmer 2010). This is an important issue because, as the scale of event design shifts from single events to event programmes or portfolios, so the need arises to design beyond the confines of the event itself, into infrastructure and orgware (organizational structures and processes). Events themselves then become structures which in turn shape social, economic and cultural practices.

Thinking beyond the level of the individual event, or even event programmes, event design can also encompass entire 'eventscapes' or portfolios of events. Hall (2008) points to the profusion of 'scapes' related to events, including brandscapes, illustrating the point that event design can also contribute to the image of entire cities or regions. The collection of different events in a place may also be conceived of as an 'experiencescape', or the 'place where experiences of pleasure, enjoyment, and entertainment can be encountered, as well as where human interactions occur' (Walls 2009: 3; O'Dell and Billing 2005). These experiencescapes also influence the way eventscapes are configured, as Steijn makes clear in Chapter 11.

In this sense, it should be taken into account that in the process, as Nordström *et al.* (2010: 7–8) state:

> neither services nor experiences can be produced or delivered. Services are abstract and processual in their nature. Experiences, as do services, rely heavily upon the employees of a company in order for an actual experience of the customer to take place. Giving promises about experiences consequently involves the customer, as much as the employees, who the 'staging' of the experience rely upon. So, the fulfillment of a brand experience promise is dependent on both the customer and the staff.

In the backstage then staff is an essential element in the eventscape and consequently in the event design. Hede and Kellett (Chapter 9) touch upon this matter and make evident that, for example, human resource management of digital marketing is fundamental in event design.

Events are sites of interaction, and therefore represent archetypal experiencescapes. Most event research concentrates on the experience of the visitor, but the eventscape contains different elements (front and back stage) as well as qualities (speed, tempo, rhythm, identity production). It is also in this sense that Nelson (2009) reflects on the creation of the experience as connected to the emotional status of event attendees. Event design is therefore a holistic process of creation which involves emotional and social contexts where the event itself is a (co-creative) platform where innovation takes places. The design process has then to allow, promote and provoke the conditions for co-creative innovation to happen, for example by considering it as an interactive theatrical setting with its composite dramatic elements (Nelson 2009).

The development of dramaturgical settings for events also creates a fresh need to develop storytelling in order to link different dramatic elements into a compelling whole. Steijn (Chapter 11) gives some practical illustrations of how this can be achieved in the case of classical music events. Other strategies are also possible, such as the use of 'game thinking' or processes of 'gamification' (Huotari and Hamari 2011; Deterding 2012). Events can apply larger scale game design principles to engage participants more actively in the drama being unfolded by an event, making the personal event experience even more meaningful and symbolic. This can raise the 'emotional energy' (Collins 2004) generated to a level where the borders between tangible and intangible, physical and virtual are increasingly blurred.

Recent research on the outcomes of event experiences (de Geus *et al.* 2013) poses the question: does the design of an event produce the outcomes desired by event organizers and sought after by event attendees in experiential terms? Given the increasing rapid circulation of experience elements and the pressure to keep up with (or ideally stay ahead of) consumer trends, events have increasing problems keeping their experience design up to date. This is a major challenge for many established events, as Cardoso, Silva and Fernandes point out in Chapter 13. This makes it even more likely that event designers will look beyond the current range of physical event models into new design fields such as virtual events, hybrid events (such as the conference/festival model described by Crowther and Orefice in Chapter 10) or gaming.

These new event concepts also point to the need for new means of evaluating event outcomes and effects. Much research has emerged in recent years on visitor satisfaction and economic impact, but these are relatively limited aspects of the problem. As the forthcoming special issue of the *Journal of Policy Research in Tourism, Leisure and Events* on 'Monitoring and evaluating cultural events' (Richards and Thomas, forthcoming) indicates, there are many new possibilities for devising evaluation and monitoring strategies that can guide different aspects of event design. These include action research, visual methodologies, the use of new technologies including video streaming and podcasts, consumer panels and the creation of events designed to evaluate event programmes.

Such new evaluation strategies will also have to take on board the growing complexity of measuring event outcomes in relation to an increasingly fragmented stakeholder landscape and rapidly increasing forms of event delivery. In a broader social context, event design and evaluation will need to deal with the 'new relationality' (Richards 2013), which is leading to events that deal not only with their own output goals, but, as Bawens (2010) explains, the need to connect the individual goals of event users with a 'transcendental collective goal'. This is likely to increase the power of event design, and the potential of events as communication vehicles considerably in future.

References

Adema, K.L. and Roehl, W.S. (2010) 'Environmental scanning the future of event design', *International Journal of Hospitality Management*, 29(2): 199–207.
Berridge, G. (2012) 'Designing event experiences', in S.J. Page and J. Connell (eds) *The Routledge Handbook of Events*, London: Routledge, pp. 273–288.
Bawens, M. (2010) 'Peer-to-peer relationality: the city and anonymity'. Online, available at: http://w2.bcn.cat/bcnmetropolis/arxiu/en/pagea8ed.html?id=23&ui=424 (accessed 24 January 2014).
Bladen, C., Kennell, J., Abson, E. and Wilde, N. (2012) *Events Management: An Introduction*, London: Routledge.

Boswijk, A., Thijssen, T. and Peelen, E. (2007) *The Experience Economy: A New Perspective*, Amsterdam: Pearson Education.

Collins, R. (2004) *Interaction Ritual Chains*, Princeton, NJ: Princeton University Press.

Deterding, S. (2012) 'Gamification: designing for motivation', *Interactions*, 19(4): 14–17.

Hall, C.M. (2008) 'Servicescapes, designscapes, branding, and the creation of place-identity: south of Litchfield, Christchurch', *Journal of Travel and Tourism Marketing*, 25(3–4): 233–250.

Hall, C.M. and Page, S. (2012) 'Geography and the study of events', in S. Page and J. Connell (eds) *The Routledge Handbook of Events*, London: Routledge, pp. 148–164.

Huotari, K. and Hamari, J. (2011) '"Gamification" from the perspective of service marketing'. Online, available at: http://gamification-research.org/wp-content/uploads/2011/04/14-Huotari.pdf (accessed 25 February 2014).

Intellitix (2013) 'WOW! Smart RFID wristbands!' Online, available at: www.intellitix.com/resources/newsarticle/65 (accessed 25 February 2014).

Getz, D. (2012) *Event Studies: Theory, Research and Policy for Planned Events*, London: Routledge.

Geus, S. de, Richards, G. and Toepoel, V. (2013) 'The Dutch queen's day event: how subjective experience mediates the relationship between motivation and satisfaction', *International Journal of Event and Festival Management*, 4(2): 156–172.

Kammeier, H.D. (2002) 'Coping with "pulsar effects" in the context of sustainable urban development: towards a conceptual framework', Paper presented at the 38th ISOCARP Congress, Athens, September 2002.

Kiger, P. (2013) 'Crowdfunding a new urban identity', *Urbanland*, 14 August. Online, available at: http://urbanland.uli.org/economy-markets-trends/crowdfunding-your-way-to-an-urban-identity/ (accessed 24 January 2014).

Kritzer, A.G. (2012) 'Creatives seek crowdfunding for festivals', *Jacksonville Business Journal*, 7 December. Online, available at: www.bizjournals.com/jacksonville/print-edition/2012/12/07/creatives-seek-crowdfunding-for.html?page=all (accessed 24 February 2014).

Mueller, P. (2009) 'The logic of open value creation'. Online, available at: www.philippmueller.de/the-logic-of-open-value-creation-2/ (accessed 25 February 2014).

Nelson, K.B. (2009) 'Enhancing the attendee's experience through creative design of the event environment: applying Goffman's dramaturgical perspective', *Journal of Convention and Event Tourism*, 10(2): 120–133.

Nordström, C.S., Alsér, M. and Bergström, F. (2010) 'The backstage experience room: a space for development and integration of brand promises. A case study of Norrgavel', in S.-B. Arnolds-Granlund and P. Björk (eds) *The Nordic Conference on Experience: Research, Education and Practice in Media 2008: Conference Proceedings*, Vaasa: Tritonia, pp. 112–137.

O'Dell, T. and Billing, P. (2005) *Experiencescapes: Tourism, Culture and Economy*, Copenhagen: Copenhagen Business School Press.

Owinski, B. (2013) 'The beats music guide to music curation', *Forbes*, 22 August. Online, available at: www.forbes.com/sites/bobbyowsinski/2013/08/22/the-beats-music-guide-to-music-curation/ (accessed 24 February 2014).

Prentice, R. and Andersen, V. (2003) 'Festival as creative destination', *Annals of Tourism Research*, 30(1): 7–30.

Richards, G. (2007) 'Culture and authenticity in a traditional event: the views of producers, residents and visitors in Barcelona', *Event Management*, 11(1/2): 33–44.

Richards, G. (2013) 'Creativity and tourism in the city', *Current Issues in Tourism*, 17(2): 119–144.

Richards, G. and Palmer, R. (2010) *Eventful Cities: Cultural Management and Urban Revitalization*, London: Routledge.

Richards, G. and Thomas, R. (forthcoming) 'Monitoring and evaluating cultural events', *Journal of Policy Research in Tourism, Leisure and Events*, special issue.

Richards, G. and Wilson, J. (2006) 'Developing Creativity in Tourist Experiences: A Solution to the Serial Reproduction of Culture?' *Tourism Management*, 27(6): 1209–1223.

Richards, G., de Brito, M. and Wilks, K. (2013) *Exploring the Social Impact of Events*, London: Routledge.

Rihova, I., Buhalis, D., Moital, M. and Gouthro, M.-B. (2013) 'Social Layers of Customer-to-Customer Value Co-creation', *Journal of Service Management*, 24(5): 553–556.

Rojek, C. (2013) *Event Power: How Global Events Manage and Manipulate*, London: Sage.

Rojek, C. (2014) 'Global event management: a critique', *Leisure Studies*, 33(1): 32–47.

Sewell, W.H. (1996) 'Historical events as transformations of structures: inventing revolution at the Bastille', *Theory and Society*, 25(6): 841–881.

Van Ingen, E. and Dekker, P. (2011) 'Dissolution of associational life? Testing the individualization and informalization hypotheses on leisure activities in the Netherlands between 1975 and 2005', *Social Indicators Research*, 100(2): 209–224.

Walls, A. (2009) 'An examination of consumer experience and relative effects on consumer values', PhD Thesis, University of Central Florida.

Wiszniewski, D. (2010) *Florence: Curating the City: 3 (Cityspeculations)*, Edinburgh: University of Edinburgh Press.

Index

Andanças (Portugal) 6
Antwerpen Open 7
Arenal Live 168
ATLAS Events Group 3, 186
atmosphere 94, 148, 199
audio-visual 145–6
authenticity 105; vernacular 72

Barcelona 7, 19–20, 203
Bari 96
Bilbao BBK Live 168
blurring 112
Bowie, David 201
branding 65–76; emotional 39
business: event industry 37–48; models
    46–7

changes in event design 206–7
Christmas 30
city 175; branding 66; eventful 1
classical music events 137–60
Coachella 169, 171
co-creation 28, 47, 125–34, 161, 199–200
co-creative: events 122–34; spaces 125–6
collaborative design 200–1
Collins, Randall 14, 104, 106, 204, 207
Commonwealth Games 109
community involvement 105
communitas 93, 126
competitive identities 66
concept, high 39
concerts 137–8
confraternities 95–6
Copenhagen 140
corporate social responsibility 128
'Creative Europe' 141
creative: industries 67; tourism 29
crowdfunding 206–7
curation 201–2

customer journey 55
cyberspace 163–4

Denmark 137–59
design 65–76; and the city 67–8;
    collaborative 200–1; -lab 143, 146–9;
    level 204–5; methodology 110;
    production 144–6; purpose 198;
    sensorial 66; service 4–5, 25–34;
    students 142–3; thinking 5
development 86–7
digital technologies 137–59
DNA 2
Draaksteken Beesel 78–89
dramaturgy 143–4
Durkheim 97, 100, 106
Dutch Design Week 70–5, 205
dynamic marketing communications 113–19

Easter 95, 101
Eindhoven 68–76, 205
e-leisure 163, 175
emergent design 9
emotional energy 18, 122, 199, 201
engagement 8, 123, 199, 204
European Capital of Culture 204
event: design 40–2; evaluation 126;
    marketing 39–48; networking 61–3;
    organizations 110–12; platforms 127;
    research 207–10; scale 205–6
eventful cities 1, 198
eventfulness 71
eventscapes 126, 209
events industry 2
experience 122, 182–5; design 5–6, 127–6,
    140–2; festival 168, 190–2; memorable
    161; outcomes 192; planned 78;
    prototype 30–3; service 28–30; tourist
    182; visitor 51–2

experiencescape 27, 209
experiential marketing 124

Facebook 113
facilitation 131
Festas de Gràcia (Barcelona) 19–20
festivals 166–8
festival experience 168, 190–2
Festival Internacional de Benicàssim 169
FIFA World Cup 111
Finland 25–34
flash mobs 200
flow 56
FRESH conference 128–30
future research directions 207–10

gare 99–100
gastronomy: events 181–95; experiences
    182–4
generation Y 124
Glasgow 1990 17, 202
Glastonbury 6, 131
globalization 113, 184

Heineken MyFestival 171–4
Helsinki 17, 71
heritage 79
Hieronymus Bosch 500 20–2
High Line Festival 201
high performance work systems 110–19
holistic approach 124
Holy Week 95–106, 199
Hoyle, Joy Sun-Ra Pawl 153–4
human resource management 111, 115

identity, urban 67
imagineer 123
imagineering 4, 15, 37–48, 109–10, 126,
    128, 132, 161; definition of 40, 110
innovation 65–76
installations 156
intangible cultural heritage 101
interactivity 172–3
interaction ritual chains 18, 97, 199
Italy 92–106
iteration 110
iterative: events 110–11; organizations 116

Lapland 25–34
legacy 124
leisure 71; experience 162–6
Lille 17
liminality 94
liveness 137–59

live streaming 170
Lollapalooza 170
London 71

MADE Entrepreneurs Festival 130–3
Malmö 140
marketing 39–48; communications 41,
    113–14
mediatized 143
Meeting Professionals International 126
mega-events 202
metro station 156–8
Mezzogiorno 97
Minogue, Kylie 203
mobile apps 170
MOMA 67
motivations 165
music 127, 130; events 137–59, 161–74;
    festivals 161–74

narrative 144
Netherlands 38, 42–5, 65–76
network: approach 207; society 18, 123
networking events 61–3
Newport Folk Festival 169–70

Oerol Festival 204
Olympics 203
One Spark Festival 206
online: community 130, 172; events 129
orchestra conductor 149–50
Øresund region 137, 140–1

Paaspop Den Hout 56–61
pace 127
Paris 65
Philips 68–9
place branding 65–7
pop-up 110
Portugal 181–95
post-event: involvement 117; phase 174
production design method 144
Puglia 92–106
pulsating events 110–11
purpose of visit 195

quality of life 98

Rasmussen, Josephine Farsø 153–4
Ranua Zoo 30–2
recruitment 111, 116
religious celebrations 93–5
RFID 170–1, 200
rituals: concert 137–40; design 17–19

ROI 126
role ambiguity 113
Roskilde Festival (Denmark) 6
Rotterdam Festivals 7
Royal Danish Theatre 155
Rugby World Cup 109

Santarém Gastronomy Festival (Portugal)
    181–95, 198, 206
scenario 32
self-organisation 129
sequencing 41
service: design 4–5, 25–34; experience
    28–30; prototype 33
Sheffield 130–2
's-Hertogenbosch 20–2
slow: cities 81; events 82–3; food 80–1;
    travel 81–2
social: cohesion 101; context of events
    15–17; design 6–7; impacts 78; media
    112, 113, 129, 164, 200; media
    platforms 109, 119; practices 7–9
socio-economic impact 101–5
Sørensen, Sarah Gad Wøldike 150–2
space 145, 163, 202–4
Spain 171
sponsorship 133
sports events 111
stakeholders 125, 126, 131, 198
stakeholder centricity 126
Stamatin, Bogdan 149–59
storyboarding 31

storytelling 127, 129, 209
surprise 127

Taranto 95–106
technology 29, 128, 130, 161, 162–6, 200
time 85–6, 145, 158, 163, 202–4
Tomorrowland festival 6
touch, high 39
touchpoints 52–4, 185
tourism 101, 104, 182–3
tradition 104
transformation 161–2
triple helix 69
troccola 99–100

unconference 128
University of Sheffield 132
users 174

value creation: platforms 2, 106, 199;
    spaces 124–6
Vans Warped Tour 169
vernacular authenticity 72
video 152–4
virtual reality 173
Visit Denmark 130
visitor: experience 51–2; journey 50–63

Web 2.0 109–19, 124
work–life balance 113
World Design Capital 72

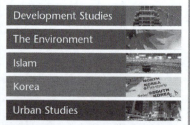